George Moore: A RECONSIDERATION

George Moore:

A RECONSIDERATION

By MALCOLM BROWN

University of Washington Press

SEATTLE · 1955

© 1955 BY THE UNIVERSITY OF WASHINGTON PRESS
LIBRARY OF CONGRESS CATALOG CARD NUMBER: 55-10802
MANUFACTURED BY THE COLONIAL PRESS INC., CLINTON, MASS.

FOR M. AND B.

He wends unfollowed, he must house alone;
Yet on he fares, by his own heart inspired.
                         —Matthew Arnold, THYRSIS

              . . . nigh founder'd on he fares
Treading the crude consistence, half on foot,
Half flying. . . .
                         —John Milton, PARADISE LOST

The wolves came from the mountains; and led by the carrion
scent, devoured the dead bodies which had been hastily
buried during the plague, and emboldened by their meal
crept, before the short day was well past, over the walls of
the farmyards of the Campagna. *The eagles were seen driv-*
ing the flocks of smaller birds across the dusky sky. Only,
in the city itself the winter was all the brighter for the con-
trast, among those who could pay for light and warmth.
The habit-makers made a great sale of the spoil of all such
furry creatures as had escaped wolves and eagles, for presents
at the Saturnalia; *and at no time had the winter roses from*
Carthage seemed more lustrously yellow and red.
                         —Walter Pater, MARIUS THE EPICUREAN

Preface

*It is difficult for me to believe any good of myself.
Within the oftentimes bombastic and truculent appearance that I present to the world, trembles a heart
shy as a wren in the hedgerow or a mouse along the
wainscotting.*

—HAIL AND FAREWELL

To his contemporaries George Moore was a very great writer.
In the 1920's one of the certainties of literary criticism was the
view that he was "the greatest living master of English prose."
The little circle of partisan champions who gathered around him
in his old age in Pimlico of course held this view. But it was no
less the opinion of reputed critics outside his *cénacle*, critics like
Rebecca West, whose praise, though reluctant, was hardly less
sweeping than that of Moore's disciples. One of his detractors,
Ford Madox Ford, said: "When it comes to writing, George
Moore was a wolf—lean, silent, infinitely sweet and solitary."
Such pronouncements are rarely heard today, for his reputation
has emerged only slowly from the long hibernation that commenced with his death in 1933. We have books on Sheridan Le
Fanu and Mrs. Gaskell, and French, German, and English publishers issue new biographies of Oscar Wilde with regularity;
but, since the publication of Joseph Hone's splendid biography
of Moore nearly two decades ago, no study of his work has
appeared.

The collapse of Moore's reputation was unquestionably related to the fact that he collected, in the course of a long lifetime,
an extraordinary number of distinguished enemies, including
Yeats, Hardy, Henry James, Conrad, Middleton Murry, Sir Walter Raleigh, his own cousin Edward Martyn, his own brother,

Colonel Maurice Moore, and Whistler, who once "called him out," though Moore was not in a dueling mood and had the good sense to ignore the challenge. In the two decades since his death, the victims of his spleen have nearly all left the stage, carrying the original force of their loathing with them to the grave but leaving behind their testimonials of scorn. To Yeats he was "a man carved out of a turnip"; to Yeats's father he was "an elderly blackguard"; to Middleton Murry, "a yelping terrier"; to Susan Mitchell, "an ugly old soul"; to Ford Madox Ford he was repulsively, inhumanly cold; and even the anonymous authors of Moore's epitaph, carved on a rock on an island in Lough Carra, remind the passing vacationist that for art Moore "deserted his family and his friends."

One can understand these antipathies and may perhaps be moved to extend back through the years a sympathy for those who were driven almost to distraction by the tireless reiteration of Moore's childish, frenzied, and often cruel compulsions. Yet one no longer feels acute distress in the presence of Moore's weaker self. A generation has gone by since his death; the time has passed for composing another of those outbursts that would undertake to scold Moore for being the man he had to be, and for offering with condescension advice about how he might better have invested his talents. Our ambition seeks only to bring to his work the sort of detached curiosity with which he scrutinized it, and to seek the sort of understanding he sought.

We see him, much as he saw himself, as a stubborn and fact-minded seeker, torn by violently contradictory impulses, periodically incapable of moderation in discourse. We see him as the most uninhibited, and hence the most valuable, of the commentators to testify upon the motives, satisfactions, frustrations, and persistent, incurable longings of a practicing artist of talent in the opening phase of the modern age, when the ideals to which the artistic world has since given full allegiance were in process of delineation. His story is the story of the painful demise of the Victorian age and the equally painful birth of the age which succeeded. His adventures summarize this entire epoch of transition, and he represents his time rather more fittingly, though with less lurid interest, than Wilde or Beardsley.

One does not hesitate to label him a very important literary figure. His *Esther Waters* and *A Mummer's Wife* stand as two of the dozen most perfectly wrought novels to appear in the English realistic tradition since the high noon of Victorian genius, novels not out of place in the company of the best novels of the language. At least six of his other novels seem assured of "permanence." These are *A Modern Lover* and *A Drama in Muslin*, which brought the first vivifying transfusion of French realism into the ailing late-Victorian English novel; and *The Lake, The Brook Kerith, Heloise and Abelard,* and *Ulick and Soracha,* the novels of his final "melodic line" manner, narratives in which he hoped to bring to the novel the languid, mellifluous flow of mythic streams and the disembodied melancholy of the Celtic twilight. None of these latter novels fits a pattern that is modish just now, and all lie awaiting their eventual rediscovery and resurrection after today's dominant tastes have passed with the mutation of things.

Perhaps his autobiographical writings will carry his fame longest. He found that he was able to study, if not to control, his outrageous personality, and it occurred to him that his own character provided a subject for literary treatment. He set up as his own Boswell and passed the time spying upon himself with mingled affection and malice. He was not, it is true, capable of the sort of candor that Gide has accustomed us to expect. Readers searching Moore's autobiographies for scandals proportionate to his public reputation for wickedness will conclude that he was a very mild sinner after all, being mainly addicted to small petulancies rather than to scarlet flaws. His habit of comparing his confessions to Rousseau's was rather on the boastful side; one is more particularly reminded of Augustine's anticlimax: "And besides that, I stole things from my parents' root cellar and dinner table." Yet one of the most palpable self-portraits of all literature arises out of the pages of his autobiographies and confessions—first in *Confessions of a Young Man* and the anecdotes of *Memoirs of My Dead Life,* and later and more impressively in *Hail and Farewell,* which relates Moore's part in the Irish literary revival and makes the definitive statement of the results to be expected when a fatigued talent, searching for lost innocence, stumbles into a condescending alliance with a mass political and literary resurgence.

It is a commonplace of literary history that Moore held the decisive point in the line of attack against the tyranny of antiquated Victorian ways in art and literature. If Victorian prudery and evangelical priggishness were a dragon to be slain, Moore, as much as any literary figure, deserves to be remembered as the Siegfried who did the deed. As Ruth Zabriskie Temple has shown, he was not only the most knowing critic of living French and continental culture in late-Victorian England but also its most influential publicist, broader and more generous than his illustrious predecessor, Swinburne, and more authoritative and perceptive than his dedicated contemporary and friend, Arthur Symons. He discovered Laforgue before Ezra Pound was born; and a generation before T. S. Eliot made Bloomsbury familiar with Gérard de Nerval's unhappy Prince of Aquitaine of the fallen tower, Moore was quoting with glittering eye the sestet of the same sonnet:

J'ai rêvé dans la grotte où nage la sirène.

How many readers owe their discovery of Balzac, Flaubert, Zola, Turgenev, Huysmans, Verlaine, Manet, Degas, and even Wagner to the infectiousness of Moore's enthusiasms?

Moore's allegiances were both fanatical and mercurial. He was totally devoid of loyalty to yesterday's absolute and ruthless in casting off ideas and emotions, not to say friends, when they no longer served him. The variety of his aesthetic adventures was unparalleled. Every important literary and artistic circle of late-Victorian and Edwardian times saw him arrive—and depart.

At one time or another he considered himself to be a pre-Raphaelite, a "decadent," a symbolist, a naturalist, an Ibsenite, a Wagnerian, a Gaelic Leaguer, an imagist, an impressionist, and at last the creator and sole practitioner of his own late literary manner. He embraced no fewer than seven distinct literary styles and manners. This was the peculiarity that occasioned Oscar Wilde's famous jibe, "Moore conducts his education in public," and that led other contemporaries to mutter angrily about his opportunism and meretriciousness. "He stands for nothing," said his estranged brother Maurice somewhat oversimply. The same trait was applauded by his friends as a "passion for self-renewal." He was the most adventurous of the important artistic figures of his time, and his career was an incomparable aesthetic journey, ranging more widely than the careers of Shaw, or Bennett, or Wells, or even Joyce and Yeats, though he did not always return from his expeditions as enriched as they.

Moore's collected works are of course one's first concern. But these volumes might better have been called "selected," since they were painstakingly sorted and polished in old age to present his best to posterity. Of the thirty-five volumes that Moore took to press during his career, some fifteen volumes were subsequently disowned. Such vigorous culling is unusual, especially since Moore had no Grub Street phase to renounce, but was seemingly a serious writer from first to last. One turns with curiosity to the disowned volumes and finds there other abundant riches. Three of them are essential for understanding Moore, though many commentators have shared Moore's embarrassment in their presence and have tried to put them out of mind. One is *Pagan Poems*, an attempt to Anglicize the poetry of Baudelaire, notable for a failure whose enormity casts suspicion on Moore's motives. A second is *Parnell and His Island*, a hysterical anti-Irish pamphlet published at the height of the Home Rule agitation in the late 1880's shortly before the fall of Parnell. The third is *Mike Fletcher*, a forerunner of the *fin de siècle* novel, the first exhibit in English fiction of the moods that later flowered in the English decadence of the 1890's. One might perhaps agree that these volumes are without literary merit; yet it is not possible to maintain that they are uninteresting or unimportant.

Such lapses into absurdity make the tasks of the critic delicate and difficult. A reader approaching Moore for the first time is likely to be dismayed by his perversity. He introduces himself as a fool caught in the grip of a compulsion to degrade all good things into noise and vulgarity, and one is impatient to dismiss him as at best no more than amusing and at worst simply unspeakable. Eventually one learns the inadequacy of this first impression and comes to glimpse behind his absurdity a rare and complex talent, gentle, perspicuous, and not without an austere dignity and poise.

Still, his absurdity cannot be laughed off or argued away. Like Rossetti's chloral glass and Gide's cape, it casts its shadow across pages where it is unwanted, distracting the mind from pure consideration of art. Unquestionably Moore was hounded by a frightful inner disharmony, as Charles Morgan pointed out many years ago. His absurd manner was a symptom, though an enigmatical one, puzzling to his friends and contemporaries and obsessing his own endless self-searching meditations.

Among his oddities, Moore possessed an incorrigible taste for bluntness. "I haven't enough talent to be obscure," he once said. Like the French, whom he admired above all other people, he had a way of forcing tendencies to yield up their ultimate polar implications. These he would embrace and flaunt, loudly scornful of the timid straddlers who begged him to remember common sense. This was the peculiarity of his temperament that led Yeats to house him in the same phase of his well-known astrological system with H. G. Wells and George Bernard Shaw, the three representing for Yeats the absolutely earth-bound anti-mystical temperament.

But a second look at Moore's "clarity" warns that it was not always as innocent and ingenuous as it sounded, and further scrutiny suggests that he had invented a way of approaching sensitive issues that was sly, intricate, and oblique. What is one to make of a pronouncement like this:

> What care I that some millions of wretched Israelites died under Pharaoh's lash or Egypt's sun? It was well that they died that I might have the pyramids to look on, or to fill a musing hour with wonderment. Is there one amongst us who would exchange them for the lives of the ignominious slaves that died?

This is a specimen of a "Moorism," a violent rhetoric of mingled self-assurance and self-mockery peculiar to his vision. In his lifetime it was commonly believed that this mannerism betokened simple crudeness of mind. That it was a kind of excess is clear enough; but its simplicity is illusory, a part of a trick so successfully played that it seems to have disarmed most of his contemporaries. Even Yeats, though an expert on "masks" and the convolutions of irony, was deceived. "Violent and coarse of temper," was the last of his many denigrations of Moore, a man he hated but could not drive from old-age memories and dreams. Yeats's judgment was understandably vehement, since a long history of enmity lay behind it. New readers of Moore are forewarned and should be cautious in inferring behind Moore's peculiar manner either outrageous candor or, on the other hand, ordinary spoofing. More than one scholar, including the present writer, has found himself led into the swamps by failing to be constantly suspicious of Moore's rhetoric.

During the past generation the memoirs of literary and artistic folk in Dublin and London have teemed with anecdotes about Moore. These are an "original source," and in America, at least, they are the principal vessel of his reputation at the present time. They have a certain importance; though, when one collects them all together, one is struck by their repetitiveness and suspects that we have inherited almost too many George Moore anecdotes. Invariably they depict a foolish Moore, and to support this impression they commonly mention his receding chin and white walrus mustache, his female pelvis, his champagne-bottle shoulders (Moore's own phrase), and his china-blue eyes peering icily at his fellow men. Many of the anecdotes deal with his uncontrollable urge to make scenes in public and tell how he would swoop down upon some innocent and unsuspecting waitress, taxi driver, or mere passer-by, pouring out a torrent of unmotivated abuse, a habit that grew more ugly as senility took hold of him. Most of all, the anecdotes deal with his grandiose boasts of sexual adventure, but without creating a clear impression. Some hint broadly that his boasting cloaked a condition of sexual impotence—hence Susan Mitchell's well-known report that he was a lover who "didn't kiss, but told"; others imply that he was a veritable Priapus strolling the boulevards. The somber, muted artist who stands behind his best creative work does not often appear in the memoirs of his acquaintances.

MALCOLM BROWN

Seattle, Washington
May 6, 1955

Acknowledgments

ANYONE WRITING about George Moore must confess a great debt to Joseph Hone's two biographies. One deals with George Moore himself, the other with the extraordinary history of the Moore family through two centuries. Hone's gleanings from the fabulous material in the records of the Moore family will long stand as one of the richest sources of information for students interested in the breakup of Victorian culture. Hone's ability to maintain both his good humor and his detachment toward his subject was an accomplishment not duplicated by any of the other commentators who had "known Moore personally" and strolled within the range of the explosive personality, or by very many of those who have known Moore only through his writings.

I also take pleasure in acknowledging the kindness of three of my colleagues at the University of Washington: Professors Giovanni Costigan and Joseph B. Harrison, who took the time to read the manuscript when they were already overwhelmed with more important obligations, and S. K. Winther, who has in many ways shown good will toward the study.

I wish to thank Mrs. Eleanor Widmer for her assistance in research.

Special thanks are also due to Mr. C. D. Medley for permission to quote from Moore's letters and published work.

Other copyright owners who kindly granted me permission to reprint from their work are extended my thanks, as follows:

Browne and Nolan Ltd., Dublin, for permission to quote from Lennox Robinson's *Palette and Plough.*

Jonathan Cape, Ltd., London, for permission to quote from Joseph Hone's *The Moores of Moore Hall.*

Harper and Brothers, New York, for permission to quote from Grant Richards' *Memoirs of a Misspent Youth.*

ACKNOWLEDGMENTS

William Heinemann, Ltd., London, for permission to quote from William Archer's *Real Conversations.*

Matthew Josephson and Emerson Books, Inc., New York, for permission to quote from Mr. Josephson's *Zola and His Time.*

Alfred A. Knopf, Inc., for permission to quote from Ernest Boyd's introduction to *Germinie Lacerteux,* by J. and E. Goncourt.

T. Werner Laurie, Ltd., London, for permission to quote from Maurice Moore's *An Irish Gentleman, George Henry Moore.*

The Macmillan Company, New York, for permission to quote from W. B. Yeats's *Dramatis Personae* and Joseph Hone's *Life of George Moore.*

George Weidenfeld and Nicholson, Ltd., London, for permission to quote from J. M. Cohen's translation of Flaubert's letters.

Contents

George Moore: A RECONSIDERATION

The Irish Landlord

Scene: A great family coach, drawn by two powerful country horses, lumbers along a narrow Irish road. The ever-recurrent signs—long ranges of blue mountains, the streak of bog, the rotting cabin, the flock of plover rising from the desolate water.

—CONFESSIONS OF A YOUNG MAN

The thin meagre aspect of the marshy fields and the hungry hills reminds you of the smell of poverty— the smell of something sick to death of poverty.

—PARNELL AND HIS ISLAND

ALL IRISHMEN KNOW that the mountains and glens of Connemara are separated from the main body of Ireland by a long chain of shallow lakes stretching northward from Galway Bay for some forty miles into county Mayo. The longest and most southerly of these lakes is Lough Corrib, the scene of the mythical battles of ancient Irish gods at Moytura, and of the tiny but famous village of Cong, which gave to the world both the Cross of Cong and Oscar Wilde. Adjoining it on the north is the second link in the chain of lakes, Lough Mask; here at Mask House in 1880 there lived a certain Captain Charles Boycott, whose name was to add a new word to the English language through his chance role in the Land War in Mayo. At the upper end of the chain, deep in county Mayo, is the smallest of the lakes, Lough Carra, George Moore's lake. To the north and east of Lough Carra lie pleasant flatlands, bogland, and fertile farms, but to the west is a wild and rugged country like the Scots highlands, fastnesses that have sheltered fleeing remnants of defeated peoples since before

3

history and that have preserved, in isolation, the last native Gaelic speakers and the last relics of the primordial Celtic culture. In search of the primitive, Synge chose a village on Lough Carra as the setting for *The Playboy of the Western World*, making Pegeen Mike and Christy Mahon fellow villagers of George Moore, who was born in 1852 in sight of the lake and of the Partry Mountains across on the western shore. On a beautiful spring day in 1933 his ashes were brought back to the lake and deposited, pagan fashion, in a great rock on an island just across the water from the bones of his ancestors lying in consecrated Catholic ground on the mainland. Thanks to police protection and the tact of the parish priest, who quieted the growlings of villagers, no ugly incident marred the funeral service of Lough Carra's most far-famed son.

The Moores were originally English Protestants who had come to county Mayo sometime during the seventeenth century as part of the garrison of strong-armed landlords planted by the Stuarts and the Commonwealth to hold the native population in subjection during the anarchic interludes between formal military campaigns in the field. Nothing is known of the Moores during this period except that they were regarded as contentious, even among Irishmen, and that they perpetuated about themselves the reputation that, "if you scratch a Moore, your own blood will flow."

In the middle of the eighteenth century the first George Moore known to history, the novelist's great-grandfather, embraced Catholicism and left Ireland to seek the company of the "wild geese" in exile abroad. He moved to Spain, where he grew wealthy in the Alicante wine trade. After the easing of the Penal Laws in the days of Grattan and the Volunteers, Ireland seemed less inhospitable to the emigrated Catholic wine merchant, and with easier times promised he felt a call to return to spend his last years on his native sod. In 1785, three years after the seating of Grattan's parliament, he reappeared in county Mayo buying lands around Lough Carra, acquiring by purchase and inher-

4

itance some twelve thousand acres with a tenant population of about five thousand persons. On a slope overlooking the lake he built a great square Georgian country house, which he named "Moore Hall," and on the stone lintel above the main entrance door he had carved the words: *Fortis cadere cedere non potest,* advising all the world of Ballinrobe that this family was able to resist but not to surrender, a genteel reminder of the Moores' traditional love of fighting.

No sooner was the great country seat established than the family began to show signs of advanced demoralization. The recklessness of the Irish gentry was taken up by the Moore family with almost suicidal gusto. John Moore, the wine merchant's eldest son, died in the Rising of Ninety-eight. In Joseph Hone's uncharitable account of his adventures, he appears as a silly and pompous lad, yet tragic, too. Hearing of the landing of the French troops in Mayo, a quixotic whim, a "lonely impulse of delight," impelled him to dash across Ireland to join up with the invaders at Castlebar. He arrived in time to receive the title of "President of the Republic of Connaught," but a few days later found the rising crushed and Moore a prisoner of the Crown charged with high treason. He died while awaiting trial for his life, achieving a small measure of immortality as a fellow martyr with Wolfe Tone.

The wine merchant's second son, George, the novelist's grandfather, lapsed from the family's reckless tradition. Early in life his temperament hardened into a Whiggish mold. He married a strong-minded Catholic girl from the patrician Browne family. In county Mayo it was said of this family that "if you want anything from a Browne you have to give him a kick," an outsider's version of the wine merchant's fine Latin motto. Finding the collection of rents unbearably tedious, George turned all his business affairs over to the former Miss Browne and retired to an upper room in Moore Hall, where he surrounded himself with books and whiled away the years composing a voluminous but never published history of the French Revolution. He expressed

5

the warmest affection for the political ideals of the Protestant Ascendancy, which his brother had died trying to destroy. He believed that the salvation of Ireland would come only with the universal acceptance of English customs and deplored all manifestations of Irish patriotism. "If the whole bundle of Irish MSS, pedigrees, histories, and traditions were finally to perish," he said, "abundant good would be done to the country. These serve to foster vacuity, idleness, and habits pernicious to industry." [1] These sentiments were insufficient to give any meaningful direction to his life, and his character was fixed in the memory of his family as that of a mild and weary cynic, sitting in the upstairs room and habituated less to "industry" than to gazing at the bland landscape and brooding on the fleetingness and ennui of life in a great country house set beside the reedy lake in the midst of the savagery of west Ireland bogs. In later years his famous grandson was to discover that the nineteenth-century Russian novelists had perfectly delineated the type to which the old historian belonged, and their success seemed to him one of the ultimate achievements in the creation of beauty. In his own old age he always associated the beautiful with the mood of the world-weary Irish gentleman looking at the "melancholy line" of the Partry Mountains and at the "mild and gracious lake amid low shores vanishing into grey distances"; such was the charm he found in Chekhov, Turgenev, Landor, Corot, and in his own last novels.

Among the sons of George Moore the historian, demoralization took the form of a suicidal passion for horseflesh. One son, John, was killed at an early age in a riding mishap. A second son, Augustus, showed a mathematical gift so extraordinary that his tutors at Cambridge imagined they had discovered a genius. But before his training was finished he left Cambridge and took up the arrogant and idle pursuits of an Irish squireen, hunting, riding, and defending his touchy pride. He was killed in early manhood when his horse fell at a barrier in the Aintree steeplechase.

George Henry Moore, eldest son of the historian and father of the novelist, was compounded of a similar mixture of the gifted and the erratic. It was said in the family that he had talent both as a writer and as a painter, but if so he took no trouble to cultivate it. He was hardly out of childhood when he became entangled with a married woman, and in order to escape both the lady and his overweening mother he dashed off in Byronic fashion to Damascus. When he returned to Moore Hall, he had purged himself of all his interests except for the stable, the stud book, and the race track. The old historian died in 1840, leaving George Henry Moore an income of about four thousand pounds based on rents at Moore Hall, an income sufficient to inflame his passion for what he liked to call "the noble pastime of the course." His stable became famous, and three of his greatest horses, Wolfdog, Anonymous, and Croagh Patrick, were sentimentally remembered by racing Irishmen for half a century. Meanwhile his income from rents, supplemented by occasional purses and lucky bets, did not keep pace with his spending, and the family watched with alarm the steady rise of his debts, secured by mortgages on Moore Hall.

The Irish famine was sufficient to sober him. In 1846 he began to perceive the frightfulness of the disaster, and sadly he put his horses up for sale and closed his stables. The suffering of the peasants distressed him, and in an old-fashioned paternal way he felt that he had a feudal responsibility to come to their aid. When he heard, for example, of two thousand starving people waiting outside the Castlebar workhouse for two days in the rain, without a shilling of relief being offered them, his impulse was to do something about it. His neighbors saw the famine in a more ironic light; they of course deplored suffering but were quick to seize the opportunity the famine provided for "clearing the land" of uneconomic small holdings. They evicted tenants methodically and turned their land to more profitable use as pasture for beef cattle. George Henry Moore was constitutionally unable to carry out such cold-blooded measures. Instead of evicting

7

tenants he forgave their unpaid rent. He volunteered to serve on the government relief committee without pay. Desperate because of the inadequacy of funds and the slowness of bureaucratic machinery, he paid a thousand pounds out of his own pocket at one time to ship in corn meal from New Orleans. At the height of the famine he learned that a neighboring Anglican bishop who controlled some relief funds was withholding food from the famine victims until they had renounced Catholicism. Moore was furious; he spoke of "the return of the times of Cromwell" and took up oratory and political canvassing. Under the spell of his new solemnity he married a good Catholic girl, a neighbor of his own class. When the famine had passed he found himself possessed of the dignity of a seat in the House of Commons and the cares of a growing family. His mortgages were more portentous than they had ever been before, but he was able to say that not one peasant at Moore Hall had died of starvation.

Yeats once remarked that the landed gentry in Ireland had prepared its own doom when it lost its "hereditary passion." Did he mean that it was deficient in honor, or recklessness, or paternalistic impulse, or did he mean only that it lacked style? George Henry Moore's history suggests that the defeat of his class resulted from forces more prosaic than Yeats could recognize and that hereditary passion, or its absence, finally determined little more than the pitch of eloquence it gave to its valedictory. Hereditary passion led George Henry Moore into politics, but his behavior seemed to his neighbors and relatives to be calculated to speed their mutual doom rather than to avert it. In the hopeless days between O'Connell and Parnell, he set out to build a Repeal opposition in the House of Commons even though his interests as a great landlord seemingly required the continuance of the Union. His militant Nationalist agitation cost him a painful severance from his own class and brought no compensatory gain other than the good will of Fenians, whose extremism he feared (remembering the death of his unhappy uncle John in

'98), and the affection of peasants, whose self-interest, as he was to discover, ran counter to his own.

When the crisis of the famine had passed, he returned to his stables, though without forsaking politics. Through the 1850's and 1860's he was in and out of Parliament and in and out of luck at the race track. His debts grew, and at last he found himself in such a tight corner that any interruption of his income from Moore Hall would bring ruin. Precisely at this point a world-wide fall in the price of wheat made rent reduction unavoidable. In the early spring of 1870 the peasants on his property organized and pledged themselves to pay only what they considered a fair rent. Moore, sitting in the House of Commons, was handed one day a piece of paper sent from Moore Hall. It was a notice, written in red ink, that had been posted to a tree, and it read:

IMPORTANT   CAUTION

Notice is hereby given that any person who pays rents to landlords, agents, or bailiffs above the ordnance valuation will at his peril mark the consequences.

By order,
Rory.

TO THE TENANTS
OF MR. MOORE'S PROPERTY AND
WHOM IT MAY CONCERN

Coming from peasants to whose service he had sacrificed his life, this show of force seemed the blackest ingratitude and treachery. Bewildered, hurt, and desperate, he wrote to a populist-minded priest in his home parish:

If it is supposed that, because I advocate the rights of the tenants, I am to surrender my own rights as a landlord; if it is suspected that I am so enamored of a seat in Parliament that I am ready to abandon my own self-respect rather than imperil its possession; if it is hoped that because I alone of all the landlords in the parish of Ballintubber have not cleared my estate of the people, the people are to send me to jail—those who count upon taking this base advantage of my political position will find that they have mistaken their man.

9

. . . I am determined to vindicate my own rights without fear or flinching, and if it be necessary to evict every tenant who refuses to pay his rent in full—whatever be the consequences—I will take that course.

At Easter he left for home with the intention of settling matters. From Moore Hall he wrote to his family in London: "The climate and the air are delicious, and it seems to me as if it were good for us to be here, and that if we could build tabernacles for ourselves in this world we could find a paradise for ourselves here." [2]

Two days later he was dead under somewhat puzzling circumstances. The local doctor diagnosed his fatal illness as apoplexy; the populist priest spoke of a heart broken by ingratitude; his son George, the novelist, declared he "should like to believe" his father a suicide. According to the tradition of the family, a Moore would prefer to fall rather than to yield, and he fell, seemingly unable to survive the opening skirmish of the frightful economic warfare that was to be the curse of his native bogs for the next half century. His Ascendancy neighbors pointedly declined to attend his funeral.

George Moore the novelist was born shortly after the crisis of the famine, and he was thus the first substantial fruit of his father's serious phase. His childhood spanned the period when his father was gradually drifting back to his old sporting passion for horseflesh. Like many children in the families of the gentry, the boy was subjected alternately to tyrannical discipline and to no discipline at all, with anarchy winning out at last, and lapses into strictness occurring just often enough to sweeten the value of his freedom. His mother had learned from observing the family life of her class that when females of the Irish gentry attempted to guide the males, either sons or husbands, they commonly produced results the opposite of those hoped for. Accordingly she relied upon the warmth of her affection as her one means of exercising family control and made no effort to mold her children by sternness. When George announced as a boy that he had decided to take up atheism, the expected explosion did not occur, and his mother merely observed dryly that she was sorry. In manhood George felt free to report to her on his adventures, real or imaginary, with mistresses. Yet hope was not abandoned that George might be made respectable, and sporadically his father or some schoolmaster took up the task of trying to shape him into some conventional pattern.

The boy was mostly left to range as he pleased, bringing out the Moore Hall hounds to hunt and kill the laundry cat; boating up and down Lough Carra for months on end, rowed by two peasants, fishing for eels; jumping his pony over the stone walls into the peasants' gardens. Once when his father's horse, Croagh Patrick, was entered in the Goodwood, George was left with the wife of the stable trainer for many weeks, forgotten, as he later claimed, by his parents in the excitement of the race, which Croagh Patrick won at odds of forty to one. Occasionally he was snatched out of his delightful idleness and ordered off to school, sometimes with the parish priest, sometimes to Birmingham, where he attended Oscott, the Catholic school for boys. George remembered his hatred for Oscott for forty years and finally unburdened himself in one of the most memorable chapters of *Hail and Farewell*. The father was much shamed by the boy's obstinacy and lack of progress, and he eventually had to face the fact that Oscott was not for George. Amid a minor scandal having to do with George's childish advances to an Oscott kitchen maid, he was hurriedly taken home. Once again he became his own master, dividing his time between Mayo and London, where his father had again been returned to the House of Commons.

"At Moore Hall," he recalled in old age, "there was no life except the life of the stable-yard, and to it I went with the same appetite with which I went to the life of the studio afterwards; if I had remained at Moore Hall I certainly should have ridden many steeplechases, and perhaps succeeded in doing what my father failed to do," that is, to win the Liverpool.[3] In London

11

he passed his time in elaborate surreptitious betting on the races and in idling about the music halls, the taverns, and such gay resorts as the Cremorne Gardens. One day his father discovered a picture of a girl in tights among the boy's things lying about the house. He determined to get him at once into military school, a gentleman's last hope for dealing with wayward sons. Unlike Victor Hugo, who had said:

> *J'ai des rêves de guerre en mon âme inquiète;*
> *J'aurais été soldat, si je n'étais poète,*

George was not attracted to military glory. He was sullenly awaiting the military examinations when his father left London on his last trip to Moore Hall, and his father's death instantly closed his incipient military career.

These years brought George Moore to manhood equipped principally with innocence, ignorance, and independence. He was totally uneducated. Except for his familiarity with a few "atheistical" poems of Shelley, he was devoid of the slightest knowledge of the world of art and letters in which all of his mature years were to be spent. He came "straight from his father's racing stables," said Yeats contemptuously, "from a house where there was no culture as Symons and I understood the word." [4] Moore was never to regret either the racing stables or the lack of "culture," but thought of them as necessary links in his destiny, superior for him to the orthodox routes to self-realization.

The most striking trait of his childhood had been his slowness, and particularly his slowness in articulation. He was slow to talk, slow to read, hopelessly slow in school. In the family his utter want of precocity was thought shameful, and among his acquaintances in later years it occasioned much merriment. Oscar Wilde struck off more than one epigram on the subject. It was an error, however, when his acquaintances interpreted his slowness to be mere stupidity. Moore himself correctly considered it his special strength, even though he was forced first to discover the word, then the sentence, and at last, at forty, after he had become a world-famous writer, the paragraph. It was the source of a genuinely innocent outlook given only to those whose education begins at absolute zero with the rapt discovery of the obvious. All that he ever knew, as Rebecca West once observed, was what he had found out for himself.

When George was thirteen his father commanded him to improve his spelling by writing a three-page letter home from Oscott each day. The fruits of this effort were preserved in the Moore family records and brought to light three-quarters of a century later. What reader of Hone's biography can pass by the letters without being startled at the extraordinary vividness of the child's individuality?

> Keep my pocket money if you will but dont keep me here during the vac I am sure that if I could only see you half an hour that I could convince you that I could not writ that letter of three pages besides my writing is much smaller than yours and I write much closer together than yours this letter will fill up twice as much space if I write wider apart I have made a great deel of improvement in spelling since mid-summer do not be cross with me any more I will soon know how to spill perfectly the wood cocks must have been plentiful for you to shoot so many I am sure you will change your mind and take me home next summer just you try and write a letter every day and you wont find it so easy.[5]

In punctuation and spelling this lad had much to learn, but he could have been thought stupid only by insensitive persons.

George was eighteen when his father's sudden death made him his own master forever. He found himself in possession of an income of about five hundred pounds, a mere fraction of what Moore Hall had once yielded but quite enough to provide an adolescent with a jolly time. He announced that he had no intention of trying to manage the desperately encumbered property, and he declared himself to be henceforth a landlord of the absentee variety. The unpleasant burdens of the landlord's lot, the haggling, the threats, the evictions, were dumped into the lap of his uncle Joe Blake, who was instructed not to consult, or even to inform, the young owner on the problems arising out of the affairs of the property. Immediately after his father's funeral he bade county Mayo adieu and hurried back to London. If the perplexed father had thought of Moore Hall as a "paradise" where he might build tabernacles for himself in this world, the son could not. His mother, he said, "would have liked to linger by her husband's grave a little while, but I gave her no peace, urging the fact upon her that sooner or later we should have to go back to London. Why delay, mother? We cannot spend our lives here going to Kiltoome with flowers." [6]

For the next decade, Moore Hall held no interest for young George, who had now discovered Art and felt the unhappiness of youth. When he had uttered "a cry for Art," his cousin Jim Browne, an eccentric painter of gigantic melodramatic canvases, had told him that the place to seek Art was Paris. Immediately upon reaching his majority he set out for Paris and commenced his education, which was to begin in a stodgy and philistine painter's studio and conclude in the cafés of Montmartre, where he would sit bewitched by the voluminous passionate talk of French writers and painters. He visited his mother at Moore Hall occasionally, but otherwise Ireland in the 1870's was merely a distant abstract source of income, not worth the attention of the new devotee of art.

In 1880 his Parisian idyll was interrupted by an "odious" letter from Joe Blake in county Mayo, announcing that financial disaster had come to Moore Hall. Letters from his manager had always produced a sensation of repugnance in him, even when he knew "the envelope contained a cheque." [7] This letter announced that there would be no more cheques. Blake could not collect the current rents. The peasants had once again, as at the time of the death of George Henry Moore, refused to pay rent until a new reduction had been granted by the landlords. Blake's letter also demanded payment of three thousand pounds advanced to Moore against future rents, now found to be uncollectible; he asserted that he no longer intended to risk assassination

14

trying to administer Moore Hall affairs and that he was forthwith handing all responsibilities back to the owner.

The traumatic shock of Blake's letter was the most memorable experience of Moore's life. *Confessions of a Young Man* describes him sitting at the breakfast table of his Montmartre apartment, holding the "odious epistle" in his hand and crying: "That some wretched farmers and miners should refuse to starve, that I may not be deprived of my demi-tasse at Tortoni's; that I may not be forced to leave this beautiful retreat, my cat and my python—monstrous." [8] This is the most famous of all Moorisms and the most frequently misunderstood. It does indeed, as anyone can see, assert an immorality. At the same time, however, it denies its own proposition, the denial arising in the self-mockery of an overassertion couched in the style of a provocateur in the enemy's pay. The statement is a genuine ambiguity, asserting a genuine contradiction. It does not, however, "master reality," as ambiguous constructs are sometimes thought to do. It was Moore himself who was mastered; and the contradiction, being stubborn and importunate, refused to dissolve in the magical flux of the verbalization which acknowledged its existence.

From Paris Moore wrote his uncle a bewildered reply: "The question of the tenants refusing to pay any rent is terrible. What does it mean Communism? If I have never looked into my business at all events I have never committed any follies. I never spent more than five hundred a year and I was told when I came into the properties I had ever so much." [9] He packed up and went home to Moore Hall. He found another agent and rode out with him to the tenants' cabins to listen to complaints about "watery potatoes" and to negotiate new rent agreements. Eventually he put his affairs into a sort of shape, and once again he bade Ireland adieu. Convinced that he was but one step from the workhouse, he went up to London and set about grimly to earn his living as a writer, peddling to the London publishing market the literary oddments he had picked up in Parisian cafés.

In London his latent attitudes toward Ireland began to move

15

toward articulation. He declared himself to be possessed of a violent loathing for Ireland and Irishmen, and he proceeded to express himself on the subject in language of rare savor, echoing the untempered verbalization of such a masterful Celtophobe as Swinburne. An understanding of Moore's mission in art begins with an examination of these first shrill declarations about the place of his birth, the source of his income, and the home of his distinguished forebears.

Joe Blake's letter flashed upon Moore's mind a lurid vision of the extinction of the landlord class in apocalyptic holocaust. He began to annoy his family and neighbors with a tireless reiteration of his opinion that the landlords of Ireland were doomed, that nothing could save them, that they should instantly capitulate and accept whatever terms the peasants chose to offer. As we now know, his prediction was slightly alarmist. When Moore Hall was finally broken up many years later, a government subsidy shielded him from loss, and he died a wealthier man than his father. Still, the over-all soundness of his vision was supported by historical fact, whose unfolding gave him continual, if sardonic, satisfaction. Proof of the accuracy of his foresight did not, however, fully assuage his own discomfiture at being caught up in the common fate of his class; indeed, it intensified his own sense of danger. He "sought refuge in art," to use his favorite phrase, pursuing a hope that he might recover, in some more permanent form, values that were being rapidly extinguished before his eyes.

Moore's predicament as an Irish landlord was the source of an uncommonly blunt contradiction in his view of his own share of human freedom. On the one hand he insisted that he was a person marked by no prejudices or commitments. "I may say that I am free from original qualities, defects, tastes," says the well-known opening of *Confessions of a Young Man*. He believed that as a writer his special virtue was "disinterestedness." This is a claim that many readers would instinctively reject in any case, particularly when made by the last heir of so distinctive a family in so critical a time. His feeling was not baseless, however, but was a tribute to Moore Hall for affording him so powerful a *sense* of freedom, his most valuable inheritance next to his father's property. The great squire's eldest son, whose boyish whims might annoy a thousand Moore Hall peasant families, necessarily grew up to be a very stubborn, unsuggestible, and "free" observer. But in another sense, as he understood, he was not free at all. His imagination never broke out of the spell of the nightmare which began when he opened Joe Blake's fateful letter. When that memory returned, he veered around to the position of an absolute determinist, and he would argue that life was without either choice or the chance of alleviation. This opinion arose out of his vision of the Irish gentry moving to their destined ruin without possible interruption by any conceivable act of will, intellect, or passion. "I foresaw a disaster," he said to his brother, "and I don't think anything can be done to avert what has to happen." Even the gift of prevision appeared to be a curse, "for it does not enable you to steer a better course." In this mood he would see art as the only surviving value; for life was only to be lived when transfigured into patterns and arabesques for leisured contemplation, patterns of preordained destinies slowly evolved in languid action against a bland and somber setting.

In spite of much offensive talk, Moore was actually not a bad landlord. His tenants and their problems bored him, but he was no more given to ruthless action than his father had been. He was unwilling to evict tenants; and though he once cried: "Oh that I had, or my father had, evicted like the others in '49," he had not acted upon the wish. He was not particularly disliked by county Mayo peasants until his old age, when his anticlerical opinions were resented; and, unlike his neighbors, he did not call for a war of extermination against rent defaulters. He went to Connaught on many trips during the Land War between landlords and tenants in 1880 and 1881, but he never thought it necessary to carry arms for protection. He was endangered only once, when a bridge collapsed under him as he rode his horse across a creek. The piers had been sawed off by moonlighters, but apparently Moore was not the intended victim.

Moore's sense of identity with his own class was by no means perfect. The snubs his father had received from fellow landlords were remembered and repaid. He asserted that the Irish gentry had "dirty teeth," and that his neighbors' "brogue" offended his ear. He deplored the restriction of their interests to "the foinest harses in the harse show," and he attributed to them the belief that Richard Wagner was a race horse. But as a rent collector he could not clearly disentangle his position from that of the rest of the gentry. When he predicted the extinction of the Irish landlords he understood that he would no more be spared than any other. *A Drama in Muslin,* his first novel about the Irish scene, depicts the breakup of the gentry in terms that might have described the scattering of George Henry Moore's sons: "An entire race, a whole caste, [was] driven out of their soft, warm couches of idleness, and forced into the struggle for life. The prospect appalled them. . . . What could they do with their empty brains?" [10] Alice Barton comes, in the same novel, to "see something wrong" in the society of which she is a part, where each "big house" is surrounded, like Moore Hall, by a hundred little ones "all working to keep it in sloth and luxury." Moore's conviction of his social guilt was confessed more baldly in *Parnell and His Island:* "I see the square white houses of the landlords gleaming at the end of the vistas—handsome square white houses —each is surrounded with a hundred or so of filthy tenements that Providence and God have decreed shall unite to keep the master in affluence and ease." [11] The "master" was, of course, George Moore himself. In one passage Moore attacked himself in the revolutionary phrases of the Land League:

> The socialist axiom that capital is only a surplus-value coming from unpaid labor, either in the past or in the present, is in other countries mitigated and lost sight of in the multiplicity of ways through which money passes before falling into the pockets of the

rich; but in Ireland the passage direct and brutal of money from the horny hands of the peasant to the delicate hands of the proprietor is terribly suggestive of serfdom. In England the landlord lays out the farm and builds the farm buildings. In Ireland he does absolutely nothing. He gives the bare land to the peasant, and sends his agent to collect the half-yearly rent; in a word, he allows the peasant to keep him in ease and luxury. . . .

In Ireland every chicken eaten, every glass of champagne drunk, every silk dress trailed in the street, every rose worn at a ball, comes straight out of the peasant's cabin. . . .

. . . this plague-spot is apparent today to every eye; it is visible everywhere, even in the heart of the slums as in the most elegant suburb; it was as if a veil had been drawn revealing the boils with which the flesh of Ireland is covered.

He understood that the Land League had arisen out of the peasants' unbearable hardships, to which he was contributing no less than his fellow landlords. "Suddenly, without warning, the scales fell from the eyes of the people, and the people resolved to rid themselves of this plague," [12] he said, using the most original language ever penned by an unreconstructed landlord on the agrarian question.

In all of Moore's dozens of novels, reminiscences, and essays, no such candor on this subject ever appeared again. It is an invaluable revelation, exposing in one lucid unguarded moment the fearful dilemma of his inheritance. The testament concluded:

I am an Irish landlord, I have done this, and I shall continue to do this, for it is as impossible for me as for the rest of my clan to do otherwise; but that doesn't prevent me from recognizing the fact that it is a worn out system, no longer possible in the nineteenth century, and one whose end is nigh.

Moore's wordly-wise detachment was not rigorously maintained. A few pages farther in the same volume we find him unfilially complaining that his mother's claim against his father's estate had to be paid before he could draw his own income, and denouncing as "unjust" the provision of the Land Act of 1881 which reduced rent without reducing interest. "Is it possible," he asked in dismay, "that the entire upper class of a country will be deprived of all its worldly goods and turned adrift out on the world to starve, and that we shall soon have a country composed exclusively of peasants?" [13]

A country composed exclusively of peasants would have been, according to his viewpoint, considerably worse than the Ireland of the Protestant Ascendancy. His contempt for himself and for his neighbors among the gentry was vigorous but measured; his language grew more extraordinary when he turned to contemplate the Irish peasant:

> Mickey Moran is a strong-built man of forty-five; a pair of corduroy trousers, a frieze coat, a dark discolored skin with scanty whiskers, a snub nose, blue eyes set deep under a low forehead, receding temples, and square-set jaws. His face is expressive of meanness, sullenness, stupidity; he is obviously nearer the earth than the Saxon; he reminds me of some low earth-animal whose nature has not yet risen from the soil. He is evidently of a degenerate race—a race that has been left behind—and should perish, like the black rat perished before the brown and more ferocious species. Mickey is not a Celt, he is a Fin. Ages ago the Fins were defeated by the Celts and driven into the outlying districts of Connaught; there they should have died, but owing to their extraordinary power of reproduction they are now making headway against superior races.

Not that the Celt made a much better peasant. "The Celt," he observed, "is a savage, eminently fitted for cattle-lifting, but ill suited to ply the industry of farming." The idyll continued in the same vein:

> Down in the wet below the edge of the bog lies the village. The cabins . . . are not so large as a railway carriage. And in these dens a whole family, a family consisting of husband and wife, grandfather and grandmother, and from eight to ten children herd together as best they can. . . . At each doorway there is a dungheap in which a pig wallows. . . . The interior . . . is a dark place from which exudes a stink; a stink which the inmates describe as a warm smell! . . . A large pig, covered with lice, feeds out of a trough placed in the middle of the floor. . . .[14]

When Joe Blake's letter called Moore home, he appeared in county Mayo in Parisian *artiste* regalia, and for several days he went about the countryside chattering in French and implying that he had lost the English tongue. *Parnell and His Island* described his return: suddenly there "appears a singular individual. . . . His tiny hat, his long hair, his Parisian-cut clothes and his Capoul-like beard gave him a very strange air. . . . On the boulevard he might pass muster, but where he stands he is *un être de féerie.* . . ."[15] The contrast between Montmartre and county Mayo was staggering, and he added to his description of the Irish countryside and its peasant "inmates" a last definitive detail: "Never have I observed in these people the slightest aesthetic intention."

Moore's sense of separation from the Irish peasant was perhaps not exclusively aesthetic in origin. When George Henry Moore was alive, the peasants walking along the country roads would tip their tall Irish hats to the carriage from the big house, shouting "Long life to yer honor!" But after the Land League agitation started, the custom was supplanted by arson, boycotting, and moonlighting. "I was born in Irish feudalism," Moore said wistfully in old age, "and my world is over and done." There had been a time when the Irish gentry were kings; it was Moore's destiny to witness their dissolution and to see the bottom rail on top.

> . . . we often sundered wife and husband, sister from brother; and often drove away a whole village to America if it pleased us to grow beef and mutton for the English market. . . . I remember one day up in the mountains while grouse-shooting stabling my horse in a man's cabin. But we shall never be able to do it again. The landlords have had their day. We are a disappearing class, our lands are being confiscated, and our houses are decaying or being pulled down to build cottages for the folk. All that was has gone or is going.[16]

As Moore watched this change, his irony and his detached melancholy would sometimes desert him and it would be difficult to distinguish his reaction from that of his less sophisticated neighbors. "In the mist and mud of the slum," he wrote darkly, "plots and counterplots were hatched [against the landlords] and, breaking their shells, they emerged like reptiles into a terrible and multiform existence; out of the slime they crawled in strange and formless confusion." [17] As the Bartons' carriage in *A Drama in Muslin* passed through the countryside, it met "surly" peasants with "obtuse brain," and here and there as it moved through the dusk one could see "in a doorway full of yellow light the form of a man often sketched in menacing black." In his opinion the achievement of Parnell and Davitt was to elevate murder to a fine art and repudiation of debt into a cardinal virtue.

> Murder and repudiation of debt, such is the doctrine of the League, and insidiously in veiled phrases, in euphemisms of all sorts, the doctrine is preached at land meetings and brooded over, as we have seen, by the cottage fireside. Imagine the ferment produced by these teachings in the minds of a primitive people—and worse than primitive, a people in a retrograde state. Imagine the disintegration of all simple associations of belief, the discarding of all familiar ideas and usages; it is as if the fiber and nerve of a body were destroyed, pus oozes, and the gases of decay are exhaled, and all the phenomena of dissolution begin—such was Ireland in 1882.[18]

The same statement observed that the past was "holier, purer, and fitter," and uncorrupted by "deceptions and changes."

The Irish politician seemed to have degenerated since the days when George Henry Moore sat in the House of Commons. The patrician had now stepped aside for the peasant, "a little sharper than his cousins who remain in the Western bogs . . . but he is cunning, selfish, cruel, even as they. . . . In London this half-animal . . . is bewildered . . . the low peasant nature ferments, and the foul imaginings of gross gratifications bubble and burst in his brain. . . ." Moore stalked this new politician in his rounds of the fleshpots of London, saw him sicken with "the strong perfume of gardenias" in "nostrils filled with the rank smell of the dungheap, the pig, the damp cabin"; and Moore concluded that to make the pleasures of life available to such a nature was equivalent to attempting "to feed a hyena on chocolate creams." [19]

The Irishman's religion had also grown more formidable and sinister in Moore's eyes. Church and country were always inseparable in his mind; and the two dominant notes of his character, as announced in *Confessions of a Young Man,* were the twin sentiments, "an original hatred of my native country, and a brutal loathing of the religion I was brought up in." The identification, more exactly stated, was between church and peasant, the two forming in his mind an image of ignorance wedded to filth. He was inclined to attribute the successes of the Land League to the support of meddlesome village priests, the imputation being that the church had deserted the landlords in their crisis and thrown its support to the peasants out of a cynical wish to be on the winning side. The "fat priest" thus appears in the early Irish sketches as a sort of villain and conspirator. Though sometimes reluctant, the priest blesses the tenants' rallies, speaks in incendiary phrases about "loosing the dogs of war," preaches that murder is justifiable on the grounds that "self-preservation is the first law of the land," and generally compounds Mickey Moran's felonies. Tenant conspiracies were plotted under the sheltering walls of the village churchyard. Cromwell, Moore decided, was right: "Catholicism is eunuch-like, dirty, and oriental. . . . Look at the nations that have clung to Catholicism, starving moonlighters and starving brigands." [20]

Peasant and church were obsessively connected in his mind with an image of sputum. He insisted that the priest of the chapel at Ardrahan had spat upon Edward Martyn's carpet at dinner in Tillyra castle; he depicted a gathering of priests on the curb in Dublin solemnly discussing spitting as a problem of every parish; and in *Parnell and His Island* his apprenticeship to Zola led him to compose this account of the peasants' attendance at Mass:

> The peasant women wrapped in their long black cloaks are bent double over the pews; their thin, long yellow hands extended beyond

23

their faces clutch a rosary feverishly; some of the men are down on their hands and knees grovelling, some kneel with straight backs, chins lifted, breasts advanced—poses that recall those of martyred saints; they groan, they strike their breasts, their hearts are full of the gross superstition of the moment, they address God in the coarse language of the cabin; out of their torn shirts, revealing the beast-like hair of their breasts, rises the rancid sweat of the fields; and the sour smells of frieze and the heavy earthy smells of the cabin are as an almost palpable dust in the intense morning light as it flows through the windows. They cough and groan as they pray, and the spittle splashes on the floor.

All this verbal ferocity was easily expandable into a kindred statement about mankind in general. Moore, as is well known, declared himself possessed of a fierce disdain for all humanitarianism, and indeed for humanity, too. His declaration, however, was cast in the form of a Moorism stating his conviction in satanic rhetoric so violent that it cast ridicule and doubt upon itself:

> Humanity be hanged! Men of inferior genius, Victor Hugo and Mr. Gladstone take refuge in it. Humanity is a pigsty, where liars, hypocrites, and the obscene in spirit congregate; it has been so since the great Jew conceived it, and it will be so till the end. Far better the blithe modern pagan in his white tie and evening clothes, and his facile philosophy. He says, "I don't care how the poor live; my only regret is that they live at all"; and he gives the beggar a shilling.[21]

A fusion of his repugnance for the "stench" of "the cant of human humanitarianism" with his fear of "the blind, inchoate, insatiate Mass," led him to a denunciation of pity, "that most vile of all virtues," and of justice: "Hail, therefore, to the thrice glorious virtue injustice. . . . I say that all we deem sublime in the world's history are acts of injustice; and it is certain that if mankind does not relinquish at once, and for ever, its vain, mad, and fatal dream of justice, the world will lapse into barbarism." The twentieth century, he said, would be a century of darkness because it would be an age of pity and justice. It would suspend the "terrible austere laws of nature which ordain that the weak shall be trampled upon, shall be ground into death and dust, that the strong shall be really strong,—that the strong shall be glorious, sublime." [22] The same view survived his youth and persisted into his old age, when he predicted that fifty years after his time "men will hang like pears on every lamp-post, in every great quarter of London there will be an electric guillotine that will decapitate the rich like hogs in Chicago . . . and blood shall cover the face of the earth." And he added, the elderly little Irish man of letters speaking out of Pimlico the words of Louis XV, "I laugh, I rub my hands. I shall be dead before the red tide comes." [23]

This melodrama is in part half-hidden farce, a mummery plagiarized out of Montmartre, where the invention of spooks for the astonishment of philistines was a fixed local custom. And yet the figure of the worried landlord of Moore Hall cannot be totally erased from the reader's impression of these passages. The humanitarianism that Mr. Gladstone was "taking refuge in" was embodied in his Home Rule Bill for Ireland, which seemed to promise the abandonment of the Irish gentry to the fury of the Irish peasant. The word "justice" was much used in Land League pamphlets and oratory: "Hail, therefore, to the thrice glorious virtue injustice." Balzac had observed in *Les Paysans* that there was a *"conspiration permanente de ceux que nous appelons encore les faibles contre ceux qui se croisent les forts, du paysan contre le riche"*; converted into Moorism: Mickey Moran should understand that "the weak" were created "to be trampled upon," not to annoy the "strong," though hard-pressed, young squire and aesthete called home from Paris by a rent strike.

Moore saw Dublin as only a wretched provincial capital where the ugliness of the peasant, politician, and church was brought into full evil flower. His favorite metaphor of the time envisioned Dublin as a body covered with sores. "The castle is the head, the Shelbourne Hotel the body, the Kildare Street Club and Mrs. Rushville's [dressmaking shop] the members of the miserable creature that is called Dublin Society." The Ascendancy cringed in Dublin behind barred entry doors. "Today it trembles with sullen fear, and listens to the savage howling of the pack [of Fenians and Land Leaguers]." As Gladstone's program for Home Rule grew stronger, "the barking springs to meet him; the fierce teeth are heard upon the woodwork. Will he lift the latch and let the hounds rush in on the obscene animal?" [24] Dubliners, like their "dirty city," wore unintermittently a "look of melancholy silliness." In Dublin he saw the dreary images that Joyce was to immortalize a generation later: "the weary, the woebegone, the threadbare streets," "melancholy Merrion Square," "broken pavements, unpainted hall doors, rusty area railings." He sighed: "how infinitely pitiful." [25]

Pitiful, but also loathsome; wistfully sad, yet repulsive. He was guilty with the rest of the gentry; yet he was victimized by his victims. As a pamphleteer he could talk about the "rat-faced peasants"; but as a novelist he could achieve no such ferocity. The low-born characters of his novels have no resemblance to the more abject targets of Huysmans' or Maupassant's hatreds, nor to Mickey Moran. He saw clearly that the peasants' objectives were reasonable; yet he felt them to be very wrong. His writings about Ireland in the 1880's showed him to be, in short, confronted by a hopeless intellectual and emotional impasse. This fact he recognized, and, with his characteristic bland shamelessness, he called his readers' attention to his confusion. But he suggested that the chaos could be unscrambled in one way: by retreat into the quiet stillness of art. Summarizing the schizophrenic tone of *Parnell and His Island*, he said:

> Ireland is a bog, and the aborigines [the Fins] are a degenerate race—short, squat little men—with low foreheads and wide jaws. But the bog, its heather and desolation, and the Fins in their hovels and dirt are as good a subject for brush or pen as an English village clustered round a green—red roofs showing against the foliage of the elms, rows of great sunflowers flaring in the gardens, and quaint windows overgrown with roses.
>
> Picturesque comfort or picturesque misery, *l'un vaut l'autre* in art, and I sought the picturesque independent of landlords and Land

Leaguers; whether one picture is cognate in political feeling with the one that preceded it I care not a jot; indeed, I would wish each to be evocative of dissimilar impressions, and the whole to produce the blurred and uncertain effect of nature herself. Where the facts seem to contradict, I let them contradict.[26]

A careful searcher might discover, even amidst Irish ugliness, places of refuge and rest, that is, of beauty. In the 1880's Moore spent a few days as the guest of Lord Ardilaun, the great Dublin brewer, in his Victorian-Gothic castle at Cong, not far from Moore Hall. Moore's younger brother Julian wondered whether a fortune built on ale and stout was to be admired, but Moore rebuked his sauciness and added: "I crack the Ardilauns up to the skies." *Parnell and His Island* devoted a chapter to the visit. "This strangely beautiful castle," he said, "renders me singularly happy."

> To awake in the cool spaces of a bedroom, beautiful and bright with Indian curtains, and musical with the rippling sound of the lake's billow, is also full of gracious charm and delicate suggestion of poetry to him who is alive to the artistic requirements of today. . . . Here we are almost shut out of the storm and gloom of crime and poverty that enfolds the land.

There had been a cruise down Lough Corrib on Lord Ardilaun's yacht, and, as Moore warmed to the job of describing it, the germ of his famous later style appeared for the first time in his writings:

> The day is breathless, but the sky is full of a soft grey light; and in the fairy-like silences of the lake, when nothing is heard between the pauses of the conversation but the ripple of the water along the vessel's side, and the subdued panting of the machine, the many aspects of this noble wilderness, the wild outlines of the guardian mountains, the dark promontories covered with rough wood, the marshy shores where the heron stalks, arise as supernaturally still and calm as the visions of an Icelandic god, and in the exquisite clarity every detail is visible; the shadows of the pines fall like ink into the smooth mirror. . . .
>
> The scene is now supernaturally still. The day dies in pale greys and soft pink tints, and harmonies in mauve more delicate and elusive than

27

the most beautiful Japanese water-color; the lake hangs like a grey veil behind the dark pine-woods through which we wander, making our way to the yacht; and at the vistas we look on the long wavy lines of mountains that enclose the horizon, and they seem now like women sleeping the sleep of enchantment, and the mountains whose precipitous bases rise out of the lake are as fabulous creatures in a northern legend guarding the solitude. Our eyes follow the black flight of the cormorant along the smooth greyness of the water, and our souls are filled and stilled with sadness that is at one with the knowledge that the dear day we have lived through is now a day that is over and done. . . .[27]

Moore felt an urgent emotional need to bring the "graciousness" of Lord Ardilaun's castle to Moore Hall, where the cows left their droppings on the gravel walk beneath his great-grandfather's Latin inscription. With substantial sums of money, Moore Hall might have been made adequate to his needs; without it, fantasy offered the more ready solution. Joyce said that the shortest way to Tara was via Holyhead; and Moore fell into the habit of staying away from the Moore Hall of actuality and of dwelling constantly in the Moore Hall of his imagination. "My dreaming house," he called it, and it provided him, once he learned how to exploit it, with an unfailing cue for nostalgic evocation of "the sadness of ruined things" and the mood of the past, in which his imagination would be increasingly immersed.

In 1923 terrorists of the Irish Republican Army burned Moore Hall in an act of reprisal directed, ironically enough, not against the author of *Parnell and His Island* but against his patriotic brother, Senator Maurice Moore. Although Moore had not troubled himself to visit county Mayo for years, and although the Irish Free State underwrote the fire loss with generosity, the news of the fire was a staggering shock. "The burning of Moore Hall," he said a year later, "affected me more deeply than anything else could, more than anything I thought could; it has gone to the roots." [28] At other times before and after the burning, he was more insistent to state his hatred of Ireland, no longer a "gentleman's country" but a "swamp of peasants with a priest here and there," a land devoting itself to the "exaltation of sacraments and whiskey," its legislators "united only in protecting monkeries and nunneries from secular inquisition." [29]

> Today is the life of the peasant,
> But the past is a haven of rest—
> The things of the past are the best.

So he wrote when poetically moved. And looking into the future he sadly envisaged the destruction of the last remaining vestiges of the Ireland of the Penal Law days, which very few other writers have been sufficiently audacious to pronounce "the greatest epoch" of all Irish history.

The excessiveness of this attitude is obvious enough, perhaps too obvious. Its real point was sometimes lost in the commotion it created. For Moore's blustering verbalizations mask a profound duplexity in his reaction toward Ireland. Moore, like Joyce after him, did not part company with his homeland painlessly. But he did reject all its ambitions. He foresaw that the separatist movement—for which his great-uncle and his father spent wasted lives—would in its turn beget ironies not then clearly perceived by its adherents. And he scornfully renounced the fatal lures of Irish sentimentalism, whose emotions and ideas he simply inverted to create his own unpatriotic rhetoric.

The Parisian

My dear Mama, I cannot I am sorry to say pay you a visit at Christmas. I am working so hard that I have not time. I have only one bit of news. I am completely changed.
—George Moore to his mother, from Paris, 1875

ACCOMPANIED BY a "savage," a peasant valet called in from the potato patches of Moore Hall, George Moore arrived in Paris in the early spring of 1873, only a few days after his coming of age. He had not yet formed any particular shape. "I developed upward from the sponge," he said, and his progress along the scale of human evolution was altogether leisurely. When he first saw Paris he was not without predilections, but they drew him in the direction of nihilism and drifting as a principle of behavior. His clearest commitment was to the precept *non serviam;* hence he was potentially fitted to become another Prince Kropotkin or James Joyce, had talent and chance so decreed. Paris formed his protoplasm into another shape. The amorphous Irish squire became the George Moore of history as he sat listening to café talk, absorbing his education by osmosis from Parisian painters and writers.

His immediate Parisian mission was to search for art, "art" meaning to the twenty-one-year-old lad the activities, professional and personal, of his cousin Jim Browne, who painted large crowded canvases with rare empathic verve. Once Moore found him at work in his London studio on a picture called "Cain Shielding His Wife from Wild Beasts" and stood nearby to watch the mystery of artistic creation:

All the beasts in the picture were roaring, Jim roared in accompaniment, while whirling a mass of vermillion and white upon his palette; and then, uttering a deep growl, he would rush forward and a red tongue would appear; and when he had mixed emerald green with white he would advance some paces, cat-like, and then, snarling, would leap forward, and a moment after a great green eye started out of the darkness.[1]

A man of energy and talent, Moore decided, but unfortunately born in the wrong place at the wrong time, in county Mayo at the beginning of Victorian times. To the boy, Browne's life seemed voluptuous and seductive, and Moore never forgot the day Browne showed him a six-foot-by-four-foot painting of a satyr capturing a nymph in a wood. "My eyes dilated and I licked my lips," and shortly afterward he was in Paris searching for a studio that would undertake to teach him to paint.

Seven years passed between Moore's arrival in Paris and the time when the "odious epistle" called him home at the commencement of the Land War in Mayo. Most of these years were spent in following what seemed at the time to be blind alleys and misadventures with humdrum minds and inferior talents. Much time was lost in attempting to paint under many different teachers, mostly in Paris, but including an unexciting session making charcoal sketches of plaster casts at South Kensington. He concluded one day that he was without talent as a painter. Humiliated to tears, he put away his brushes and resolved never to take them up again, convinced that his years of dabbling in studios must be written off as a total loss. This was a hasty judgment, for the knowledge gained had prepared him for his future role as the "highest paid critic of painting in England," besides sharpening his pictorial eye and giving him a number of characters and incidents for future novels. More energy and money were wasted in trying to nurse the talent of a young English painter named Lewis Weldon Hawkins, whose flashy knack was mistaken for genius. Hawkins never arrived, and, when Moore discovered that his taste was incorrect and passé, he abruptly dropped him. Again he was to recover on his investment by exploiting Hawkins as a character in two novels and a play and as an important background figure in the autobiographies.

For a time Moore's artistic life in Paris seems to have been overshadowed by the pursuit of rather exalted social ambitions. His letters home spoke of his closeness to princesses and countesses, hinting that he had been favored in ways not called for by the usual social courtesies. He wrote to his mother:

> I was at the famous Princess Ratazzi masked ball the other day they are the most famous things in Paris. Her hotel is something wonderful and she spends between sixty and eighty thousand francs on a fete they are something extraordinary in their splendour.

Later he reported more exciting triumphs:

> I am playing my cards now to become the lover of the Marquise d'Osmond, she is very swell if not very young but I don't mind that (I mean the latter). The first thing a young man who wants to get on in Paris must do is to get under the wings of some lady with a good name and in a high position that done with tact he can wriggle himself anywhere.[2]

He wrote of having poisoned himself *"avec les reveries,"* enervating like a deadly intoxicating flower *"exquise et sinistre";* this enigmatic statement may have referred to his dining twice a week with the Duchesse de la Tremoïlle at her "most select" dinners, where "everyone speaks with the sweet Racine elegance, that exquisite choice of expression."

Moore did not stumble upon the outer fringes of the magic circle of Parisian art and letters until he had been several years in Paris. Late in 1875 he made the acquaintance of a playwright by the name of Bernard Lopez, who had written a hundred and sixty plays and collaborated with more than a hundred writers, according to Moore's interesting tally. He had collaborated with Hugo, Gérard de Nerval, and even Gautier, "the master himself." Lopez had not been notably successful in subduing Paris and was ready to try an assault upon London. He imagined that the brash young Irishman might be used to gain access to the English stage, while Moore on his part hoped that his acquaintance with Lopez might lead to more profitable French connections. The two began to take their meals together, and schemes for their joint efforts were proposed.

One day in the Café du Rat Mort they found a "dishevelled and wild-eyed fellow," a friend of Lopez who turned out to be Villiers de l'Isle-Adam. Villiers told Moore that he ought to know Mallarmé and gave him a note of introduction. Mallarmé introduced him to Manet, who in turn led him to the Café de la Nouvelle Athènes, a nightly gathering place for impressionist painters, naturalistic novelists, and Parnassian poets. There he met Degas, whose well-known painting, "L'Absinthe," depicts the terrace of the Nouvelle Athènes. Shortly before leaving Paris in 1880 he met Zola, who later introduced him to Edmond Goncourt, Daudet, Heredia, and Turgenev. Moore's entrance into this esteemed company was apparently made in late 1877, and his association with it occupied the last three years of his seven-year stay in Paris.

Now his letters home dwelt upon the contrast between the elegant life in the salon of the Duchesse de la Tremoïlle and his concurrent life in Montmartre. He wrote his mother:

> Sometimes if I get away early I go to a low artists cafe, where with my two elbows on the beer-stained [table] I scream the beastliest and slangiest french to groups of bohemians.[3]

This was the pose that Manet's pencil caught in his famous drawing of Moore slouched over his beer glass in the café. At the moment, however, Moore was not so much concerned with having achieved that immortality as with the insecurity and excitement of "climbing up and down the social ladder" between Montmartre and the Champs Elysées and living in two compartmentalized worlds. Philosophically he observed to his mother: "There is such an abime between the two," and he hoped that "the low society I have so much cultivated has not spoiled me."[4]

The time would come when he would not be at all averse to standing in the reflected glow of his great French contemporaries.

Paris in the seventies had a world to offer the curious young Irishman. In later years Moore was to speak of his time in Paris as the "wonderful seventies," betraying the foreigner's viewpoint. Frenchmen, as Joseph Hone has pointed out, were inclined to think of the seventies as the time of their greatest national misery and humiliation, the time of Sedan, the siege of Paris, the tragedy of the commune, and the tawdry first years of the Third Republic. But through all its trials Paris remained in perpetual artistic travail, and the seventies saw many of the important modern movements of art and literature in gestation or in birth. When Moore and his valet arrived in Paris, Baudelaire, Gautier, and Ingres had been dead only a short time, and the ancients, Hugo, Flaubert, and Corot, were still at work. At the zenith of their powers were Goncourt and Zola in the novel; Manet, Degas, Sisley, Pissarro, Renoir, Monet, and Cézanne in painting; Rimbaud, Verlaine, and *le parnasse* in poetry; and Rodin in sculpture. Moore was quickly intoxicated by the excitement generated in contact with living genius and with the great artistic movements in their full creative phase, and he was overcome by the heady emotions arising from marching *dans le mouvement* that he would feel once again when Ireland called him home in 1900.

> It pleases me to recall . . . the seventies and the intellectual atmosphere in which these men lived, going about their business with comedies in their heads—an appointment at ten to consider the first act of a vaudeville; after breakfast another appointment, perhaps at the other end of Paris, to discover a plot for a drama; a talk about an opera in the café at five, and perhaps somebody would call in the evening . . . for they wrote on into the night, tumbling into bed at three or four in the morning.[5]

He was dazzled by the freedom enjoyed in the Parisian artists' community, a freedom almost incredibly generous to a subject of Queen Victoria. Since the early 1830's Parisian writers had been struggling to establish the sovereignty of the artistic individuality. By the time Moore appeared in Paris a large measure of success had been won and the artist's freedom from molestation had taken on the status of an institutional right, grudgingly acquiesced in by the nonartistic French public. In Montmartre and the Latin Quarter the right was asserted everywhere and unceasingly, with warm remembrance of past victories, especially of the defiant opening of *Hernani* forty years before and the more recent failure of the prosecution of Flaubert for indecency; with legends of the Promethean heroes of art, Hugo, Gautier, and Baudelaire; and with a rich literature of impudent manifestoes, in which Moore's own *Confessions of a Young Man* was eventually to be one link in a chain reaching from *Mademoiselle de Maupin* down to the modern call of the French anarchist André Breton for "total resistance," or of André Gide for *"l'imperatif opposé,"* the doctrine that "no individual shall resemble any other person whatsoever," on pain of sin against the Holy Ghost.

One is tempted to try to find particular artists as sources for various strands of Moore's "French influence," but the search is not fully rewarding. Except for his technical imitations, which bear clear—sometimes too clear—evidence of debt to particular writers, he took his most important borrowings from the store of ideas that were the common property of a broad intellectual movement rather than from the special wisdom of individual teachers. Many of his ideas, for example, sound like plagiarisms from Flaubert's letters. Yet he never laid eyes on Flaubert in the flesh and did not read his letters until his own opinions had been expounded in a dozen books. One infers that Flaubert's ideas were in the public domain and that what Moore picked up in his "rag basket," to use his own metaphor, was the common property of Flaubert, Hugo, Baudelaire, and Gautier in the older generation, and of Zola, Manet, Mallarmé, Degas, and their satellites in his own circle of acquaintances. The ideas

35

belonged, in short, to all faithful Montmartre partisans, great and small, under Louis Philippe, the Second Empire, and the Third Republic alike.

For purpose of emphatic statement Moore did assign a particular source to the key ideas about art which the French gave him, invoking the authority of a noted Parisian personality in their behalf. In one instance the parent named was Manet, who was said to have uttered in Moore's hearing words that he was never to allow his readers to forget: *One should be ashamed of nothing but to be ashamed.* The other imputed parent of Moore's intellect was Gautier, who had written—twenty years before Moore was born—the other two most-quoted tags in Moore's works: *The correction of form is virtue* and *The visible world is visible.* The transplantation of these three precepts to English ground was Moore's basic lifework.

To be ashamed of nothing but to be ashamed was a doctrine that cut two ways. It was on the one hand an enabling act for genius, a necessary condition for the achievement of the great French artists of the nineteenth century. At the same time, often in the same person, it was an incitement to the crank and the bore. In his compulsion to "resemble no other person whatsoever," the Parisian artist had paradoxically invented the perfectly predictable clichés of the bohemian and dandy, and stamped them with the well-known trademarks: the stylized exhibitionistic manner, the savage verbal petulance, and the self-conscious and fickle excesses of taste. Like all callow pilgrims to Montmartre during the past hundred years, Moore was instantly convinced that the one thing needful was to assume this stance.

He acquired a Parisian beard and hat, the artistic uniform then current. He redecorated his apartment in Turkish décor. He spoke often of his cat, à la Baudelaire, and announced that he had acquired a python. He embraced Lust, also Cruelty, in pursuit of "intensity of feeling, fervor of mind." He suggested to Mrs. Kendal that her acting might improve if she would emulate Sappho, Sara, and George Eliot and take a lover. "If long locks and general dissoluteness were not an aid and a way to pure thought, why have they been so long his [the artist's] characteristics?" he asked his readers, half-consciously burlesquing Rimbaud's formula for reaching the unknown by a planned derangement of the senses.

His early work took up bohemian sloganizing as its major burden. There was the inevitable denunciation of the machine:

> The world is dying of machinery; that is the great disease, that is the plague that will sweep away and destroy civilization. . . . Look at these plates; they were painted by machinery; they are abominable. Look at them. In old times plates were painted by hand. . . .[6]

This prejudice was to linger to the end of his life, so that in old age he avoided the dead mechanistic touch of the telephone and the private automobile and only compromised his principles to the extent of using taxis, trains, steamships, and typewriters. There was also the usual statement on marriage:

> Marriage—what an abomination! Love—yes, but not marriage. Love cannot exist in marriage. . . .

There was the expected sentiment about the passing of folkways:

> Respectability is sweeping the picturesque out of life; national costumes are disappearing. The kilt is going or gone in the highlands, and the smock in the southlands. . . . Too true that universal uniformity is the future of the world. . . .

There were the necessary paradoxes, always ferocious: "injustice we worship," "art is sublime excrement," "the philanthropist is the Nero of modern times," and so forth.[7]

He studied the technique of the aggressive confession, the French literary convention which, after "shamelessly" professing to practice the vices antithetical to each virtue in the philistine's publicly proclaimed moral code, thereupon embraces the philistine and calls him brother. The import of Baudelaire's taunt: *"Hypocrite lecteur! mon semblable! mon frère!"* was not wasted on Moore, who said:

> And now, hypocritical reader, I will answer the questions which have been agitating you this long while, which you have asked at every stage of this long narrative of a sinful life. Shake not your head, lift not your finger, exquisitely hypocritical reader; you can deceive me in nothing. I know the baseness and unworthiness of your soul as I know the baseness and unworthiness of my own. . . . I hold out my hand to you, I embrace you, you are my brother.[8]

Gautier's hero, D'Albert, had succeeded in "completely losing the knowledge of good and evil," in recapturing the innocence and ignorance of a savage or a child through "sheer depravity." This achievement Moore found congenial to his taste. He announced to his "exquisitely hypocritical reader": "I am feminine, morbid, perverse; but above all perverse," and he turned to Baudelaire to admire the "clean shaven face of the mock priest," the "cunning sneer of the cynical libertine." *"Les Fleurs du Mal!"* he cried, "beautiful flowers, beautiful in sublime decay." [9]

A balanced judgment of Moore's bohemianism is not easy. It is difficult to pass it in silence, so large is its scope throughout his early work, or to deny its occasional puerile quality, although some of his admirers have been able to do so. In retrospect, one can see that bohemianism served him in part as a practical asset, a perfectly reliable reserve, always on call whenever all other literary subjects failed or whenever his other talents proved incapable of breathing life into his writing. In this function it was frequently summoned to his rescue until he approached full mastery of his craft. It was further a venerable, not to say a shopworn, device for producing astonishment and was commonly referred to as a "weapon" against bourgeois vulgarity; hence the bohemian slogan, *épater le bourgeois*. As applied to Moore's manner, this explanation is plausible only in part. It is not certain that astonishment actually constitutes a weapon; as witness both the rise and fall of Oscar Wilde: whom did the Oscarian "weapon" ever defeat? Moreover, though himself a landed gentleman, Moore was demonstrably sporadic and contradictory in his animus against the bourgeois; and he was quick to catch and expose the sentimental note in Yeats's "antibourgeois" gestures of defiance, when the poet, dressed in his great fur overcoat, climbed upon the speaker's platform and stamped his foot in wrath at the Dublin merchants who refused to interest themselves in Lane's collection of paintings.

Moore's detractors have always been excited by proof that he was strictly a verbal bohemian, that prudence was never allowed to lose the direction of his practical affairs. Judged by the standards of ordinary respectability, his personal life was almost exemplary, and the impression of orgy conveyed in his first published work was unquestionably a distortion for literary effect. Acquaintances like Frank Harris, who actually believed the stories Moore circulated about his adventures, were surprised to learn that in private life he was almost a teetotaler, a very niggard in guarding his money, and unfailingly circumspect, if not always chivalrous, in his relations with women. He felt no urge to follow in the fatal paths of his more consistently bohemian contemporaries, such as Lionel Johnson, Ernest Dowson, or Aubrey Beardsley. His Parisian acquaintances of the seventies, when they remembered him, called to mind a bohemian with reservations, that is to say, no bohemian at all. "He tried to shock and astonish people," said one, "but he was always the gentleman, and would never associate with those whom he thought to be below his rank as an Irish landlord." [10]

Oddly enough Moore's enemies scarcely laid more stress upon the meretricious element in his bohemianism than he did himself. He told the story that as a child in Dublin he had once broken away from his nurse and

. . . inspired by an uncontrollable desire to break the monotony of infancy, I stripped myself of my clothes, and ran naked in front of my nurse or governess, screaming with delight at the embarrassment I was causing her.

"How little the soul of man changes," he added, "it declares itself in the beginning and remains with us to the end." [11] The confession suggests that his bohemianism embodied not only youthful combativeness but a mingled element of self-defilement as well. It allowed him to judge and yet to bring the judge to judgment, producing the sort of equivocation found in *Martin Chuzzlewit*, where Dickens' lampoon against American meanness is accompanied by a sweet-tempered apology for his savagery. Moore achieved this effect by a habitual impudence which simultaneously expressed his repulsion of the object under discussion and his identification with it. This was no mean feat, but the device was not permanently satisfying. After 1900 his self-assertiveness became more tempered and his self-defilement more mellow, though his work was always likely to revert to strange atavistic spells of uncontrollable absurdity, which he labeled the work of *"amico Moorini,"* his impish double. He maintained that he knew of no origin for these impulses, indicating that he had forgotten the imperious dual impulse that had forged the rhetoric of his early work.

Manet's precept on shame gave Moore attitudes more solemn than bohemianism. If it was not an antibourgeois dogma, it was unquestionably antievangelical. Having once escaped from the half-repressive moral code of the Irish gentry and finding himself moving relentlessly toward a battle of great historical importance against the meddlesome prurience of the Anglo-Saxon, he was to make Manet's liberating advice into the happiest of his French acquisitions. It encouraged him to pursue interests previously kept in quarantine by social custom operating in the name of the morality of the Absolute; in particular it opened the subject of sex to scrutiny and declared it to be proper for a man of letters to exploit it without molestation, in accordance with the French precedents set in literature by Baudelaire and Flaubert and in painting by Manet. Later he was to assert: "I invented adultery," meaning that he was the first English novelist in a century to demand and to win the sort of freedom in choice of literary subject and treatment that his French masters had taught him to expect as his due.

The doctrine that *the correction of form is virtue* paraphrased Victor Cousin's more familiar and more incendiary slogan, *l'art pour l'art*, a phrasing Moore generally avoided, though it occurs once in his first novel, *A Modern Lover*. There "the love of art for art" is described as "that most terrible of maladies"; in context the phrase simply denoted perfectionism, the terror of art lying in its power to drive the artist to attempt the impossible. In old age he allowed the phrase to appear once again; it had been invented, he incorrectly asserted, by some "flippant unthinking journalist" to provide the "tea shop and bus with a convenient catchword," and he defended with some heat the reasonable proposition that art cannot be produced "for other than aesthetic reasons." In any case, Gautier's phrase was superior to Cousin's in precision, and in that form Moore proclaimed the doctrine in season and out of season.

If the correction of form *is* virtue, it must displace the rival contenders for that title. Flaubert accepted this logic as a matter of course and blandly announced that the world existed in order to make his book. Gautier's followers were committed to denigration of the popular virtues, particularly the prudential virtues, whose perpetual rejection has kept the artists' quarter of Paris ceremonially busy for more than a century. The doctrine that *l'immoralisme* is an essential accompaniment of art has never lacked vigorous spokesmen among French writers from Stendhal to Gide. Peace, comfort, and happiness were declared to be incompatible with the virtue practiced by the artist, mere trivialities and irritations not worthy of the concern of *le poète maudit*. "You are a happy man," Baudelaire wrote in a letter, "I feel sorry for you, sir, for being happy so easily. A man must have sunk low to consider himself happy." [12] Moore echoed this sentiment, contrasting the vulgarity of common happiness with the excruciating rewards of art:

> How to be happy!—not to read Baudelaire and Verlaine, not to enter the Nouvelle Athènes, unless perhaps to play dominoes like the bourgeois over there, not to do anything that would awake a too intense

41

consciousness of life,—to live in a sleepy country side, to have a garden to work in, to have a wife and children, to chatter quietly every evening over the details of existence. We must have the azaleas out tomorrow and thoroughly cleansed, they are devoured by insects; the tame rook has flown away; mother lost her prayer-book coming from church, she thinks it was stolen.[13]

If the correction of *form* is virtue, it follows that didactic purpose, topicality, and realistic imitation deserve no consideration in art. Moore's teachers adopted the distinction between "form" and "content" that had been invented by their enemies, the utilitarian philosophers; but unlike the utilitarians they insisted that "content" was the minor partner and that "form" was supreme. Thus Flaubert had declared that the most beautiful works are those in which there is the least content, and Degas had said with Moore's approval that he could spend a pleasant and profitable lifetime refining his skill in "indicating" fingernails.

Gautier's followers authorized the epithet "pure" to describe art which seemed to them to embody form abstracted from content. Moore declared himself in favor of artistic purity at the beginning of his career, and late in life he published *An Anthology of Pure Poetry*, defined as "poetry devoid of ideas." This charming volume proceeded in seeming innocence to turn the concept of the pure in art into a patent absurdity; since Moore's death it has been useful to academic critics for illustrating the extremes of critical opinionizing.

Moore's French masters delighted in repeating the dogma that art is useless and that beauty and utility are incompatible. Baudelaire, in the fragment of his confession, *My Heart Laid Bare*, had said: "Usefulness to the community has always seemed to me a most hideous thing in man," arguing that utility was "natural," hence depraved, just as "commerce is 'natural,' therefore infamous." Gautier announced that nothing could be thought beautiful unless it be of no use whatever: "Everything useful is ugly, for it is the expression of some need, and man's needs are ignoble and disgusting like his own poor and infirm

nature. The most useful place in the house is a water closet." [14]
It happens that Moore was not impressed by the premises of
this conclusion, for when he escaped from Oscott he left behind
his interest in the theology of natural depravity, except as an
aesthetic proposition. The conclusion itself, however, he accepted
as a natural part of his French education.

The ideal of amorality in art originated in this dogma, morality
being the most "useful" of the "impurities" by which beauty was
thought to be put to flight. It made little difference in the result
whether the amoral attitude was "scientific," as in Flaubert,
Zola, or Stendhal, who had said: *"Je ne blâme ni n'approve;
j'observe"*; or whether it was "pagan" in the manner of Gautier.
Gautier's hero said:

> Nothing touches me, nothing moves me; I no longer feel, on hearing
> the recital of heroic deeds, those sublime quiverings which at one time
> would run through me from head to foot. . . . I see the tears of my
> fellow creatures flow with as indifferent an eye as the rain, unless in-
> deed they be of fine water, and the light be reflected in them in pic-
> turesque fashion, and they flow over a beautiful cheek.[15]

Moore turned D'Albert's speech into the following paraphrase,
almost faithful, though the Moorisms he added gave to Gautier's
idea a clownish piquancy not quite achieved in the original:

> What care I that the virtue of some sixteen-year-old maiden was the
> price paid for Ingres' *La Source*. That the model died of drink and
> disease in the hospital, is nothing when compared with the essential
> that I should have *La Source,* that exquisite dream of innocence, to
> think of till my soul is sick with delight of the painter's holy vision.
> . . . Oh, for excess, for crime! I would give many lives to save one
> sonnet by Baudelaire. . . .[16]

To Gautier's basic doctrine Moore eventually added further
eclectic ornamentation aimed at increasing its palatability to the
English reading public. Sometimes he argued that art is power-
less to affect life in any case; hence to force morality upon art is
"useless." "A flower," he said, "may influence our conduct, but
not literature, or rarely"—a truth he believed to be known to all

Frenchmen but beyond the grasp of the Anglo-Saxon, who persisted in his folly that "the moral conduct of his race is dependent on the last novel published." [17] The Englishman's shortsightedness on the subject reminded him of "the old woman who was afraid to relieve herself in the sea lest she bring about an inundation." Joseph Hone has aptly remarked that this contention does not accord with Moore's grandiose boast that *Evelyn Innes* is the most powerful aphrodisiac ever written.

At other times Moore would explain to Englishmen that the artist working as an amoral agent created beauty, which thereupon paradoxically caused good acts. Thus Turgenev, he said, had been passionately interested in the emancipation of the serfs but had retained qua novelist a strictly amoral view on the subject. The implication was that all this oblique behavior somehow helped emancipation, since the novelist "with beautiful images and ideas . . . may draw men's minds from baser things." This line of argument led to the proposition that Verlaine was by paradox more evangelical than the chapel.

Gautier's dictum has a final permutation: The *correction* of form is virtue. This sounds tame enough at first glance, but its implications were as devastating as anything Moore learned in Paris. If the essence of the artistic experience is contained in the "correction" of form, it follows that, the more correction expended, the greater the virtue. The dictum thus put the most extreme stress upon the value of the expenditure of artistic energy and led to a doctrine of work so joyless and tyrannical that it seemed to have come from the murky pages of Carlyle rather than from the "pagan" Gautier, who had loved "gold, marble, and purple; splendor, solidity, and color." Yet the grim compulsions were well understood by Flaubert, who declared: "I would sooner die like a dog than hurry my sentence by so much as a second before it is ripe"; and who built his plan of living around the same precept: "Compel yourself," Flaubert said, "to regular, exhausting work." [18]

Moore's response was to drive himself into an almost super-

EDOUARD MANET. *George Moore at the café Nouvelle Athènes*

human diligence in work. Of his many enemies, not one ever questioned his devotion to art as he had understood the term. Whistler thought his incapacity for friendship to be the result of the fact that he "thought of nothing but his work." Douglas Hyde concurred. Æ presented Moore's example to his disciples as the model of pertinacity; he had seen "Moore's face pale with anguish after a morning's unsuccessful wrestling with his work." St. John Ervine spoke of his "most pure devotion" to "incessant labor"; and even Yeats could not conceal an admiration for his extraordinary standards of craftsmanship, though he did question whether the total achievement had been worth the effort. Yeats once told Moore: "You will work so hard that, like Lancelot of Tennyson, you will almost see the Grail," an opinion he later retracted as too kindly.[19]

Taking Gautier perhaps too literally, Moore developed a philosophy of revision, which he came to consider not as a drudge chore but as an essential creative act, and at times he suggested that it was the only creative act. Thus *The Brook Kerith* was composed in fourteen months but revised and polished over a period of ten years. The little novel, *Vain Fortune*, was corrected to death. It was published, then completely rewritten, republished, rewritten again, republished once more, and finally disowned and suppressed. *Evelyn Innes* had a similar history, and all of Moore's early work was revised or rewritten one or more times.

If the virtue of art is located in the correction of form, it is available only to the corrector, the artist himself. The alienation of the artist is thus rendered complete, and Gautier's dogma half proclaimed and half demanded a barrier separating eternally the artist and the layman. Only a slight shift of emphasis was required to create the doctrine that the audience is wholly unnecessary, a point of view commonly associated with late nineteenth-century French painters and exemplified in the legends that Cézanne threw his completed canvases into roadside ditches and that Degas silenced a dilettante by shouting, "Don't bother me! Is painting meant to be looked at?" Moore made his own minor contribution to this tradition in an anecdote about Manet painting his portrait:

> The color of my hair never gave me a thought until Manet started to paint it. Then the blond gold that came up under his brush filled me with admiration, and I was astonished when, a few days after, I saw him scrape off the rough paint and prepare to start afresh.
> "Are you going to get a new canvas?"
> "No; this will do very well."
> "But you can't paint yellow ochre on yellow ochre without getting it dirty?"
> "Yes, I think I can. You go and sit down."
> Half an hour after he had entirely repainted the hair, and without losing anything of its brightness. He painted it again and again; every time it came out brighter and fresher, and the painting never seemed to lose anything in quality. That this portrait cost him infinite labour and was eventually destroyed matters nothing; my point is merely that he could paint yellow over yellow without getting the colour muddy.[20]

One understood that it was hopeless for the unsanctified to seek access to this virtue. Gautier's animosity was especially fierce against the dilettanti, those young men "who have as yet slept only with their charwoman." But he also habitually excoriated all critics, denying them the right to hold any opinion of their betters, the creators, and scorning their pompous sterility. "With all my heart," Gautier said, "I pity the poor eunuch who is obliged to be present at the diversions of the Grand Seignior."

Following his cues with normal fidelity, Moore devoted hundreds of pages to the chastisement of the dilettanti. His first novel, *A Modern Lover,* is mainly concerned with their degrading influence upon art, their incessant bickering and factionalism, their lack of taste, their failure to help artists in need, their fickleness, their pretentiousness and dishonesty. The theme runs through *A Drama in Muslin,* in which the dilettante, the fatuous Mr. Barton, an amateur painter and guitar player, flees Ireland during the Land War in Mayo in cowardly haste in order to study gargoyles in Bruges on the money his wife received from her noble lover. *Mike Fletcher* returns to the theme, and in *Evelyn Innes* the breed is again numerous. All England seemed, indeed, a nest of amateurs, fittingly ruled, he thought, by a royal family of dilettanti, "a staid German family dabbling in art in its leisure hours—the most inartistic, the most Philistine of all Royal families." [21] His scorn, however, was not absolutely sweeping. One remembers the amateur, Lady Ardilaun, whose hospitality in Cong castle was the only oasis in all Ireland. In that barbarous land where a "race harse" was more interesting than a Manet, Lady Ardilaun was yet worthy of art, "sketching with a free hand a long range of jagged mountains—one of the mountain prospects she loves so dearly and with which her London drawing-room is so beautifully decorated." In later years Moore found other exceptions in Sir William Eden and in Lady Cunard and her daughter, and of course in himself, for his lack of authority—according to his own standards—to speak about painting was not a deterrent to his incessant opinionizing on the subject.

The scorn that Gautier had spent on critics Moore reserved for university dons, especially those who wrote on Shakespeare. "The din of adoration," he complained, "is so loud that we might as well be in a chapel full of Negroes striving to catch the ear of the Deity. By any chance do the critics of Shakespeare imagine that he can hear them?" [22] He took up the Baconian cause and pursued "all the many Sirs"—for all students of Shakespeare's text had been knighted—with his argument that Shakespeare could not have written the plays because he was an actor, and actors, in Moore's opinion, were necessarily without intelligence. Baconism was one of those compulsory dissents rooted in his jealousy for the purity of art.

In terms of sheer numbers most of the enemies of art were thought to be among the great legions of the indifferent public at large, who seemed to threaten, in their depraved millions, to overwhelm art, artist, and aesthetic virtue. Gautier feared them; he had linked poetry with royalty as "the two greatest things in the world," and prophesied that neither could be preserved. "Poor dear Théo," said Flaubert at Gautier's death, "he died of disgust for modern life; September fourth killed him." On that day, "the most damnable in the history of France," the Third Republic was proclaimed.[23] Baudelaire and Flaubert both suffered intense obsessive fear of the masses. Flaubert dreamed of being drowned in the "bottomless gulf" of human stupidity and, turning the metaphor about, said to a friend shortly after the collapse of the commune: "I should like to drown humanity under my vomit." [24] This emotion, one of the constant properties of bohemia beginning with Barbey d'Aurevilly, was not altogether unfamiliar to the young Irish landlord.

Like Flaubert, Moore declared theatrically that "the human is very despicable vermin" and that those who failed to recognize the true human condition were deficient in genius, for example, Victor Hugo and Mr. Gladstone. Knowing that the correction of form is virtue, one could go to art hopeful that one would not be followed by the hordes of the insensitive. But even that security was not guaranteed. When very young, Moore was certain that he felt a "mysterious something" lurking in the "Mona Lisa," but, after it had been seen and praised by every tourist in Paris, he felt its charm no more; and he was forced to scold even the great Walter Pater himself for insensitively writing nonsense about "the vampire older than the rocks on which she sits."

Noting the rise of popular literacy, Moore declared:

> The old gods are falling about us, there is little left to raise our hearts and minds to, and amid the wreck and ruin of things only a snobbery is left to us, thank heaven, deeply graven in the English heart; the snob is now the ark that floats triumphant over the democratic wave; the faith of the old world reposes in his breast, and he shall proclaim it when the waters have subsided.[25]

This famous taunt, invoking for art in the most naked possible terms the sanction of what Thorstein Veblen called invidious distinction, is in a sense the core of Moore's aesthetics. It is the sentence that finally exhausted the patience of Malcolm Elwin, who drew from it the title for his valuable, if sometimes humorless, book on the perfidy of Moore's age, called *Old Gods Falling*. On this rock was to be built one part of Moore's artistic career, the less substantial part, one may add. Yet the sentence does not convey the firmness of Moore's conviction with perfect confidence. The declaration would appear to be essentially a Moorism, burlesquing itself, mocking its author in terms no solemn affirmation could allow, and betraying thereby fundamental doubts about the center of his system; yet simultaneously, almost heroically, it confronts the source of his doubts and, if nothing more, at least refuses the usual self-deceptive means for quieting them. Proust's efforts to dispose of this same stubborn problem by the invention of the concept of "inverted snobbery" was more ingenious, perhaps, but hardly as enlightening as the crude, implacable force of Moore's peculiar rhetoric.

Moore's contemporary, George Gissing, had a similar respect for art as the supreme instrument of invidious distinction, as the best force available for combating "sordid transaction" and "plebeian compliance"; but Gissing was so demoralized that he feared snobbery itself to be doomed. Moore's retreat was more spirited. To the end of his life he continued to hope that the British public would rise up some day and repeal the Flementary Education Acts of 1870, replacing them with a new statute that would require that "not more than one child in a hundred shall be taught to read, and no more than one in ten thousand shall learn the piano."

The visible world is visible, said Gautier, *"je suis un homme pour qui le monde extérieur existe";* and this dictum encouraged Moore to affirm that the sting of immediate sense experience is superior to all other competing values whatsoever. This was the tie that bound Moore to the French impressionists, a tie that seems genuine despite doubts cast upon it by Douglas Cooper several years ago in *Horizon.*[26] Cooper rejects Moore's claim that he was one of the first Englishmen to champion the impressionist painters, and he argues that Moore, out of uncertainty as to the course the public taste would take, delayed identifying himself with the impressionists until they had won widespread acceptance many years after he had left Paris. Yet Moore's acquaintance with Manet could hardly have been either casual or tenuous. The three portraits of Moore that Manet painted in 1879 or 1880 are unforgettable, and had there been only one, or even two, Cooper's argument would have been strengthened. In any case, once Moore declared himself for impressionism, he never again forsook it. Since renunciation of old loyalties was one of the dominant principles of his life, his constancy in this instance was a remarkable fact in itself. His stubborn fidelity to Manet could indicate "naturally cheap taste" and a "reactionary" cast of mind, as Cooper claims. It could also betoken a true affinity between the ideals of the impressionists and his own temperament, in that he and they were among the last of the self-conscious *avant-garde* artists to defend the view that the visible world is visible before the drift toward solipsism, to which they had themselves contributed, began at last to dissolve the visible world itself.

Moore did not ordinarily approve of that dissolution. The most advanced aesthetic position in Paris during the seventies was occupied by the symbolists, to whom the visible world was not visible. Moore had established friendly connections with them, having discovered Mallarmé before he knew Zola. He attended Mallarmé's Tuesdays, and thirty years later he recalled elfishly that besides himself very few came: "We generally spent Tuesday night together tête-à-tête." Mallarmé gave him a folio edition of *L'Après-Midi d'un Faune* on Japanese paper with tassels, and Moore was delighted in later years to read in the report of book auctions how his gift had increased in value. He identified himself casually with the symbolists and published from time to time in their journals. One of the "fads" he reported bringing to London, when he left Paris in 1880, was symbolism; he carried it, he said, "like a toy revolver in his waistcoat pocket, to be used on an emergency," in overpowering London editors. It is clear, however, that he only partially approved of Mallarmé and did not understand what he was attempting to do.

To a person like Moore, who was compelled by temperament to fire always point-blank, the symbolist ideal of suggestive evocation was altogether foreign. Mallarmé had attacked the Parnassians because they composed too clearly and told too much, leaving no enigma. Moore, who hadn't enough talent to be obscure, stood by the Parnassians; the propagation of the impalpable and enigmatic did not interest him, and he declared with impatience: "I am an objectivist, reared among the Parnassians, an exile from the Nouvelle Athènes," that is, from the café associated with *le parnasse*, naturalism, and impressionism. "And what is symbolism?" he asked. "Vulgarly speaking, saying the opposite of what you mean"; and a character in his play, *The Bending of the Bough*, disposed of the issue with the epigram: "Whenever people shrink from saying what they mean, they call it a symbol." He condemned Mallarmé for obscurity; Browning was, by comparison, "mere child's play." [27]

Moore had not been prepared to make the leap either from Heredia and Banville to Mallarmé and Rimbaud or, in painting, from impressionism to postimpressionism. He was irritated that people should go about crying, "Cézanna! Cézanna!" and undertake to paint "the archetypal poppy which is in heaven" rather than the "poor poppy of the fields and garden." To the American playwright Balderston he confessed a wish to "persecute" the postimpressionists and was glad that the means to do so were not available. In choosing between suggestion and delineation as literary ideals, Moore's temperament spoke consistently for the latter, molding his Parisian literary loyalties accordingly and preparing him for his adventure with Zola.

But if symbolists failed to understand that the visible world is visible, they still believed that one should be ashamed of nothing but to be ashamed and that the correction of form is virtue. Moore recommended Verlaine to the British public principally for his "licentiousness" of both verse and emotion; "hate is to him as commonplace as love, unfaith as vulgar as faith." "And that man Gustave Kahn," he said warmly, "takes the French language as a violin, and lets the bow of his emotion run at wild will upon it producing strange acute strains, unpremeditated harmonies comparable to nothing that I know of but some Hungarian rhapsody . . . a music sweet, subtil, and epicene." [28]

All these various aesthetic attitudes fuse in the metaphor, "the religion of art," used to denote an extremely fervent devotion to an art-centered system of values. The metaphor was a commonplace to Moore's French masters. Thus Flaubert spoke naturally of Baudelaire's poetry as "the blood of Christ that flows in us"; and he informed Louise Colet: "We must love one another *in Art,* as the mystics love one another *in God,* and everything must grow pale before that love. Let all life's other lamps (which stink, one and all) vanish before this great sun." [29] Moore employed the religious metaphor incessantly. In his old age he said to Geraint Goodwin:

> Men put their faith in many things. One can, let us say, put one's faith in humanity. I cannot do so. To begin with, there are too many people born—and too many of an inferior type—for me to take much interest in them. For my part I have done with seeking. . . . I have sought and found and taken refuge in art. Art to me is elemental. . . . Art to me is sacred. It is my religion.[30]

At the time of Moore's death the metaphor came to Æ's mind as he worked at the delicate task of composing a funeral oration to be read at the burial service at Muckloon. "It is possible," he wrote, "that faithfulness to art is an acceptable service. That worship, that service, were his. If any would condemn him for creed of theirs he had assailed, let them be certain first that they labored for their ideals as faithfully as he did for his." [31] Among his disciples, the terms "priest," "priest of letters," and "priestlike devotion" to art were habitually employed in reference to him.

The metaphor made several significant indirect assertions for

Moore. It implied, for example, that religion and art were by nature competitors, struggling against each other for the right to serve man's symbolic needs. To Moore's delight, art seemed to have moved into the rival's territory and found business there very good. The metaphor was thus related to his direct attacks upon religion, as in the last volume of *Hail and Farewell,* which lengthily defended the anticlerical position on the grounds that Catholicism was unartistic. It was similarly related to his playful mannerism of defending art by half-blasphemously presenting its case in transposed religious terms. He called *The Brook Kerith* "the fifth gospel," and like Paul on the road to Damascus he heard voices calling to him in Chelsea Road and repeating three times: "Go to Ireland!" With Newman in mind, he composed an *Apologia,* but for the artistic rather than the religious vocation. His *Epistle to the Cymry* parodied the Pauline manner. He began a book of aesthetic martyrs with a sketch of the "angelic" Cabaner, an obscure sculptor, "our high priest," whose mission was to denounce commercialism and who sheltered the homeless of Montmartre in his garret studio, where on cold nights sleepers were tenderly covered with plaster casts for warmth. This was farce, of course, but other religious parallels to the artistic experience more treated with full respect. There was no lack of solemnity in his exposition of his belief in aesthetic original sin, atonement, and election.

All men were cursed, Moore thought, with instinctive bad taste. Nobody was ever born with the choice of liking or disliking Degas; everybody naturally disliked him. Doré was the painter one instinctively liked, even George Moore. "Titian and Holbein conveyed but little meaning to my youthful mind, and Doré did; and my stages of comprehension were many before I understood why Ingres is a greater painter than Cabanel." But while he was struggling upward, everybody else lingered in unregenerate complacency. "The aesthetic sense of the working man does not develop; he likes the same false, crude, emotion at forty as he did at twenty. Nor are 'women, ecclesiastics and persons of quality' more erudite in art. It is open to doubt if there are very many Dukes in England who could tell a Titian from a Veronese." The public distinguishes between good and bad art only to choose the bad, for "the original taste of man is always for the obvious and commonplace, and . . . it is only by great labor and care that man learns to understand as beautiful that which the uneducated eye considers ugly." [32]

When the natural man comes to knowledge of his depraved taste, he seeks atonement through sacrifice for art. Atonement commences with a condition of humility and submission. "If Degas were to tell me that a picture I had intended to buy was not a good one I should not buy it; and if Degas were to praise a picture in which I could see no merit I should buy it and look at until I did." [33] One thus made the tormented choice to leave the ways of depravity; this step required an absolute break with popular aesthetic unrighteousness. Moore's critical dicta about other writers were concerned to an extraordinary degree with their failure to walk this straight and narrow path. Among those he accused of unholy surrender of his jealously guarded standard were Maeterlinck, Rossetti, Tolstoi, Yeats, D. H. Lawrence, even his friend the painter Sickert. But he praised Meredith for having "no trace of the crowd about him," and he predicted with convoluted irony that Pater's and Landor's readers would fortunately always remain few and sanctified. "The thought is a sad one that the next generation will be more concerned with my writings than with Landor's or Pater's, and merely because they are inferior." [34] He seems to have been first attracted to Balzac by the conviction that he was inaccessible. "There is a vulgarity about those who don't know Balzac," he said in *Evelyn Innes.*

On leaving the way of transgression, one could expect only sacrifice, even martyrdom. Flaubert's letters dwelt constantly on this somber theme:

> You cling to your religious ideas that make you suffer, and I to my chimaera, style, that wears me out, body and soul. But perhaps it is only by our sufferings that we acquire any value. . . .

Advising young Maupassant on the life in art, Flaubert explained that for the artist there is only one principle, "to sacrifice everything to Art. Life must be no more than a means to an end, and the last person he must consider is himself." [35] When Moore took up the theme, he observed that it was always the "purest" and least commercial writers who were threatened with jail for their writings; then, with the studied egregiousness that was his special gift, he announced that the three in England who "loved literature most purely" were "driven into exile"—Byron, Shelley, and George Moore. The shading of this rhetoric was not quite satisfactory to his taste, however, and later editions deleted "George Moore" from the list of martyrs, allowing the other two names to stand in solemnity.

Moore's early novels were abundantly peopled with martyrs and saints of art. There was the painter Frazer; encumbered with a wife and five children, he lived in a garret, "unable to prostitute his talent to the public taste." The artist Howell "had unfortunately blown his brains out in despair." The artist Thompson was presented as having sacrificed all the felicities of life to "that most implacable god," artistic creation:

. . . he thought of the past; there it lay before him, concentrated into a few yards of canvas, but of the cost and the worth, who could speak but himself? What could his friends tell of? A few years of privation, but only he knew of the terrible drama of abdication, of the life that might have been, of the life he had let lie in the limbo of unborn things, of the love, the dreams, the joy and sentiments that he had ruthlessly torn out of his heart and flung like flowers under the resistless wheel of the chariot of art, that most implacable god, that most terrible of Juggernauts.[36]

The theme recurs as the central subject of the novel, *A Vain Fortune,* which will be examined later. Moore's fascination with these tragic destinies appears to have arisen out of his need to probe into the potential contained in his own belief, which held sacrifice to be an essential step toward aesthetic atonement.

Obstacles, however, merely sweetened one's final election. Believers in original sin may insist that salvation is ever so hard to win, but they rarely imagine their own place in the struggle toward it to be a poor one, competitively speaking; and it is not uncommon for believers to allow themselves a monopoly on the means of access to grace. Moore's system was a sort of aesthetic Calvinism. The difficulties in the way of earning one's vision were so exacting that when he had arrived at the state of aesthetic beatitude he discovered it almost uninhabited.

How shall one know who are the chosen? Moore championed the "poem in prose" as the supreme test of literary sensitivity. This odd little genre, which Tolstoi singled out for his most savage satire and which seems to many Anglo-Saxons to be the one flaw in French taste, aroused Moore to the heights of enthusiasm. He translated one of J. K. Huysmans' exotic pages in praise of the genre, explaining that Huysmans' prose was "like a dose of opium" or "a glass of some exquisite and powerful liqueur." Moore's version of Huysmans was as follows:

> The poem in prose is the form, above all others, they prefer; handled by an alchemist of genius, it should contain in a state of meat the entire strength of the novel, the long analysis and the superfluous description of which it suppresses—the adjective placed in such an ingenious and definite way, that it could not be legally dispossessed of its place, would open up such perspectives, that the reader would dream for whole weeks together on its meaning at once precise and multiple, affirm the present, reconstruct the past, divine the future of the souls of the characters revealed by the light of the unique epithet. The novel thus understood, thus condensed into one or two pages, would be a communion of thought between a magical writer and an ideal reader, a spiritual collaboration by consent between ten superior persons scattered through the universe, a delectation offered to the most refined, and accessible only to them.

Moore then offered his reader a translation of two of Mallarmé's poems in prose, the second of which ended: "Oh, calm child, I will speak with thee for hours; there are no fields, and the streets are empty. I will speak to thee on our furniture. Thou art abstracted?" Forgetting his prejudice against symbolism, Moore concluded by seconding Huysmans:

> To argue about these forgotten pages would be futile. We the "ten superior persons scattered through the universe" think these prose poems the concrete essence, the osmazome of literature, the essential oil of art; others, those in the stalls, will judge them to be the aberrations of a refined mind, distorted with hatred of the commonplace; the pit will immediately declare them to be nonsense, and will return with satisfaction to the last leading article in the daily paper.[37]

To join the ten most sensitive persons, one must have a knowledge of *questions de métier*, must smear his "fingers in the *galipot*," must respond to art with the sensitivity of the craftsman rather than the prejudices of the villa and the scullery kitchen. But above all one worked, as Flaubert worked, as Moore worked, "like a Negro or like Balzac." Moore said in an address to the Gaelic League: "We believe that we should make sacrifices for art as we do for religion, that part of the joy of art is the sacrifice." The sacrifice could take more than one form; one witty recommendation he made in Dublin was that "in artistic enterprise there should be, if possible, a slight monetary loss at the end of the year." But mainly he embraced sacrifice through a grim, ceaseless, perfectionist creative struggle. Driven on by sheer force of will, he pursued as earnestly as Gladstone or Dr. Arnold the goal of salvation through good works.

Art grew so important in his eyes that all other values were made contemptible by comparison. Art was the yardstick by which all societies and all human endeavor were measured. Art seemingly devoured all other values. Had Sir Walter Scott dedicated his pen to the payment of his debts? A reprehensible thing, said Moore, showing that Scott had accepted "the morality of the grocer as applicable to the artist." Was Ireland an unhappy land of abused, benighted, and hungry people in the first half of the nineteenth century? Irrelevant, said Moore, the yardstick is art, and: "I remember one of Mayo's carpenters designing and making a handsome wardrobe; he could not read or write, but it may be doubted if Mayo's newspaper-reading peasantry could show so excellent a craftsman; and of this I am sure, that Mayo is a drearier country, for landlords and peasants alike in the twentieth century, than it was in the first half of the nineteenth." [38] That the Webbs should have spent a lifetime writing "a literature people will never read again" was a fact his imagination could not grasp. He was shocked to learn that Nancy Cunard was taught to recognize the industrial products of England, for what could be more stupid than for this beautiful girl to engage in a colloquy like this: What is Leeds famous for? or, How many knives does Sheffield make?

He was not afraid to propose the Moorism that art is greater than humanity itself. Geraint Goodwin told an anecdote about Moore's conversation on this subject with a fellow citizen of London during the Zeppelin raids. A Georgian hospital had been hit, and Moore expressed anxiety for the architecture only, ignoring the bombed-out patients. The citizen, who presumably was unacquainted with Moore's rhetorical habits, was shocked and protested against such cold-blooded sentiments. But Moore assured him that the brick and mortar could never be restored, while "any kitchenmaid and scullion" could produce a human life in five minutes.[39] Gautier had stated a willingness to renounce French citizenship if it should be the price of seeing an authentic picture by Raphael. Moore's paraphrase said that he could "in all sincerity" decapitate all the Japanese in Japan "and elsewhere" to save from destruction "one drawing by Hokee." Moore had little direct knowledge of Nietzsche and probably did not know that he had once said that "the misery of the men who struggle painfully through life must be increased to allow a small number of Olympian geniuses to produce works of art." But the doctrine that the artist is Superman was one that his French tutors had led him to embrace, though in his own dubious and inimitable way.

First Assault on London

. . . a dilettanti poet I
Gratify the febrile whim.
—PAGAN POEMS

To be ridiculous has always been mon petit luxe, *but
can anyone be said to be ridiculous if he knows that
he is ridiculous? Not very well. It is the pompous that
are truly ridiculous.*
—HAIL AND FAREWELL

In the year 1880, at the age of twenty-eight, Moore left
the France of Gambetta, Verlaine, Zola, Degas, and Renan and
moved to the England of Gladstone, Browning, Spencer, Arnold,
and Pater. He found that the gospel of the Nouvelle Athènes
had crossed the Channel ahead of him and that in proclaiming
the word of Théophile Gautier he had been anticipated. A generation had passed since Swinburne had first brought over the
"paganism" and "sensuality" of *Mademoiselle de Maupin.* Later
travelers had imported other assorted French items. Whistler,
"the butterfly with the barbed tail," had already challenged the
Royal Academy's elephantine authority over British taste and
was busy propagating the creed that Art is for the Artist alone,
an opinion that he had definitively stated in the "Ten O'Clock
Lecture." "The Master," said Whistler, "towers above all; and
in their intimacy they revel, he [the Master] and she [Art] in
this knowledge; and he knows the happiness untasted by other
mortal. . . . Art seeks the Artist alone." Oscar Wilde, four
years younger than Moore, had precociously outraced him in the

59

return from the cafés of Paris. Merging the aestheticisms of Ruskin and Gautier, he was already dazzling the West End with Oscarian paradoxes. Whistler and Wilde were more accomplished publicists than Swinburne and Rossetti had been, and between them they had stirred up more artistic scandal and commotion than England had heard since the days of Lord Byron. In the wake of their furor had gathered a group of young poets, painters, and journalists, all eager to join in the assault.

Victorianism was under general attack in 1880. It had passed its grand climacteric in the 1850's, but its decline was leisurely, and its great distinguishing traits persisted with monumental inertia. Yet, by the time Moore left Paris, its difficulties were so many and so sharp that there was no phase of the old order that did not find itself challenged. On the surface it might seem that these attacks were unified, for all were directed against a single target, the hide of the man Matthew Arnold called "Mr. Bottles," the powerful, pious, tasteless, self-confident *nouveau riche,* the zealous, suburban middle-class man of affairs who had dominated the world for more than half a century and who was, from the point of view of Cheyne Walk, Hammersmith, and Denmark Hill, the enemy of light and of the chosen people. Actually the critics were a heterogeneous collection, without cohesion and more often at odds with each other than with the enemy, as witness the Whistler-Ruskin lawsuit or the threatened duel between Whistler and Moore. The Fabians were interested in the socialization of Mr. Bottles' factories but were not led to anxiety by the condition, bad though it might be, of his metaphysics. The suffragettes were absorbed in the need for extension of the franchise, reform of the divorce law, and the end of prostitution in Mr. Bottles' East London tenements, all without impugning his aesthetic condition. Ruskin and the Oxford Hegelians deplored Mr. Bottles' materialism, but Tyndall and Huxley had attacked him for not being more materialistic than he was. The Prince of Wales himself was a sort of anti-Victorian in his sluggish disregard of the Ten Commandments and the Sabbath, but otherwise he had no perceptible resemblance to William Morris or George Bernard Shaw.

Within the loose confederation of dissidents, the so-called "aesthetes" held to very limited and specialized aims, seeing Mr. Bottles' shortcomings strictly from the viewpoint of the practicing craftsman in literature and art. Their criticism was based on two observations: first, that neither Mr. Bottles' person nor his suburban villa nor his possessions could be judged to be aesthetic objects. Wilde's program for the beautification of Victorian clothing was motivated by this conviction; and Ruskin's and Morris' passion for reform was originally aesthetic, growing out of a revulsion against the ugliness they saw everywhere around them. Second, Mr. Bottles and his agents occupied the strategic control points in the literary and artistic world, and they had decreed that all artistic expression must reflect Mr. Bottles' own inner and outer image. Mr. Bottles knew exactly what he wanted. He wanted a simple story, both in literature and in painting; he wanted piety, utilitarian morality, adventure, amusement; he liked to hear himself and his achievement admired; he would countenance no sex, no pessimism, and no fancy business. The commodity he ordered was to be delivered punctually and at economical prices. Artistry, in short, was to be industrialized like textiles and pottery.

Mr. Bottles wielded great power in New Grub Street, where most fell into line with his wishes with or without grumbling. But he could not bring all artists into his system, and the more talented they were the more disobedient they proved. A rebellion formed among a small wing of writers and painters, and there ensued a verbal turmoil of great violence, motivated by the same desperate impulses that had led to the smashing of the Midlands power looms seventy-five years earlier. Self expression, it was discovered, does not make a reliable market commodity. The happy times when talent wanted to say what respectability wanted said, when the aging Tennyson and mid-Victorianism could walk together in accord, were now only a memory. The new generation of talent had its mind on unpleasant things. It was not impressed by the power of those who might take offense but, relying on the superior verbal skill and resourcefulness of the artist, impatiently called its challenge and confronted the issue.

The immediate grievance was the evangelical and academic dictatorship, not only in publishing but in the libraries, theatres, and art galleries. Evangelical prudery was found to be well organized. The National Vigilance Association had taken upon itself the guardianship of public morals and demonstrated its zeal through surveillance of published material and ruthless legal pursuit of any author or publisher suspected of obscenity. This organization specialized in French literature, especially French novels. Its greatest victory was the jailing of Vizetelly, the septuagenarian publisher of George Moore, for printing Zola's novel on rural fecundity, *La Terre*.[1]

More formidable guardians of piety were two circulating libraries, Mudie's, with an enormous book mart in London, and Smith's, a network of railway-station bookstalls. The two libraries together purchased such a large number of copies of new issues of books that their opinion had almost the authority of law, for few publishers dared risk a printing without circulating-library sales assured. Both libraries studied with great caution the prejudices of their clientele. They refused circulation to *The Ordeal of Richard Feverel* as condoning illicit affection. They rejected Charles Reade's novel *Cream*, but Mudie magnanimously announced that, if Reade would write with "anything like his old delicate and sparkling freshness," he would pay "a good round sum for the first edition." At times, however, the libraries seem to have been more urbane than their subscribers. They had circulated *Adam Bede* over the protest of many subscribers, and they circulated all the published novels of Thomas Hardy.[2]

In sophisticated literary circles, timidity was no less frequently encountered than at the circulating libraries. Stevenson had destroyed his first novel on the advice of a publisher's reader who thought it indecent. Hardy's first novel came to the same end for the same reason; and, as everyone recalls, the enlightened Leslie Stephen thought *The Return of the Native* "too passionate" for publication. *The British Quarterly Review* found itself profoundly shocked by an incident in *Far from the Madding Crowd* in which Bathsheba's father suggested to his wife that if she removed her wedding ring he would find marital fidelity more easily accomplished. "Coarseness," said the *Review*, "is not a necessary attribute either of strength or reality." After listening to such criticism for a generation, Hardy was finally provoked to reply to his attackers in a famous essay on candor in the English novel, which raised the question whether the creation of art might not be impossible in England, since art cannot exist without honesty. The preface to *Two on a Tower* again complained of the abuse he had received, recalling that the critics had described his work as "repulsive," "hazardous," and "a studied and gratuitous insult." In defense he reminded readers that the novel contained "hardly a single caress" outside legal matrimony.[3]

Yet the Victorian press had treated Hardy with relative generosity. Clarence R. Decker has collected some of the Victorian reactions to Zola and French naturalism: "Nothing more diabolical has ever been written by the pen of man"; naturalistic novelists were "shameless purveyors of hideous garbage" and "hyenas delighting in carrion"; their novels were "the obscene ravings of delirium tremens," "unclean fruit," "ordure." The introduction of Ibsen into England was likewise a signal for general hysteria in the London press. These epithets were collected by Miriam Franc, who discovered an incredible list running into dozens of items ranged along the spectrum of abuse from the more restrained—"unhealthy," "coarse," and "morbid"—to the near demented—"crapulous," "putrid," and "bestial."[4]

The abject behavior of such an unquestionably gifted writer as Andrew Lang reveals the state of affairs. One of the most influential book reviewers at the close of the century, Lang used his prestige in puffing the extroverted romances of Rider Haggard and his school. His reviews called constantly for "more fighting rather than free love," and derided the more thoughtful novelists like Olive Schreiner, whose people, he said, were "always tackling religious problems, or falling in love on new and heterodox lines, instead of shooting deer, and finding diamonds, or hunting up the archeological remains of the Transvaal." When Hardy protested against Lang's bigoted condemnation of *Tess of the D'Urbervilles,* Lang replied with a lengthy extension of his original remarks, ending with the sentiment of Mudie's words to Charles Reade: "So I have ventured to say my say, though I had not intended to speak again about any work of Mr. Hardy's." When George Moore's *Esther Waters* appeared in 1894, Lang announced to his enormous audience that he would refuse to read it.[5]

Victorian surveillance also kept the London theatre throttled during the 1880's and 1890's and had brought its level of imagination and craftsmanship to the lowest ebb in four centuries. For two decades the common level of mediocrity was broken only by two plays of Wilde, one of Pinero, and the early work of Shaw. Even the "advanced" William Archer, the most vocal Ibsenite in England, was only another sort of Mr. Bottles. In 1900 he had graciously conducted an interview with George Moore on the subject of the new Irish theatre, and Archer's published version of the interview, which seems anxious to demonstrate Moore's absurdity, is more eloquent in recording Archer's own limitations. An incongruous tone of undue excitement arises from Archer's defense of the ornate stage settings of the London theatre, from his attack upon simplified spelling, and—in keeping with the spirit of the Boer War—from his lecture on the racial superiority of the Anglo-Saxon over his Teutonic cousins. Like Mudie and Lang, Archer exuded on all subjects a pharisaical self-assurance, the great thick-skinned armor of orthodoxy against which nothing but the impudence of paradox and epigram seemed effective.

George Moore's revulsion against these Victorian institutions and his alignment with Wilde and Whistler in their rebellion was fitting, if not inevitable. Like Wilde, Shaw, and Whistler, he was a foreigner and a cosmopolitan. His religious freedom was singular. As a Catholic renegade he was unmoved by the charms of conversion to Catholicism that tempted so many of his aesthetic contemporaries. At the same time, his Catholic boyhood had immunized him against the evangelical outlook. The ethical beliefs of the Victorian positivists, "the religion of humanity" as practiced by George Eliot and her circle, thus offered him not the slightest attraction. As for the evangelical conscience and sense of sin, his introspective probings could discover no such entity as belonging to himself. "I had never been able to do anything that I thought wrong," he said in old age, and, since with him "thought and action are at one," [6] his conscience had disappeared through atrophy, like eyesight among moles. "My conscience is deaf and dumb." Among one's Victorian neighbors, however, one observed an interesting tic or reflex pattern that might be called "conscience," and this pattern the novelist could profitably dissect. As for belief, he believed in art. But art to him was not exactly what it was to the Victorian readers of Ruskin and Arnold, the praise of God and the best that had been thought and said. Among the important artistic figures of his time, he was probably the most ignorant of the English literary tradition and the most free of its influence. He also believed in himself: "Self, and after self a friend," [7] such was his stated creed. But he had no friends. Finally, although he thought his Irish property lost and imagined himself on the verge of poverty, time was to prove his fears unwarranted. Thus he gathered the rewards of both poverty and comfort without experiencing the debilitating effects of either. He was the perfect recruit for the anti-Victorian brigade.

Moore's assault on London did not wait for his final departure from Paris in 1880. At the time of the Land War in Mayo, he had already published three volumes in London and had a fourth in preparation for the press and a fifth projected. The first volume, a play called *Worldliness,* has disappeared. His second volume, a little book of verse called *Flowers of Passion,* was published in 1878. It is now a very rare collectors' item, and a single copy has been known to fetch more than two hundred dollars at auction. The third volume was *Martin Luther,* the play he wrote in collaboration with Bernard Lopez and printed in 1879. The fourth volume was a collection of verse, *Pagan Poems,* printed in 1881, the year after he moved to London. The projected volume which was to have become the fifth missile of his assault was never finished.

The preface to *Martin Luther* relates that Moore met Bernard Lopez in December, 1875, at about the time he made up his mind to abandon painting. He confessed to Lopez that his thoughts were turning to poetry, and he asked that incredibly experienced man of letters to explain how one proceeded in that direction. Lopez replied:

> . . . choose subjects that would astonish the British public by their originality—for instance, if instead of inditing a sonnet to my mistress's eyebrows I were to tell the passion of a toad for a rose. Not that, of course not that, but poems on violent subjects. "A young man's love for a beautiful corpse," I interjected.[8]

In keeping with his lifelong habit of precipitate action, Moore apparently resolved instantly to make thought and action one, for upon opening *Flowers of Passion,*[9] his first surviving work, one finds on the very first page the title, "Ode to a Dead Body," and the opening lines:

> Is it a garden of eternal sleep
> Where dreams laugh not or weep?
> A place of quiet below the tides of life
> Afar from toil or strife?

The corpse appears and reappears through the volume, and, while composing a later sonnet on the subject, the neophyte poet had kept his copy of *Les Fleurs du Mal* open on his writing desk:

> Wondering I gaze upon each lineament
> Defaced by worms and swollen in decay,
> And watch the rat-gnawed golden ringlets play
> In hideous grimace. The bosom rent
> Is opening rose-like 'neath the sun's warm ray.

But "where dreams laugh not or weep" is Swinburne rather than Baudelaire, and most of the verse is English in derivation, consisting in a close imitation of all the decadent hints Moore could discover in nineteenth-century English poetry. His long dramatic poem "Annie" is an imitation of Tennyson's "Maud." A dramatic monologue "Bernice" seems to have borrowed its title from Poe's story, "Berenice," and its manner from Browning's "Porphyria's Lover," which it parodies with delicate malice just sufficient for the destruction of his model:

> The perfume of the roses
> Drove me mad. I know not how it was,
> In kissing her I held her face beneath
> The pallid water-flowers until it grew
> More wan than they. The roses were asleep,
> The moon saw not between the darkling trees,
> Only lilies saw her drownéd face.

Following Shelley's example in *The Cenci* he wrote a blank-verse play on incest, called "Ginevra," in which the hero complains that:

> Custom's bitter mouth had cursed the love
> That might 'tween brother and a sister grow.

The little play is noteworthy for containing the first expression of one of Moore's curious lifelong interests, the escape of a nun from a convent, a theme which recurs in more than half of his works, including both this first book of verse and the novel he was writing at the time of his death. "Ginevra" shows at times a youthful verve and flow of language and, despite much adolescent nonsense, faintly delineated the writer who would eventually appear. Thus one of the characters, one Orisino, on hearing that his fiancée has been engaged in incest, declares with striking rhetorical abundance:

> I am like one in loathsome charnel pit
> Where things are veiled in pestilential haze.
> Pah! what nauseous hell-born infamy!
> My hand would stab him in the very mouth,
> Would pluck forth by the roots the fetid weed,
> His tongue and cast it to the dogs. But no,
> The dogs would vomit sick with loathing hate.
> No mouth could hold a thing so poisonous
> Except his own. And this is whom I loved.

Flowers of Passion contains clear echoes of Rossetti, especially in two sonnets, "Summer" and "Summer on the Coast of Normandy," in which the poet lolls in the meadow where "the tedded grass breathed fragrance of crushed thyme" and the "linnets from the flowerful closes gave/ Forth sweetly songs in sad uncadenced rhyme," giving way to sensations that achieved, in the last line, a Rossetti-like trance "hushing the pain of every memory." Anticipating Oscar Wilde, the volume includes two poems exploiting the epicene, "Hendecasyllables" and "A Sapphic Dream." *Mademoiselle de Maupin* had authorized this subject, and Moore continued to play with it, though apparently merely out of a sense of duty to art.

> I love the luminous poison of the moon,
> The silence of illimitable seas.

After the fall of Wilde, the note disappeared completely from his work. Finally, the volume contains a sonnet on Moore's abandonment of painting, a prosy exercise but interesting for stating doubt that he could write better than he could paint:

> I now must start
> Upon another path, with other eyes

And hands to beckon me. Will they despise
Me as thou didst? my sweet, my own lost Art.

Flowers of Passion was reviewed in London by Edmund Yates, who plunged heavily into Moore's trap. He labeled Moore "a bestial bard" and offered his famous recommendation that the author "should be whipped at the cart's tail, while the book is being burnt in the marketplace by the common hangman." [10] Moore was delighted and wrote to his uncle: "Have you seen my little volume of poems? They made quite a little success. I am terribly abused for immorality but not for bad writing. . . . None could make out that I write badly although very indecently." [11]

Meanwhile *les séances de collaboration* between the young and old playwrights were under way, and *Martin Luther* was completed in December, 1878. Early in the following year Moore crossed the Channel to try to find a producer. All his life he was to reiterate his belief that the London theatre was hopelessly corrupt, a view for which he could offer impressive evidence. However that might be, it did perceive that *Martin Luther* was not a play, even though its co-author had collaborated with Dumas, Gautier, and Scribe. No producer would undertake the play, and Moore thereupon paid to have it printed.

The play was published with a long preface consisting of eighteen letters exchanged between the two collaborators on the subjects of censorship, literature, painting, play construction, art history, religious history, and the connections between religion and art.[12] Hone observed that the letters were not a practical necessity, since the two authors lived around the corner from each other. He also noted the remarkable vigor and freshness of the preface as compared with the play itself. Looking at this little volume after the passage of nearly three-quarters of a century, one senses what Moore must have felt as he took it from the press: that at twenty-seven years he possessed notable ability in the line of critical demolition, but that much struggling and suffering would lie between him and the achievement of creative power, when, as Whistler had said, he might revel with Art in "happiness untasted by other mortal."

As befitted the religious subject, the doctrines of the religion of art were foremost in the collaborators' minds in the opening apparatus of the volume. A Latin epigraph cites the authority of St. Gregory the Great to the effect that, even though truth cannot be spoken without offense, truth must be spoken. There are two dedicatory poems to Swinburne in French; one, a sonnet by Moore, envisions Swinburne as a sort of Old Testament patriarch of aesthetics, preparing to destroy the altars of Evil that smoke in the night, the destruction to be accomplished by the *"divin cri de chanteur, le tien!"* Lopez composed an ode linking Swinburne to Luther as a teacher and prophet and as the speaker of the Word, *"pareil à l'étoile des mages,"* which would pierce the clouds and give light to nations. Moore attributed to himself an epigram on the rivalry of art and religion: "To art ecclesiasticism is as deadly as arsenic to the body."

The preface of *Martin Luther* dealt at length with mechanical problems of dramatic form. The analysis of these problems was assigned to the letters from Lopez, who was naturally the better informed expert on the art of construction, the *théâtre bien fait*, which the French had "pursued to its furthest limits." Lopez' final conclusion on the subject was simple and brief: "To violate the unity of subject is the negation of all art." The precept left an indelible mark upon Moore, whose lifelong effort to tame his own discursiveness and to forge new forms for the English novel was based at all times upon Lopez' observation.

The letters exhibit a pattern of critical discourse which Moore's later essays on literature and painting adopted as their permanent form. The sweeping denunciation, the savage exposure of artistic cant, the unbounded range of reference, the freshly perceived detail, and the vertiginous transition—all appear first in the letters of Lopez but are quickly taken over by the pupil, who had chosen for the first victim of the method the English drama. He was eventually to proceed through all the genres of English and other literatures in the same manner, "swinging his stick at the heads of flowers," as Malcolm Elwin once complained, "like a larrikin let loose," [13] and always the method would echo Lopez' flight through the history of painting in the preface to *Martin Luther*.

All this prefatory material is delightful enough, but the epigraphs, list of collaborators formerly associated with M. Lopez, dedications, prefatory letters, and the rest of the fifty pages of preliminaries could not make up for the weakness of the work itself, a play on the life of Martin Luther. One needs to inspect only a few lines of the blank verse to realize that the authors were in serious trouble. The opening scene is in Rome, and the curtain discloses relic sellers haggling with peasants. A travel-worn pilgrim enters:

> My name is Luther, and from Wittenberg
> I come, the intervention of the Pope
> To seek, for the adjustment of some questions
> Pertaining to my convent.

Apparently Moore believed that his subject was self-vitalizing. But as he grew more intimate with the material he seems to have discovered that as melodrama Luther's life strictly presented could fill only a couple of acts in a five-act play. The obviously dramatic incidents occupy Acts I and II. Act I ends with Luther's decision to make an open break with Rome. There is a long soliloquy picturing the putrescent condition of Rome and ending:

> Lo! erubescent suddenly it grew
> As with a double dawn, and then methought
> A great voice spake from out the end of space
> Words which I could not save at first from tumult,
> And strange confused murmuring of sounds,
> But which at last swelled forth distinct and clear,
> And filled mine ears with it. I heard! I heard—
> Yea, reformation was the word!

Act II ends with Luther receiving the summons to the Diet of Worms. His mother asks: "And wilt thou go?" Luther replies:

71

> Yes, I will, my mother,
> As I did go to Augsburg, when there called
> For the same cause. Yes I will go to Worms,
> Even if I find as many devils there
> As roofs!

Outside, a chorus of students is heard singing Moore's translation of *"Ein feste Burg ist unser Gott"*:

> Our God, a right fast tower is He
> A sword and shield unshaken.

The students light a fire and burn the papal excommunication and the Bibles of Luther's enemies as the curtain falls.

The dramatic resources of the subject were now spent. Two items remained, both fascinating for Moore. One was Luther's marriage to the former nun, Katherine Bora. The other was the Peasants' War, a subject on which Moore naturally held strong opinions. These incidents were insufficient to occupy the actors through three more acts, and neither Luther's theology nor Lopez' mastery of *l'exposition de la pièce selon la formule de M. Scribe* could fill the vacuum.

The play was rescued by large borrowings from Villiers de l'Isle-Adam and Edgar Allan Poe. A second escaped nun, the decadent and tragic Elsa, was introduced and presented with Luther's bodyguard Bernstorff for suitor. The happy fortunes of Luther and Katherine Bora were thus given a somber parallel to carry down through the well-made acts, the blighted love and the fertile union neatly setting off each other. The subplot begins to operate in Act II when Bernstorff saves the two former nuns from a band of marauding soldiers, whom he challenges in these striking words:

> Stand back,
> Ye ruffians, or perfay my sword shall bleed
> You of some lecherous blood.

When Bernstorff suggests marriage to Elsa, the action rests while she explains in fifty lines how she had been buried alive in the convent cellar, and how, lacking the athleticism of Villiers' Princess Sara, she had been saved only by the intervention of Sister Katherine. "But listen to my dolorous story," she says, and she proceeds to tell that the heir of a "stern feudal family" had sought to rescue her from the convent where her parents "did shut me." But he "perished miserably," having slipped in climbing up the walls, for "foothold there was none."

> They found me by
> The dead. I was adjudged to be interred
> Alive. They placed me on a bier, and threw
> A shroud upon me, reading burial rites.
> Then I was carried down below the ground,
> Where the deep night was almost palpable;
> Unto a vault, whose entrance was a stone
> Trap, set above a very narrow flight
> Of steps, that led unto a silent darkness.
> They thrust me down, first placing in my shroud
> A loaf of bread to lengthen out my dying.

For an additional seven lines she lay "in the passion-baffling dark," suffering "in fiery frenzy of flaming fears," and beat her bleeding hands against the "heedless walls." Then

> I hear the chill, cold words condemning me,
> I feel the darkness of the dungeon still,
> The slimy walls and floor, where strange things crawl
> The utter emptiness. Against all law
> The tears and prayers of sister Katherine
> Did move the stern old abbess unto mercy:—
>
> Perhaps she thought to find me dead! They came
> After two days. Oh, speak not of them! One
> I hardly knew, and disentombed me, half
> Deprived of sense, with eyes that stared aghast
> Thro' films of blood, and wandering tangled strings
> Of hair, that my pale, trembling hands did twist
> Half listlessly.
>   Now that you know my sad,
> Sad tale of suffering, can you say again:
> "I love you."

To this enquiry Bernstorff clearly can make only one reply:

> I did only know before
> Your beauty. Since I learn your awful past
> I love you with a ten times greater love.

Elsa is disposed of at the end of Act III by martyrdom. When Cipriano, a "representative of the Inquisition," hands Luther a goblet of wine that has been secretly poisoned, Elsa seizes it and drinks it. But before dying she persuades Luther that he should marry Katherine Bora, in whose attractions he has been inclined to suspect a trap set by the devil. Elsa's spirit, according to the laws of *le théâtre bien fait*, thereupon passes intact to one of Luther's children, also named Elsa, who continues the tragic perverse activity of her namesake. In Act V she announces that she has decided to become a nun. The expected flux of language fails old father Luther. He commences his denunciation:

> Unhappy child, I ought to—ah!

After four iambic feet apoplexy stops him, and a bystander explains: "The slightest/Emotion may prove fatal to him now."

But Bernstorff tells the wayward girl of the poisoning of the first Elsa. The convent is then renounced, and the marriage of Elsa is arranged in spite of the prospective bridegroom's puzzling insistence that it was he who mixed the deadly drink with which the first Elsa was killed. At the end of the play Cipriano, the papal agent, reappears leading an army of Anabaptists; the play clearly implies that both the Peasants' War and Anabaptism were plotted in Rome. When the Anabaptists attack Luther, Bernstorff shoots Cipriano and routs his followers. Luther dies peacefully, honored by a passing parade of citizens of Eisleben.

Moore expected that *Martin Luther* would create a sensation in London and planned for a *succès de scandale*. He seems to have cherished the provincial Irish belief that the life of Luther was a violently subversive subject per se. The preface dwells on this belief in comic vein, Lopez' letters expressing anxiety that his nephew, a bank clerk in Bordeaux, might be unable to find a priest to conduct his forthcoming marriage, once the play and Lopez' connection with it had become public knowledge. Yet there was no visible comedy in Moore's statement to his mother about the play: "I shall be terribly attacked, for I have attacked all." [14] But if Mr. Bottles was in any way discomfited by *Martin Luther,* or even aware of its existence, no record of the fact has survived. The play made no scandal at all, and Moore turned to reading proof on his next volume, *Pagan Poems.*

Pagan Poems is the longest and most interesting work in Moore's opening literary phase.[15] It echoes the themes of the earlier published volumes and repeats some of the poems that had appeared in the first collection of verse. But in its general scope it moves slightly ahead, enlivened mildly by the appearance of new ideas. Meanwhile it carries the old commitments to their ultimate statement, closing with an impasse Moore's first efforts to master the literary art.

The new poetic imitations, though seemingly solemn in intent, continue suspiciously to skirt the comic. A longer poem, called "The Temptation," plagiarizes Poe and shows Moore in the act of going overboard for a new idea, Baudelaire's ambivalence. It achieves one of the more remarkable statements in literature of the ancient theme of *la femme fatale:*

> Sitting in the silence, in the glimmer
> Of my window where the light was dimmer,
> Gazing in the night
> Woman fairer than all mortal dreaming,
> Weirdly lovely more than earthly seeming,
> Saw I in delight.
> . . . .
> Kneeling at my feet, her white arms over
> My face drawn down, speaking like a lover
> Words in symbols clothed
> Wooing in low quivering serpent hisses,
> Crouching by me, feeding with live kisses

> Me that longed yet loathed.
> Then she, gathering me to burning bosom,
> Gave to tempted lips the grievous blossom,
> Saying: "Taste of this."

A three-hundred-line poem, "Ode to a Beggar Girl," marks the acquisition of another new idea. In the opening lines Moore sees a beggar girl wandering through the streets of Paris,

> Holding as the Virgin holds the Child
> In the first Italian masters
> Your neglected baby.

At first he sees her sorrow as romantically charming, but on further thought the "dreams of fancy" give way to cold reality:

> You are nothing more
> Than a dirty beggar bearing
> Traces ah! of beauty past;
> You are just as vile and commonplace
> As the thousands straying
> Daily through our Paris streets.
> I can tell your fortune:
> You will bear up still a little longer
> Struggling uselessly against your fate,
> Nathless certainly the night will come—
> There is no escape for you.
> Just a look around, a splash, a cry,
> Then a sense of suffocation—
> Onward flows the river
> Through the night.

The poet then wanders on and, in a rain shower, takes shelter under the porch of the morgue. There he sees a corpse identical in appearance with the beggar he has just passed. The beggar girl arrives at the morgue and informs the officials that the corpse is her sister. The poet watches to observe if the beggar girl will weep:

> But you did not weep,
> Very weary, simply
> Looking tired of life you left the Morgue.

There follows a series of trial interpretations of the meaning of the incident. First the poet observes that the pleasures of "flesh and intellect," unavailable to beggars, are "Never to be read by you, methinks," for "None could teach you either alphabet." However, the beggar girl is offered the consolation of his assurance that "Every life is hopeless when we think/ Who will know that we have lived/ In a hundred years." Before returning to his "pleasant thoughts of pleasure," he gives the girl "a last/ Word of pity and advice," first from Schopenhauer:

> "Life," you say, "is hard to bear."
> Every day it will grow harder,
> Pluck up courage and escape
> All this misery and woe;
> Death is always kindly—die!
>
> . . . .
>
> Life ignores you,
> You are useless,—
> You were black-balled out of life,
> There is nothing for you here,
> Nothing—only Death!

Next, since Moore is now in an eclectic phase, the meaning of death takes a Tennysonian turn, and the optimistic evolution of "In Memoriam" sounds forth:

> She is absolutely clay—
> Common clay that gives us worms and flowers,
> Flowers that nourish, worms that change again,
> Insects ever seeking higher forms,
> Animals extending up to Man,
> Man aspiring, reaching up to God!
> Ever changing, changing ever,
> Wandering through the universe
> In a long progressive dream.

But Tennysonian assurances did not satisfy, either. The poem closes with a struggle to transform cosmic progress into a less officially Victorian pattern; in that effort Moore was like

77

Nietzsche, who in the same year, on an Alpine peak near St. Moritz, had stumbled upon the doctrine of eternal recurrence:

> Centuries hence, a million centuries hence,
> You will dream again the dream of life
> In a world more perfect and a form more fair.

This idea was to develop into a permanently useful acquisition. In *Memoirs of My Dead Life*, written a generation later, the circle that Moore planned to track after his death is described in exact and affectionate detail, ending with his return, after billions of years, not to "a world more perfect and a form more fair" but to his address in Pimlico, to "the same room as I sit in now, writing the same lines I am now writing," preparing, of course, to start running through the same circle again.[16] His fascination with eternal recurrence seems to have resulted in part from its philosophical aptness to his special experience, since it was in better harmony than cosmic evolution with his conviction, growing out of the situation at Moore Hall, that "life is beautiful at the moment, sad when we look back, fearful when we look forward." He would also discover in due time the practical importance of the idea as suggesting a solution for one of the larger and more stubborn problems of narrative form. He held a lifelong opinion that English novelists were constitutionally unable to conclude their tales; his own solution for the problem of ending a novel was to bring it back, according to the principle of eternal recurrence, to the point from which it had started, a solution he was to employ with perfect tact, fifteen years after the "Ode to a Beggar Girl," in the much imitated closing chapters of *Esther Waters*.

Pagan Poems occasionally shows Moore beginning to ponder themes which could not be contained in the borrowed vessels of Swinburne and Poe and which would shortly rescue him from the mistakes of his false start. One long poem, "La Maîtresse Maternelle," despite lines like *"Et dans une douce indolence/ La lune dort comme une fleur,"* still manages to state without utter nonsense the germ of his first realistic novel, *A Modern Lover*. Another, "A Modern Poem," deals with the theme of the decay of the "big house" and the attendant marriage-mart haggling, the subject of his third novel, *A Drama in Muslin*. Another, "A Parisian Idyll," was rewritten a generation later to make his famous scandalous short story, "The Lovers of Orelay."

Sometimes the volume experimented with "shameless" confessions in anticipation of *Confessions of a Young Man* and *Hail and Farewell*. One sonnet, for example, asserted that notoriety was worthwhile in a world where other values had disappeared:

> Yea, I would change my lot with anyone,
> A king, a scavenger, a courtezan,
> A priest, a murderer, an artizan,
> For nothing worth the doing have I done.
> Just once before I sleep beneath the stone,
> I want to act and not to dream, I can;
> And leave within the future world of man
> Some seed to blossom when I shall be gone.
> If I am good or bad I little heed,
> For are not all things vile or virtuous
> According to the standard of our need?
> A soldier burnt the temple of Ephesus,—
> It was, perhaps, a very dreadful deed,—
> But it preserved his name, Erostratus.

The Moorism was hidden in the rhythm of the last lines.

Occasionally there appears in the volume, as there always would in even his most perverse work, a trace of genuine individuality and freshness of outlook. Forty years before Eliot's typist home at tea time, Moore somehow succeeded in putting together this sonnet:

> Idly she yawned, and threw her heavy hair
> Across her flesh-filled shoulders, called the maid,
> And slipped her sweet blonde body out of bed,
> Searching her slippers in the wintry air.

The fire shed over all a sullen glare—
Then in her bath she sponged from foot to head,
Her body, arms, breasts, thighs, and things unsaid,
Powdered and dried herself with delicate care.
Then Zoë entered with the *Figaro*,
The chocolate, the letters, and the cat,
And drew the blinds to show the falling snow,
Upon the sofa still her mistress sat
Drawing along her legs as white as milk
Her long stockings of finely knitted silk.

Still, *Pagan Poems* mainly reveals a poverty of poetic talent. The volume was clearly the work of a writer virtually deaf to poetic rhythms; and Moore's later gift for weaving mellifluously cadenced prose demonstrates, like the combination of poetic genius with musical obtuseness in Yeats, that these special talents are not interchangeable among the genres and the related arts. The volume also showed Moore still seriously troubled with the lack of an assured direction. The theories of Théophile Gautier had not transposed well into art, and Moore's first work shows an alternation of overanxious and half-hearted allegiance. The poems frequently suggest Moorisms; in several, the self-mocking note cannot be missed. The poem "Sappho," for example, in describing the epicene setting and the "essences, pomatums, pins, and depilatories" appropriate to Lesbos, places in their midst a marble cupid "blowing from his nostrils two jets of water, one hot, the other cold." And yet Moore's "sincerity" in holding Gautier's views cannot be denied. The intermingling of pious acceptance and uncontrollable mockery of the same object, while it did not make poetry, did produce an interesting mishmash. Moore's contemporaries, however, were not interested. London took note of *Pagan Poems* only to invent a new name for the author, "Pagan" Moore, which placed him hardly a step beyond his sporting father, who was known among London toffs in the 1850's as "Dog" Moore, after the Moore Hall race horse "Wolfdog."

In Moore's twenty-ninth year the dawn of talent was still

only very faintly seen. Between the callowness of his first works, written at near mature age, and the consummate skill of his later manner, there lay a gap whose breadth is difficult to match in the history of English literature. The successful crossing of this gap provides an impressive testimonial to the power of persistence and devotion in bringing the most wayward talents home again.

4

Zola's Ricochet

> A Mummer's Wife, *strange to say, is quite a pet among the Aristocracy. All the lords and ladies want to know the author.*
>
> —Letter from George Moore to his mother, 1885

> *A man may write twenty volumes of poetry, history, and philosophy, but a man will never be born who will write more than two, or at the most three, naturalistic novels . . . if you take into consideration the difficulty of observing twice, [and] of the time an experience takes to ripen in you. . . .*
>
> —MIKE FLETCHER

MOORE'S SINISTER and exquisite flowers were half congenial to him personally, but he seems to have found *Pagan Poems* unsatisfactory in one important aspect: it could not be sold. The ragman acquired most of the edition and turned it into scrap paper, oblivious of the fact that in due time a single copy of the work would sell for two thousand dollars. Moore was destined to take up the decadent mode on two future occasions in his career, and each time would be for a brief time like a joyful homecoming; yet in 1881 it was plain that his first effort was not a success. Unless Mr. Bottles recalled Edmund Yates's attack on Moore three years earlier, he would have been innocent of the knowledge that Moore considered himself embarked upon a struggle without quarter with Mr. Bottles' world. One could hardly be said to be at war until one made contact with the enemy.

Moore already felt the grinding compulsion to slavish and

unremitting work that would drive him mercilessly until his dying day, *travaillant pour travailler,* in Flaubert's phrase. Before leaving Paris he had written to his mother: "My life is a miserable one;—*je vie dans mon o[e]uvre*—it is my only consolation." [1] If he lacked new avenues to explore, he could retrace the well-worn paths. If he could imitate Poe once, he could do it again and again, if necessary; and, if he ran out of ideas altogether, he could reprint pieces already published. One of the *Pagan Poems,* "A une Poitrinaire," pleased him so well that he reprinted it in three different works, making it as familiar to students of his work as the morning newspaper. It proclaimed the special exoticism to be derived from love for a moribund tuberculous virgin:

> . . . love perhaps is not, yet
> To see you fading like a violet,
> Or some sweet thought away, would be a strange
> And costly pleasure, far beyond the range
> Of common man's emotion. . . .

The curious word "costly" was Tennysonian, and Moore may have recalled the last line of *Enoch Arden*—"the little port/ Had seldom seen a costlier funeral." But the Parisian elements, the invidious and exotic elements, mainly account for Moore's unwavering affection for this piece.

Convinced that the "poem in prose" was a genre that one could afford to bet on, since it was preferred by the "ten superior persons scattered through the universe," Moore took up the form for the work that was to follow *Pagan Poems,* to be called *Roses of Midnight.* He intended to write thirty or forty prose poems for the volume, and in 1879 he wrote his mother from Paris that the work was about three-fourths finished. His little vignettes were, he said later, "perfectly constructed" as far as he could remember. In keeping with Gautier's precepts he had set himself a very exacting formal problem, composing in "extravagant" prose meters. The substance of the new work was, however, made of quite shopworn goods, clichés in manner if not in detail:

One of the characteristics of the volume was that daylight was banished from its pages. In the sensual lamplight of yellow boudoirs, or the wild moonlight of centenarian forests, my fantastic loves lived out their lives, died with the dawn which was supposed to be an awakening to consciousness of reality.[2]

Moore left us with a summary of only two of the thirty or forty sketches, but the two were said to be typical:

. . . there was the youth who wandered by night into a witches' sabbath, and was disputed for by the witches, young and old. There was the light o'love who went into the desert to tempt the holy man; but he died as he yielded, and the arms stiffening by some miracle to iron-like rigidity, she was unable to free herself, and died of starvation, as her bondage loosened in decay.[3]

Moore was as a rule temperamentally unable to destroy manuscript copy of any sort but would keep an unused fragment around for years in the hope of working it in somewhere. The violence of his revulsion from his initial literary manner is indicated by the fact that *Roses of Midnight* actually was destroyed. A couple of weird vignettes, one of them describing the end of the world, found their way into *Mike Fletcher*; these may have been relics of the projected volume, but the rest of the pieces have never been heard from. For Moore was now ready for the first of the aesthetic somersaults that were to become habitual in his career as a writer. "I had begun to feel," he said, "that I was working in sand, I could make no progress, the house I was raising crumbled and fell away on every side. . . . I vaguely understood that my *Roses of Midnight* were sterile eccentricities, dead flowers that could not be galvanized into any semblance of life, passionless in all their passion." Bidding Swinburne, Poe, and Baudelaire a hasty and unceremonious adieu, he turned to Balzac, Flaubert, and Zola, and declared himself a naturalist.

Balzac had appeared on his horizon a short while earlier, but as an exotic, as another Gautier. Following a hint thrown out by Gautier in an introduction to *Les Fleurs du Mal*, he had made the discovery of Balzac's *Seraphita*, "a new Mademoiselle de Maupin, with royal lily and aureole, cloudcapped mountains, great gulfs of sea-water flowing up and reflecting as in a mirror the steep cliff's side." [4] Further acquaintance with this side of Balzac's vision came through Villiers de l'Isle-Adam, who held him spellbound one night in the Nouvelle Athènes with a re-telling of "An Incident of the Terror." Pursuing these leads he came finally to *Père Goriot;* to Lucien Rubempré, in whom Moore saw a portrait of himself and his ambitions, *"être aimé et célébré";* to *Les Paysans,* which had with uncanny accuracy predicted an uprising of the peasants exactly like the Land War in Mayo; eventually to all of the *Comédie Humaine.* In time he would make his famous declaration, never to be retracted, of his debt to Balzac: "Upon that rock I built my church, and his great and valid talent saved me often from destruction, saved me from the shoaling waters of new aestheticisms, the putrid mud of naturalism, and the faint and sickly surf of the symbolists. . . . Balzac was the great moral influence of my life." [5]

One day while waiting for Lopez in a café, Moore was idly glancing through a copy of *Voltaire* and began reading an article by Zola. Amazed and excited, he read that the frightful struggle he was engaged upon in trying to compose his *Roses of Midnight* was unnecessary, and that one could become a writer by follow-ing *"naturalisme, la vérité, la science."* "I rose up from my break-fast, ordered my coffee and stirred the sugar, a little dizzy, like one who has received a violent blow on the head." [6] Moore's first reaction to his new discovery was to ask himself "how I was to participate in it," and he concluded that he would be wise to establish himself as the world's first naturalistic poet. After some consideration, however, this choice seemed to have been too hasty, and he decided to become the first naturalistic novelist in English.

His creative impasse was instantly broken. Now he need never degrade in Grub Street the ideals learned in Montmartre, by writing poor imitations of Dickens, Thackeray, or George

Eliot. He need never march lock step in the literature factories, although Gautier himself, a crucifier of journalism, had spent most of his life and talent as a journalist. He need struggle no longer to compose decadent imitations. He need only follow Zola, who was breaking ground that was *new*; and had not Baudelaire himself authorized in "Le Voyage" the most extreme actions *"pour trouver du* nouveau?"

> Naturalism, truth, the *new* art, above all the phrase, "the *new* art," impressed me as with a sudden sense of light. . . . The idea of a *new* art based on science, in opposition to the art of the old world that was based on imagination, an art that should explain all things and embrace modern life in its entirety, in its endless ramifications, be, as it were, a *new* creed in a *new* civilisation, filled me with wonder. . . . In my fevered fancy I saw a *new* race of writers that would arise . . . and at each development of the theory of the *new* art and its universal applicability, my wonder increased and my admiration choked me [italics mine].[7]

To understand Moore's attraction to naturalism, one must recall that its reputation in the middle of the twentieth century is not at all what it was when the fateful copy of *Voltaire* fell into his hands at the end of the 1870's. Naturalism was then looked upon as only the creed of another sort of *avant-garde* sect, no more peculiar than other bizarre movements that emerged out of the Latin Quarter and Montmartre. The sect's kinship with Baudelaire, and even with Gautier and Hugo and the general romantic line, was then more apparent than were its differences. The naturalists, though more especially the lesser lights of the movement, resembled Baudelaire in the prominence they gave to the sentiment of disgust, so that the affective quality of Huysmans' strange little novel *Marthe* is indistinguishable from that of Baudelaire's "Voyage à Cythère." Naturalism proclaimed its amoral outlook even more militantly than Gautier; and it was only ashamed of shame. Finally, the naturalists, like all their Parisian peers, were intensely absorbed in the problems of craft, form, and style. Moore thought *L'Assommoir* a monumental achievement in architectonics, and even after he had broken from the naturalist movement he wrote in high praise of the realists' craftsmanship:

> One thing that cannot be denied to the realists: a constant and intense desire to write well, to write artistically. When I think of what they have done in the matter of the use of words, of the myriad verbal effects they have discovered, of the thousand forms of composition they have created, how they have remodelled and refashioned the language in their untiring striving for intensity of expression for the very osmazome of art, I am lost in ultimate wonder and admiration. What Hugo did for French verse, Flaubert, Goncourt, Zola, and Huysmans have done for French prose. No more literary school than the realists has ever existed, and I do not except even the Elizabethans. And for this our failures are more interesting than the successes of our opponents; for when we fall into the sterile and distorted, it is through our noble and incurable hatred of the commonplace of all that is popular.[8]

Eventually Parisian writers discovered that in embracing, or at least countenancing, naturalism, they had committed themselves to principles not originally perceived; and they were embarrassed to find themselves being pushed by Zola into the heresy of doubting both the inutility and the divinity of art. There was then much commotion to correct the record. The inevitable philosophical break in the ancient friendship between Zola and Cézanne occurred in 1885, when Zola concluded that his former friend was a "maddened visionary . . . thrown into the exaltation of the unreal," while Cézanne was arriving at the conviction that Zola "had become a damned bourgeois." Among Zola's followers there was on the one hand a closing of the ranks; Arnold Hauser has called attention to Paul Alexis' incomparable declaration of fidelity to Zola, a telegram to Jules Huret reading: *"Naturalisme pas mort. Lettre suit."* But there were also many defections, recantations, and recriminations, climaxed by the notorious "Manifesto of the Five" in 1887, which denounced the naturalist movement on the grounds that its founder was presumed to be sexually impotent, since Madame

Zola had given birth to no offspring. Moore wrote to Zola politely deploring the attacks he had been subjected to, but Moore too was to slip out of the movement during these years of schism.

Joseph Hone has pointed out that Moore's accounts of his intimacy with Zola were somewhat inflated. Before leaving Paris in 1880 he had seen Zola only once, at a *L'Assommoir* ball given to celebrate the success of the stage version of the novel. Moore came dressed as Zola's alcoholic roofing worker, Coupeau. Manet introduced the two, but Zola was distant toward the young man and no conversation took place. At about this time Moore had become friendly with several of Zola's satellites at the Nouvelle Athènes. After a long lapse of time, perhaps as long as two years, though the date is uncertain, Moore approached Zola through correspondence from an address in London. He wrote a humble letter declaring his allegiance to naturalism and to its founder and suggesting that Zola commission him to translate *L'Assommoir*. Thus began an extended but never ardent correspondence.

The professional relation between the two writers resembled the friendship between Moore and Lopez. Moore, on his part, had no prejudice against the use of the common stratagems for securing publicity. He had discovered that his appearance in London as an English Baudelaire had been greeted by a monumental indifference. Swinburne had long since exhausted the shock possibilities of that stance and had gone his way to Number 2, The Pines, Putney. But to appear in 1882 as the English Zola was like hoisting a red flag in Piccadilly, and Moore's conclusion was the obvious one. Zola, for his part, was a proselytizer by instinct, and he welcomed the young recruit's offers to help transplant naturalism into England, particularly since *L'Assommoir* had run through forty-eight printings in Paris without having appeared at all in English. Lopez had engagingly confessed to Moore: "I should feel proud and delighted by the applause of an English audience," and Zola's ambitions were not dissimilar. The translation project did not materialize, but Moore's suggestion led to his making the acquaintance of Vizetelly, Zola's future publisher in London, who was later to join Moore in his attack upon the lending libraries.

Since the collapse of *Roses of Midnight,* Moore had been at work on a realistic novel based on the adventures of his bohemian roommate in the Rue de la Tour des Dames, the painter and genius *manqué,* Lewis Weldon Hawkins. In 1882 he published it under the title, *A Modern Lover,* subsequently changed to *Lewis Seymour and Some Women.* Moore wrote to Zola:

> I have just published a novel which has had success. . . . The fact that my novel has been successful may interest you; for, as I have already told you, I owe you everything.[9]

The homage was premature, however, and, strangely for Moore, overmodest. *A Modern Lover* is a true original, indebted finally to the vision of George Moore. It carries, it is true, an unmistakable French or "modern" tone. This trait is shared necessarily with Zola's novels, but the novel sounds less like Zola than like Balzac, Flaubert, and the Goncourts, particularly the last. In his old age Moore especially remembered the impression made upon him in his first years in London by Edmond Goncourt's *La Fille Eliza,* "a story that enchanted me in my lonely lodging and awakened new dreams of the conquest of London." One London book reviewer took pains to point out the gap that separated *A Modern Lover* from the novels of Zola, congratulated the author for it, and warned him against letting the gap grow narrower:

> One is made aware by certain passages that Mr. Moore would fain imitate the methods of Zola and his odious school, but two obstacles are in his path—the faith of a Christian and the instincts of a gentleman; the author recognizes and respects goodness, purity and disinterestedness, and if M. Zola or any of the hogs of his sty could write such an episode as that with which the story opens, the work-

girl's sacrifice for the penniless artist, one would have as much hope for their future as for that of Mr. Moore.[10]

A Modern Lover is the success story of a "mean cad," Lewis Seymour, whose rise in the world is achieved by exploiting and discarding various women in a position to advance or amuse him. Despite the possibilities offered, it is not a notably "improper" novel, even in the Victorian sense. Only a very obtuse member of the National Vigilance Association could have failed to see that, although the wages of selfishness are wealth and election to the Royal Academy, the ironic price paid for success is Seymour's moral and aesthetic decay. The novel leers frequently at the undraped female bodies on the model's dais, treats adultery openly, and engages in much bohemian chatter to make dialogue. But, compared with such a roistering treatment of the same theme as Maupassant's *Bel-Ami*, Moore's novel is pallid and unexceptionable. "I was obliged to attenuate dreadfully," he complained to Zola, "but what else could I do?"

A Modern Lover sent Moore into head-on collision with the circulating libraries. Smith's library labeled the book immoral after receiving complaints from "two ladies from the country," who took exception to the scene in which the poor but chaste Gwennie Lloyd saved Seymour from starvation by removing her dress and posing for a painting of Venus rising from the waves, the same scene that had been praised by the book reviewer who congratulated Moore on separating himself from Zola and "the hogs of his sty." Moore called on the managers at both Smith's and Mudie's and learned that they had placed his novel out of sight under the counter and only produced it upon special request. He made a disturbance at both libraries, and he concluded his interview with Mudie, "an almost lifeless man," with threats of financial ruin. "I'll wreck this big house of yours, Mr. Mudie," he shouted. Meanwhile he was able to get space in the letters-to-the-editor columns to vindicate his position and to keep the spark glowing.

The effect of this skirmish was to draw Moore closer to Zola.

He had composed *A Modern Lover* in a spirit of reasonable moderation, but, finding no reciprocal mood in the opposition, he prepared to intensify his attack. He thereupon set out to write his one strictly naturalistic novel, a tale of dipsomania, adultery, asthma, and obesity among a troupe of provincial players, *A Mummer's Wife*, printed in 1885. Anticipating that the novel would be rejected by the circulating libraries, he had persuaded Zola's friend and publisher, Vizetelly, to challenge the three-volume, thirty-one-shilling publication on which the libraries based their monopoly—the general public being unable to afford so high a price—and to bid directly for a mass market with a one-volume cheap edition of the novel.

Moore's morale improved markedly as he prepared for the showdown with the libraries. His confidence overflowed. One of his spokesmen in *A Modern Lover* had already laid down the lines of his challenge:

> Already a revolution is visible everywhere. . . . The novelist is gaining the day for the study of the surroundings; the painter for atmospheric effects. . . . A bombshell is about to break, and you open your umbrellas; but have a care, oh, you who are academicians, the bombshell will destroy without mercy all things, both the small and heavy, that oppose it.[11]

The excitement was picked up in his writing; his style improved, his eye sharpened, and his narrative began to flow under so skillful a hand that he would always look back on the time when he was writing *A Mummer's Wife* as the only effortless and joyful writing he ever did that would not later shame him.

Moore's debt to Zola now became clear for the first time. He became intoxicated with the naturalistic theory, and Zola's vocabulary added a curious fillip to his philosophizing. His heroine in *A Drama in Muslin* (1886) was doubtless the first in Victorian fiction whose "hatred of all that concerned sexual passion was consequent on her father's age and her mother's loathing for him during pregnancy and conception." He spoke constantly of logic and science as the dominant spirits of the new age, and much

91

of his rationale sounded like a direct lifting from *Le Roman expérimental*:

> How various and intricate are the questions with which we find ourselves confronted in the course of any cerebral investigation! How mysteriously they wander from their natal lines into crooked devious ways, and then suddenly, how they come flowing back in a great stream, differing absolutely in color and current. . . . And yet, if these apparent contradictions were to be pursued closely through the deeps of the night of creation, each could be demonstrated as logical as any theorem in Euclid, either by heredity, or by accidental variations of the physical nature, which in turn reacts upon the brain.[12]

Under the spell of this doctrinaire assurance, Moore unhesitatingly dispossessed the moral conscience of its Victorian prestige as the pure center of serious fiction, and into its place he put raw instinct and physiology. Lewis Seymour suffers remorse for the lives he has made miserable: has he a conscience? No, said Moore, his thin thread of conscience turns out to be merely "nervous irritability." The conscience, Moore informed his readers, "is no more than indirect laws—the esssence of the laws transmitted by heredity." Moore placed himself in all the early novels as a minor character, a wise and sardonic modern novelist named Harding. And Harding had no more conscience than the rest; he was a man "who saw and felt through his intelligence and not his conscience." By simple fiat, so it seemed, all the elaborate evangelical moral machinery of Dickens and George Eliot was simply obliterated.

If one's novels were to be built upon instinct, one must give to sex drives a more thoughtful and warm-hearted recognition than Victorian readers were accustomed to. Moore had raised the question at the opening of his career whether love, when "dissected," were not "only sensuality in disguise," and he quickly followed up the suggestion, moving into the untilled field of sexual motivation and speculation and making a spectacular reputation there for himself and for his novels. Compton Mackenzie recalled the sensation that burst upon the English literary world when the schoolgirls in *A Drama in Muslin* were overheard in their bedroom discussing their chamois drawers. It was in the same novel that Captain Hibbert, twisting his golden mustache, imaginatively undressed the waltzing girls with a connoisseur's eye. These small playful items became a sort of a trademark for Moore, and they continued to interest him down to his last novel, where the ideal contour of Aphrodite's posterior is lengthily considered.

The environmental half of Zola's theory of motivation raised more knotty problems for Moore. In *A Modern Lover* environment plays no dynamic part, but in *A Mummer's Wife* it is essential in the structure of the novel. Kate Ede, the heroine, is a woman of "lower middle-class instincts," the wife of a dreary asthmatic linen draper, a woman "admirably suited to the life she was leading" but possessed of fatal longings to escape the spiritual poverty of that life. Kate is seduced and carried away by a strolling actor, and, when thrown into the free sporting environment in which her middle-class taboos are completely swept away, she quickly degenerates into a dipsomaniac and shortly afterward dies a sordid naturalistic death, gasping alternately Wesleyan hymns and the hit song of her brief days as a vaudeville star. Moore's point seemed to be that the lower middle classes should beware of aspirations toward self-realization. This idea was of course borrowed from *Madame Bovary,* whose heroine, like Kate Ede, prepared her downfall by reading "romantic novels," according to the law that the loss of one inhibition is equivalent to losing all.

Moore prefaced the early editions of *A Mummer's Wife* with an epigraph taken not from Zola's mentor, Claude Bernard, but from a comparable authority, the historian Victor Duruy:

> Change the surroundings in which man lives, and in two or three generations you will have changed his physical constitution, his habits of life, and a goodly number of his ideas.

In later editions this arresting idea was dropped out to make room for a dedication to Robert Ross. It no longer pleased

Moore, but it remained appropriate to *A Mummer's Wife,* which took the position that, if the *Family Herald* were forbidden to publish sentimental verse or fiction in which a lady "read Byron and Shelley under the green trees to the gentleman who went to India in despair," all would then be well in middle-class kitchens and boudoirs. As a more general proposition, environmentalism did not win Moore's confidence; he suspected that it would lead to no good and preferred simply to assert that "our lives run in grooves; we get into one and we follow it out to the end," without inquiring why or how this assertion was true.

A correlative of Zola's stress on environment was the notebook method, which Moore took up in earnest. Edmond Goncourt remembered him as a strange young Irishman who scribbled notes of their dinner conversation on the cuff of his shirt. Vizetelly advised him to find the ugliest town in England and to study it with the prescribed naturalistic techniques; and, when newspapermen around the Gaiety Bar told him that this place was Hanley, one of the Five Towns, he armed himself with his notebook and a sharpened pencil and set out to learn about the potteries, just as though he were Zola heading for the Parisian vegetable markets to commence work on *Le Ventre de Paris.* Moore seems not to have been excited by his tour of the potteries, however, although the novel contains a description of a guided tour of the factories made by Kate Ede and her lover, the actor Dick Lenox. "They were now in a long lobby with big rafters overhead," et cetera. Dick Lenox, for dramatic reasons, is not convinced that "it is of the highest importance" that an "actor and dressmaker should understand the different processes the earthenware had to pass through before it was placed on toilet or breakfast table," for he is anxious to draw Kate into the darkness of the warehouse to make love to her. But Moore's projection of Lenox' boredom is perhaps too eloquent. It was not proper for Zola's pupil to be overwhelmed by "wearisome details"; he should approach a new *tranche de vie* like a Homeric horse prancing for battle.

A better yield came from his notebook study of the life of traveling actors, to which he was introduced by his younger brother Augustus. Augustus had a wide bohemian acquaintance in London and was even more adventuresome than the Moore family tradition required. He had made a name for himself as a boy by setting his schoolhouse on fire; later, he had burst into the *Irish Monthly* of November, 1878, with a sonnet entitled "To Oscar Wilde, Author of 'Ravenna,'" which closed with the following lines:

> I buried Love within the rose I meant
> To deck the fillet of your Muse's hair;
> I take this wild flower, grown against her feet,
> And kissing its half-opened lips I swear,
> Frail though it be, and widowed of its scent,
> I plucked it for your sake and find it sweet.[13]

When he came up to London from Moore Hall he became known about town as "Masher" Moore. George admired him greatly, and through him made a connection with a company of traveling actors playing Hervé and Offenbach. The two brothers collaborated in a translation of *Les Cloches de Corneville*, and Moore traveled with the company for several weeks, taking notes on the life of "mummers" and mastering with marvelous insight their peculiar experience.

A Mummer's Wife was published in 1885. Moore now called himself Zola's "ricochet" in England. He wrote to the master in Médan that *A Mummer's Wife* was "twenty times better than my first effort; and what is more important it will be printed as a single volume as you advised." As anticipated, the novel was rejected by the circulating libraries, but it achieved a modest financial success through bookshop sales. *A Mummer's Wife* received thirteen favorable notices in the London press; within a few months it ran through three editions and a translation into French was begun. This reception was well deserved. After seventy years the novel still has powerful affective force, arising in part from the remarkable, almost Tolstoian, shrewdness in observing the ordinary interplay of social creatures, in part from the tact with which Kate's "inevitable" destiny is unfolded, in part, too, from the deftness Moore displayed in the ironic characterization of Dick Lenox as he evolves from Kate's sporting seducer into a martyr who bears Kate's alcoholic cruelties and deranged jealousies with bewildered fortitude and charity. In midsummer of 1885, Moore wrote his mother: "All London has read *A Mummer's Wife*. When I enter a drawing room everyone wants to be introduced to me; I could dine out every night if I care to—I am pestered with invitations. . . . All the lords and ladies want to know the author."

The same letter concluded: "I am attacking the libraries again." He had been preparing for some time a pamphlet to be issued when another provocation should occur. As soon as the libraries announced their objections to *A Mummer's Wife*, he was prepared with his reply, which Vizetelly published shortly after the release of the novel. The pamphlet, *Literature at Nurse, or Circulating Morals* (by the author of *A Mummer's Wife*, "a realistic novel in one volume"), employed the standard stratagem developed by the French for such an occasion, namely, lengthy citation of the inconsistencies in the puritan attack. Thirty years earlier, Flaubert had sent out an emergency call to his literary friends asking for "the greatest possible number of smutty passages drawn from ecclesiastical writers." [14] Moore's pamphlet consisted mainly of "improper" citations drawn from books circulated by the libraries. For example, he took a passage from *Nadine*, by Mrs. Campbell Praed, in which the heroine came to a gentleman's room in the middle of the night and asked to have her child delivered:

> She was dressed in a loose cashmere robe that clinging to her form displayed its outlines clearly. In an instant his practical intelligence had grasped her imminent need.

Following each such excerpt Moore chimed in with an apostrophe to Mr. Mudie:

. . . tell me Mr. Mudie, if there be not in this dose just a little too much bosom showing, if there be not too much ankle appearing beneath this skirt?

This argument was buttressed with a somewhat conflicting contention that the censorship was "useless" because fundamental human drives will express themselves regardless of efforts to suppress them. In *Literature at Nurse* this idea was stated diplomatically; later, however, when he had no cause to show himself amiable, he stated with great feeling the argument that might be regarded as the definitive presentation of the view that expurgation is useless:

. . . poor human nature! when you pinch it in in one place it bulges out in another, after the fashion of a lady's figure. Human nature has from the earliest time shown a liking for dirty stories; dirty stories have formed a substantial part of every literature (I employ the words "dirty stories" in the circulating library sense); therefore a taste for dirty stories may be said to be inherent in the human animal. Call it a disease if you will—an incurable disease—which, if it is driven inwards, will break out in an unexpected quarter in a new form and with redoubled virulence. This is exactly what has happened. Actuated by the most laudable motives, Mudie cut off our rations of dirty stories, and for forty years we were apparently the most moral people on the face of the earth. It was confidently asserted that an English woman of sixty would not read what would bring the blush of shame to the cheeks of a maiden of any other nation. But humiliation and sorrow were awaiting Mudie. True it is that we still continued to subscribe to his library, true it is that we still continued to go to church, true it is that we turned our faces away when *Mademoiselle de Maupin* or the *Assommoir* was spoken of; to all appearance we were as good and chaste as even Mudie might wish us; and no doubt he looked back upon his forty years of effort with pride; no doubt he beat his manly breast and said, "I have scotched the evil one out of the villa; the head of the serpent is crushed for evermore;" but lo, suddenly, with all the horror of an earthquake, the slumbrous law courts awoke, and the burning cinders of fornication and the blinding and suffocating smoke of adultery were poured upon and hung over the land. Through the mighty columns of our newspapers the terrible lava rolled unceasing, and in the black stream the villa, with all its beautiful illusions, tumbled and disappeared.[15]

Still another facet of Moore's argument contended that it is the romantic, rather than the naturalistic, novel that is truly seductive, that *Paul and Virginia,* and not *A Mummer's Wife,* "leads to sin." Finally the pamphlet appealed to the British public to end Mudie's "dictatorship" by ceasing to patronize his libraries.

The results of the pamphlet were satisfactory. Moore received support from the respectable press, and the reverberations made his name widely known for the first time. The common sense of the pamphlet was irresistible; the British public moved slightly toward toleration for writers for the first time in half a century. Even Moore's enemies praised the novel and the pamphlet of 1885 as a decisive preparatory step leading to the creation of the twentieth-century novel. But one unexpected voice joined the outraged puritans. Swinburne, now in his reactionary phase and leading the hue and cry against Zola's "indecency," said of *A Mummer's Wife:* "It was not with a chamber pot for a buckler and a spit for a spear that I charged the philistines." [16] Moore's gratitude to Swinburne—*ô poëte sublime*—was so ample that he failed to resent the disparagement, the only such instance known to his biographers.

Moore had not succeeded in carrying out his threat to wreck Mudie's big house, but he had made it possible for novelists like himself to write without Mudie's blessing. A decade was to pass before Mudie would accept Moore's work again and bring the issue to its final conclusion. In the meantime Moore's reputation was established and his position had been made secure. His ardor for battle began to cool accordingly, and, with less need for Zola's militant methods, he began to shy away from identification with naturalism.

He was now in the midst of a "study" of the social world of the Irish gentry. Although he had grown up in this world and presumably knew it from top to bottom, he still found a need for his naturalistic notebook. In January, 1885, he wrote to Dublin Castle demanding an invitation to a state levee, explaining that he was writing a book on the social and political power of the Castle. "My books are, as you are probably aware," he wrote to the viceroy, "extensively read; this particular one will attract a good deal of attention. It would therefore be well to render my picture as complete, as true, as vivid as possible." This request was of course refused, but Moore was now a veteran in the art of extracting the maximum of newspaper publicity from small tempests, and he kept his "grievance" before the Dublin public longer than one would have thought possible, concluding it at last with a sensational personal attack upon the viceroy:

> Fame comes to us in unexpected ways, and I believe that when this somnolent earl is overtaken by that sleep that overtakes us all, and for which, it appears, he is qualifying himself daily as well as nightly, his claim to be remembered will be that he refused to invite me to dinner at the Castle.[17]

Moore now discovered that the frenetic pace expected of the naturalistic disciple was beyond his energy. Zola was capable of "working up" a new subject every year—war, railroading, the vegetable markets, the coal mines, prostitution, alcoholism, and so forth—but the subject of the Irish gentry, where Moore was most at home, began to strain him. Joseph Hone found in the family correspondence an amusing letter begging his brother Julian for help in preparing *A Drama in Muslin.* "Take a large packet and a good pencil," his instructions began, "and write me in disconnected phrases the impressions as they struck you. Don't try to imitate me too much. . . . A picture of Ballinasloe, the great meat market, would come in very well indeed." Later Moore was to assert that the human nervous system was incapable of bearing the strain of writing more than three naturalistic novels.

He was now discovering philosophical objections to Zola that weighed more and more heavily in the decision he was drifting into. In Zola's original formulation, the observation of the novelist was to be impartial, cold, and scientific. Zola had attacked Dumas *fils* for "a deplorable desire for legislation, preaching, and conversion," and for making himself "God's substitute on earth."

99

Zola thought that either plot or morality in the novel was a perversion of scientific truth, and he forbade the novelist to discuss or to resolve problems as such. "Our sole purpose," he said, "is to put the human record under the eyes of all: look, judge, and decide." The naturalists had no intention, he said, of "correcting that which is according to that which ought to be." [18] This was good, straight Second Empire aesthetics. It had an innocent sound, like the asseverations of political purity that flowed perpetually out of the headquarters of the Gaelic League. Moore was to discover that in both instances the claim to impartiality involved a good deal of self-deception. Zola's official, stated ideal was exemplified in the Goncourts' novel, *Germinie Lacerteux,* a clinical dissection of a serving girl's downfall, cold, "inevitable," and called impersonal; in actuality, however, it was a highly personal condescension by two exotics studying with inverted sentimentality the struggles of interesting specimens at the opposite end of the social scale. Antedating Zola's fame by a decade, *Germinie Lacerteux* was the first of the absolutely "pure" clinical novels, and very nearly the last, a tour de force that could hardly be repeated except at the price of increasing tediousness, irritation, and *nausée.*

Luckily for Zola his imagination overwhelmed his theory. The titanic figure of Gervaise emerges as one of the most powerfully conceived characters of world literature only because Zola was incapable of the Goncourts' view of Germinie. Gradually and logically he was driven toward an open declaration of his feelings, toward a vehement assertion that the things that he must depict as true, though true, should nevertheless not be. Since environment was in his eyes so weighty a force in the determination of behavior, he cried out at last for environment to be remade. Zola's Dreyfusard pamphlet was not so much a betrayal of the pure impartiality of naturalism as a confession that its boasted impartiality was unattainable. Moore's good friend Ernest Boyd noted this difference between Zola and the Goncourts, and in his introduction to *Germinie Lacerteux* he said:

It did not take long to demonstrate that his [Zola's] conception of realism led through monotony and repetition to the inevitable assumption of a democratic mission. Zola ended as a Messiah with a panacea and a message for humanity. Oblivion was imminent. Edmond de Goncourt remained aloof.

A weakness in Boyd's position is suggested by the fact that it was the Goncourts who were the more overwhelmed by oblivion, and the same weakness seems obviously attached to Moore's prognostication of imminent oblivion for Tolstoi's works because of their impurity.

In *A Drama in Muslin* Moore undertook to depict the frustrations of three "nice girls" who were graduated from the convent school into the seedy social life of Dublin and the "big houses" of rural Ireland during the Land War. Urged on by Zola's theory, his investigation had led him into uncomfortable places. For example, his treatment of Alice Barton's rebellion against the Dublin marriage mart led him in the direction of a sort of tentative feminism, a position absolutely at odds with his "instincts," that is, with his deepest and most consistent prejudices, which assured him that a woman's function is "the relaxation of the warrior" when he returns home from "conquering." Similarly, his dissection of the drift of Ireland toward some unimaginable disaster was leading him inescapably toward an examination of the roots of his personal predicament:

> The history of a nation as often lies hidden in social wrongs and domestic griefs as in the story of revolution, and if it be for the historian to narrate one, it is for the novelist to dissect and explain the other.[19]

This statement marks the furthest point Moore ever reached in following Zola down the road that led to "democratic mission." If that was the way naturalism led, he had been deceived, and the time was at hand for him to declare himself disaffiliated.

In the composition of *A Drama in Muslin* his imagination had already made a break from naturalism, though his theory had not yet moved so far. At precisely the time of publication,

Zola had written him a letter sparkling with energy and exhortation to battle:

> Why don't you set to work at once upon a novel about Ireland; a social novel, truthful, audacious, revolutionary? . . . England would be consternated by it; never did such an occasion offer itself to move a whole people. Think of it! Boldness, boldness, and more boldness.[20]

Too late: Moore's "social novel" had already been finished. It was, he thought, truthful, but it was certainly neither audacious nor revolutionary, and England would never be consternated by it. The raw and elemental sense of force that he had succeeded in evoking in the writing of *A Mummer's Wife* had somehow dissipated, and he found that he had written a charming, wistful, muted novel sounding like the work of a neophyte Turgenev.

Moore's struggle to master the theoretical problems of objectivity and commitment continued into the succeeding months, when the publication in Paris of his *Terre d'Irlande,* later published in English as *Parnell and His Island,* revealed his cross-purpose and confusion grown into violent proportions, resulting, as we have seen, from his dual vision of the Land War in Mayo. His picture of Ireland, extremely naturalistic in technique, closed with this curious statement on impersonality:

> The scenes in the pages of this book point to no moral. . . . They were not selected to plead any cause, or to announce the success or failure of Land Leaguers or landlords; they were chosen because they seemed to me typical and picturesque. . . . My desire was to produce a series of pictures to touch the fancy of the reader as a Japanese ivory or fan, combinations of hue and color calculated to awake in him fictitious feelings of pity, pitiful curiosity and nostalgia for the unknown.[21]

Coming at the conclusion of one of the most subjective pamphlets on Ireland's distress ever written, this declaration showed Moore to be now very close to aesthetic schizophrenia, and some new somersault, some unforeseen *péripétie,* was at hand.

When next heard of in Moore's writing, Zola had been suddenly transformed from the great genius of the age into a sort of literary anti-Christ. In 1885 Moore thought him "not inappropriately termed the Homer of modern life"; in 1888 he had become merely "the dregs of yesterday's champagne." The writer who had "conceived and constructed the framework of a complex civilization" had become a man "singularly narrow" in vision. The titan who had made language his slave, in whom "the strength and beauty of his style is an unfailing use of the right word," had become a journalistic hack: "He has no style; there is nothing you won't find in Zola from Chateaubriand to the reporting in the *Figaro*." The artist whose true virtues were delicate and evanescent and perceptible only to the "fellow worker," and hidden from the eyes of the vulgar "as the mistletoe invariably hides the oak," was found to be crude, mechanical, and unaesthetic. "I shall never read another book by him," Moore wrote to his friend Blanche. "He does not address the scholarly instincts in readers."

In the years that followed, Moore's favorite criticism against Zola's work was the familiar one that he lacked a sense of selection, a cliché not unknown even two generations after Moore's death. "Art is not nature," Moore informed his recent master, "art is nature digested. Art is sublime excrement. Zola and Goncourt cannot, or will not, understand that the artistic stomach must be allowed to do its own work in its own mysterious fashion." [22] In the 1890's the criticism was repeated: "M. Zola's books are growing more and more diffuse; it is clear that he has ceased to practice the art of omission," and "the house at Médan seems to reveal a large coarse mind, a sort of coarsely woven net through whose meshes all live things escape, and that brings to shore only a quantity of debris." [23]

That Moore could have so misunderstood Zola's method is hardly possible, although his own early novels do contain pointless details in abundance. In *A Modern Lover*, for example, he described a church interior in this way: "On the right was the pulpit, on the left the reading desk, both rich with crimson vel-

vet and oak carvings. The roof and four columns, which supported the galleries, were painted gray." The marks of the
notebook and the heavy hand are unmistakable. But Zola did not
undertake to defend such a mechanical process. Art was a slice
of life, of course, but it was seen through a temperament. In
defense of naturalism against this charge, Zola had said: "A
contemptible reproach which they heap upon us naturalistic
writers is the desire to be solely photographers. We have in vain
declared that we admit the necessity of an artist's possessing an
individual temperament. . . . We must modify nature without
departing from nature." [24]

Moore must have known Zola's position on photographic realism; and his concentration upon the point for attack served,
whether intentionally or not, to cloak more significant disagree-
ments with his late master. It was not that Zola did not select,
for obviously he did, but that he selected the wrong things,
singing not the new gospel of Huysmans and Pater, whose
aesthetics Moore now favored, but "the rude industry of the
dustman." Zola's vision and method were leading Moore toward
personal disunion. Following the same sort of impulse that had
given Swinburne a sudden access of primness on reading *A
Mummer's Wife*, Moore joined hands with his erstwhile enemy
Mr. Bottles in condemnation of Zola.

The most incisive statements of Moore's new and final opinion of naturalism were elicited by paintings. At an art exhibit in
the early 1890's Moore looked at some "naturalistic" paintings,
including one by George Clausen called "Laborers after Dinner." He wrote:

> We cry out: "What madness! were we ever as mad as that?" . . .
> Until I saw Mr. Clausen's "Laborers" I did not realize fully how ter-
> rible a thing art becomes when divorced from beauty, grace, mystery,
> and suggestion. . . . Mr. Clausen has seen nothing but the sordid
> and the mean. . . . The ordinary man's aversion to such ugliness
> seems to be entirely right. . . . The mission of art is not truth, but
> beauty. . . .[25]

Such was his dispute with those artists who had failed to leave the path along which Zola, for a few short years, had led him; and in Jean François Millet he found all the wrong tendencies concentrated:

> Millet . . . took it upon himself to explain the miserable lot of the peasant; and whoever saw it remembers "L'homme à la Houe," a detestable object, but which so stirred the loose bowels of compassion that the very world was certain something must be done. . . . Philanthropy and realism entered into art arm in arm. . . .[26]

"Were we ever as mad as that?" Moore might laugh at his debt to naturalism and to the French realists, but the debt would remain. He found his first genuine creative stimulus in Zola and Balzac, in Flaubert and the Goncourts. They taught him to write. They gave him subjects, a method, a theory for interpreting the world, and the standards of craftsmanship which permitted him to grope experimentally toward a reconstruction of the English novel. But he was not quite at home in their company. It was eventually plain to him that naturalism was not to be his resting place. He saw that *L'Assommoir* must lead to *Germinal* and that his own *Mummer's Wife* pointed in a direction he could not follow. The last heir of Moore Hall was not destined to become another Millet and "stir the loose bowels of compassion." He turned back to Gautier, hoping to rediscover an aesthetic line more congenial to his special needs.

Pater's Tide
Of Honeyed Words

> *Life in modern London even, in the heavy glow of*
> *summer, is stuff sufficient for the fresh imagination of*
> *youth to build its "palace of art" of; and the very*
> *sense and enjoyment of an experience in which all is*
> *new are but enhanced, like that glow of summer itself,*
> *by the thought of its brevity, giving him something of*
> *a gambler's zest in the apprehension by dextrous act*
> *or diligently appreciative thought, of the highly colored*
> *moments which are to pass away so quickly.*
> —Walter Pater, MARIUS THE EPICUREAN

IN THE SPRING of 1885 Moore went out to county Mayo to read proof for *A Mummer's Wife,* and while staying at Moore Hall with his mother he received in the mail a copy of *Marius the Epicurean,* just published. As soon as he opened it and commenced reading, his conversion to Cyrenaicism was accomplished. Gautier in English! It was "like the odor of dead roses." In Marius' shabby gentility, his ancient decaying house, his melancholy rustication against a background of a disintegrating society, he found a perfect likeness of his own predicament, surroundings, and emotions at Moore Hall. "At every page," he said, recalling his first impressions of the book, "this story seemed to be written for me."

. . . and when that wonderful second chapter entitled "White Nights" was reached, I sat thinking, a little overcome, reproaching myself for not having thought of the unaffected joys of the heart, the color of the great air about the yellowing marbles of the Roman villa, or that by helping one's mother with her purple and white wools, and caring for her musical instruments it was possible to win from the handling of such things an urbane and feminine refinement; or that by avoiding all that leads into desire and is evidently ugly, we can make sure of a temporal life sufficiently stable and sufficient for the soul.[1]

His sentence, which could easily have wandered on some clauses further, is a gentle Moorism, parodying Pater and his own discipleship with affectionate malice. One may be sure that he did not linger long at Moore Hall repairing his mother's musical instruments. When he finished correcting his proofs he hurried back to London "to see the press in bloom."

Pater's "urbane and feminine refinement" and his timidity, which would not allow him to look another person in the eye, were traits that Moore could never emulate. Pater's anxiety to preserve the pleasant usages of good taste were also foreign to the young man already habituated to indecorous public scenes and scurrilous newspaper battles. But the shy Oxfordian manner had its uses: as an Anglo-Saxon and a gentleman Pater was beyond public reproach and able to give new authority to the unconventional Gallic beliefs that Moore brought to London from Place Pigalle. Compared to Gautier, Pater was more dainty, more profound, more lugubrious; yet the beliefs of the two were essentially the same, and Moore's linking of the two was perfectly apt. Pater, too, thought that the earth is as beautiful as heaven and that the correction of form is virtue. He found aspect more precious than essence and the receptive powers superior to the reflective, anticipating thereby the extraordinary stress upon "thisness" and "inscape" which characterized so much of the poetry and criticism of the half century following his death. His final wisdom was: "trust the eye," a precept equivalent to Gautier's belief that the visible world is visible.

Pater's style seemed, when Moore first read *Marius* in the west of Ireland, to be *Mademoiselle de Maupin* brought into English. It was the first book he had ever read in his own language that gave him pleasure in language itself. The fabulous "tide of honeyed words preached by a divine from an ivory pulpit" set up a model in style toward which his own prose was slowly to evolve and by which the styles of other writers were to be measured. Moore's final style was not, of course, the prose of *Marius;* indeed it was superior in clarity, lacking Pater's mincing nervous need to pile qualification on qualification, to discriminate every moment in order not to sleep before evening on this short day of frost and sun. But the styles of the two writers are similar; and Moore's homage to Pater's language, "it slowly unfolds like soft silk," is equally applicable to his own.

Pater stood shoulder to shoulder with Gautier in his belief in the interchangeability of religion and art. *The Renaissance* had affirmed that the wisest spend their reprieve in art and song; and *Appreciations* found art to be a "sort of cloistral refuge from a certain vulgarity in the actual world," where "the select few," the "men of finer thread" who have "undergone exact trial," may discover a solace comparable to that of a "religious 'retreat.'" It happened that Pater's examples of the works of art which possessed such potency and perfection—"Lycidas," *Henry Esmond,* and *The Idea of a University*—were pieces that had never "fetched" Moore; the first two he had not read, and his opinion of the third may be inferred from his conviction that Newman could not, as a general proposition, be "called a writer." Still, Pater's ideal was irreproachable; and Moore, following such advice, could betake himself to the Louvre, to the British Museum, to his own writing desk, secure in the knowledge that there was a "retreat" where "a certain vulgarity" could never pursue him; where, escaped from "tears and effusion," he could commune with eternal art, which has "no other end but to make life possible." [2]

Pater's Anglicanism was something else again. One might suppose that Moore would have been repelled by it, since he had been at some pains to state his views on religion perfectly clearly and in the strongest language he could command; like Gautier, he had never bathed in the waves of blood that flowed from Calvary. Yet religious discussion and religious conflicts fascinated him unceasingly. At the time of the publication of *Marius*, Moore and Henry James had discussed Pater's religious position, and James had explained to Moore that he was displeased with Pater's ambiguous tendency to praise pagan Rome and Christianity with equal fervor. "And Henry James's point was that we cannot admire opposites equally." [3] In spite of Henry James's logic, Moore came to the conclusion that a character in fiction can indeed admire opposites equally; that the closer the balance of opposites, the greater his conflict and the better the story. A man of letters does not object to conflicts: "he sharpens his pen there," and Moore sharpened his pen permanently on the religious conflict. Out of the twelve novels that he wrote following the transference of his aesthetic allegiance from Zola to Pater, nine were primarily concerned with Pater's Christian-pagan dilemma in one or more of three standard patterns.

In one pattern the pagan is attracted to Christianity; the sensual temperament longs for asceticism. This is in part the story of Marius; and Moore was sufficiently fascinated by the theme to write three novels around it: *Vain Fortune* (1892), *Sister Teresa* (1901), and *Heloise and Abelard* (1921). The second pattern is the inverse of the first: in it the Christian ascetic rebels and embraces paganism. It has been mentioned that the theme of the nun escaped from the convent absorbed Moore in his first work and continued to exercise a peculiar hold on his imagination to the end of his life. Three novels and several short stories are built upon the theme of the recantation of religion. These include *The Lake* (1905), *The Brook Kerith* (1916), and *Ulick and Soracha* (1926). In the third pattern the Christian and the pagan simply merge, as sensuality and asceticism fuse into a single sentiment. Moore called this fusion "religious sensuality." It was the most irresistible of all the themes of decadence. Wilde used it in *Salomé*, Villiers in *Axel*, Flaubert in *La Tentation de Saint-Antoine*, Anatole France in

Thaïs, Wagner in *Parsifal.* Huysmans took it up after he had tired of the scientific study of prostitution. It stands behind Pater's high-church aestheticism. Moore's recommendation of Verlaine to the British public was made with reference to his interest in the theme, and Moore found it also in the "mediaevalism" of Rimbaud and Laforgue. It lurks in the background of most of Moore's novels and provides the chief substance of three —*A Mere Accident* (1887), *Mike Fletcher* (1889), and *Evelyn Innes* (1898).

Only three of the last dozen novels that Moore wrote fail to fit these categories. The oldest of these, *Spring Days* (1888), is a story of pallid loves in suburban villas. In setting, mood, and tempo it closely resembles *A Drama in Muslin,* though it is less distinguished. When Moore gave up naturalism, he hoped to find his new subjects in the world closest to his hand, on the other side of the bohemian coin, in the familiar world of mammas, nice girls, moderate but ample inheritances, and harmless, pleasant gentility. The banality of *Spring Days* convinced him that his expectations were mistaken. After its publication, he came to the opinion that it was a total failure, the same view taken by the literary press and the public. One reviewer called it the worst novel ever written. In later years, however, Æ and the Dublin librarian Richard Best persuaded Moore, perhaps as a joke, that it was the best of all his novels. He then revived it and allowed it to appear in Liveright's collected Carra edition; later he lost confidence in it again, and, when the English collected Uniform edition was printed, he dropped it permanently from the "canon." The other two novels written after the break with Zola which show no concern with the Christian conflict are *Esther Waters* (1894), the novel on which Moore's reputation at the present time mainly rests, and *Aphrodite in Aulis* (1931), his last published novel, written at seventy-five years of age. The significance of Moore's departure from his usual line of interest in these two novels is quite broad and will be discussed later.

With the discovery of Pater and the revival of Moore's first aesthetic enthusiasms, he was confident that he had found himself artistically at last and anticipated a new phase of increased creative power and joyful self-realization. He burst suddenly into critical activity; released by Pater from the frustrating weight of Zola's vocabulary and the restricted focus of his interests, his old delight in "aestheticizing" returned. His fresh and fluent impressionistic essays on literature, painting, and the theatre began to appear in the *Spectator* and *Academy*. Two volumes of these essays were soon collected and published: *Impressions and Opinions* (1891) and *Modern Painting* (1893). The latter volume was honored by Pater himself, who gave it a generous review in the daily press.

Moore in his new phase also developed a special talent for the art of the manifesto and the astounding statement of principles. This genre had been brought to high perfection among his old Parisian confrères, whose skill in polemics was often extraordinary and not infrequently ran ahead of their creative powers. The manifestoes of *Mademoiselle de Maupin* show more life and have more interest for some readers than the novel itself; and the authors of the "Manifesto of the Five" against Zola would not be remembered in literary history if they had depended upon their novels for their reputation. Moore's talents in this line went into *Confessions of a Young Man* (1888), whose composition during the year of the Queen's first jubilee must be regarded as a cultural coincidence of a sardonic sort. Although sometimes crass, puerile, and reckless, the *Confessions* is still a lively and youthful document, an impressive outpouring of impatience, intolerance, confusion, and real hatred felt by a disaffected artist with a rhetorical gift that retains, after four generations, a real power to arrest and challenge. This volume, too, came under the scrutiny of Pater, who abstained from public comment but wrote Moore a pleasant letter praising his "Aristophanic joy" and warning him in a friendly way against his "cynical and therefore exclusive way of looking at the world."

Pater's word "Aristophanic" was not quite precise; for Aristophanes would have had to cast himself, in the role of Socrates, as the hero of *The Clouds* before his satire would parallel Moore's in ironic complexity. But the choice of the word did show that Pater understood, as so many later readers have not, that *Confessions* is misread unless its curious humorous streak is perceived.

Moore's achievement in criticism and autobiography was, unhappily, about all he had to show for his high expectations in the new phase of his career. Pater seems to have profoundly disturbed his creative impulse and to have reduced to chaos his ability to judge the worth of his work. In the early 1890's he wrote to Edmund Gosse a strangely unconscious confession of his confusion about his own achievement:

> I send you two books. A.M.W. [*A Mummer's Wife*] is I suppose the best thing I have done. It was liked very much in France and by the best people—Zola, Coppee, Banville. It is therefore probable that you will like it more or less. My Racenian drama is what I like. I do not know that anyone else likes it, I am afraid they do not, but I do, I can't help myself.[4]

"My Racenian drama" apparently refers to *Martin Luther*, since the only other play he had written at this date was *A Strike at Arlingford*, an Ibsenite social-problem comedy bearing even less resemblance to Racine than *Martin Luther*. It is almost incredible that he should have felt any impulse to champion, after fifteen years' burial, this apprentice exercise. One can only conclude from this letter that his judgment had somehow become exactly inverted, so that his worst failure appeared to be his real achievement while his success was revealed to him only by the testimonial of "the best people" in France.

After the publication of the last of his early naturalistic series, *A Drama in Muslin,* Moore's novels began to sink, apparently without hope of rescue, into a morass of cross-purpose, fatuous idea, and vulgar sentiment. The speed of his access of creative power between *Pagan Poems* and *A Mummer's Wife* is one of the remarkable literary events of his time, but scarcely more remarkable than the speed of his plunge from *A Mummer's Wife* to *Mike Fletcher.*

The first novel written under Pater's influence was *A Mere Accident,* dealing mainly with a character called John Norton, transparently patterned upon Moore's cousin and aestheticizing companion, Edward Martyn. Martyn is remembered by many Irishmen as a patriot who supported Sinn Fein before it was popular to do so, and who gave generous bequests to the Catholic parishes of Dublin to support the revival of Palestrina's music in the church services. But Yeats despised him, and Moore immortalized him in *Hail and Farewell* as a dabbler and a fool. For many years Moore studied Martyn as a specimen possessing a notable excess of "religious sensuality," philosophical timidity, sensual self-indulgence, and celibate impulse. "Edward was a bachelor," wrote Moore, "before he left his mother's womb." In *A Mere Accident* and several novels that followed, John Norton is depicted as a timid and compromising Des Esseintes, whose taste for absinthe and Monet is mingled with a sensual attraction to Augustine and asceticism. John's mother, anxious for descendants, has browbeaten her son into an engagement which he is not forthright enough to oppose, though it is repugnant to his celibate instincts. By mischance, "a mere accident," his fiancée is caught out alone on the moor by a migratory farm worker and raped. Subsequently she commits suicide, revealing to John that he is incapable of grief, a shocking revelation whose pain is forgotten as he returns to his cloistered aestheticism.

A copy of the novel was sent to Pater, who ignored John Norton's pretty compliments on *Marius* as "delicious fragrance blown back to us from the antique world," and as bearing a "scent of beanfields mingled with incense"; but he sent Moore a tactful remonstrance against the use of lurid violence in his novel. The reviewers agreed with Pater in their lack of enthusiasm for the work, and Moore evidently agreed too, for he attempted a complete rewriting shortly afterward; then, believing both the original and the revised version to be unsuccessful, he let the novel drop from his affection and his memory.

He was now deeply involved in preparations for *Mike Fletcher,* the story of a modern Don Juan, finally published in 1889 and dedicated to his brother Augustus, who had now given up Offenbach for a connection with *The Hawk,* a sensational arty gossip sheet whose editors lived precariously between threats of libel action and bankruptcy petitions. As the novel neared completion, Moore wrote his mother:

> It is the best thing I have ever done. I do not think it can be mistaken for anything except the work of a person who has endeavored to think for himself. That it is peculiar goes without saying. I was born, I live, I shall die a peculiar man. I could not be commonplace were I to try. . . . My novel is a new method. It is not a warming up out of Dickens and Thackeray. It is a method that will certainly be adopted by other writers, but will the first effort meet with recognition. I scarcely think so.[5]

The new work was, as his letter claimed, an anticipation of the work of others. His hero, a *fin de siècle* Faust, a "strained and agonized soul of our own time," foreshadowed the stock sentiments and poses of the age of Beardsley; and Moore's novel, though vastly inferior, was five years ahead of Wilde's treatment of the same theme in *The Picture of Dorian Gray.*

Moore's belief that his "method" was something new and valuable is more puzzling. His method was the headstrong absurdity of *Flowers of Passion* and *Pagan Poems,* the reckless glibness of a writer simultaneously overwhelmed by, and uneasy with, his attachment to a new master whose doctrine he believes but cannot absorb. His novel resembles the examination paper of a pliable undergraduate, dutifully giving back the student's newly acquired convictions with such doctrinaire simplicity that their first sponsor disowns them as monsters that suggest all too clearly a tainted heredity in their parentage. *Mike Fletcher* turned out to be undeniably "peculiar," to borrow an adjective from Moore's letter to his mother. Not that it was simply incompetent as compared with Wilde's novel. "I could not be common-place were I to try," Moore had asserted correctly; and some willful urge to degrade his convictions and commitments had seized his pen and created a masterpiece of fatuousness. *Mike Fletcher* was the work of *"amico Moorini,"* his impish dual self whose intrusion into his imagination has been so often deplored. What has not been recognized is that *"amico Moorini"* was often a far shrewder critic of his talent than his other self and usually attacked and destroyed the false or commonplace impulses that, because of doctrinal confusions, Moore was not prepared to deal with consciously.

As the novel opens, Mike Fletcher, weary of life and of man-kind, is waiting in his tastefully decorated rooms in Temple Gardens for a visit from Lily Green, a nun whom he has just persuaded to flee from the convent. The conversation reveals that Mike is a man of rare gifts. John Norton, the religious sensualist from *A Mere Accident,* reports that Mike has "ruined" some "hundreds" of women and that the most ironclad virtue is unable to resist his charms. The novelist Harding, Moore's mouthpiece in the early novels, seconds this description; he has heard a lady say that Mike's influence is like "the fascination the serpent exercises over the bird." It is Harding's opinion that in a less vulgar age Mike would have outdone Casanova:

> Casanova! What a magnificent Casanova he would have been! Casa-nova is to me the most fascinating of characters. He was everything—a frequenter of taverns and palaces, a necromancer.[6]

Mike is said to possess unusual physical attractiveness, "call it magnetism, electro-biology, give it what name you will." He has "soft violet eyes in which tenderness dwelt, and the strangely tall and lithe figure was emphasized by the conventional pose— that pose of an arm and thigh which the Greeks never wearied of." His friends admire his physique enviously as he steps from his bath:

His body was smooth and white as marble; and the pectoral muscles were especially beautiful when he leaned forward to wipe a lifted leg. . . . He really was a superb animal as he stepped out of his bath.[7]

When Mike goes to the country the peasants worship him. He is a natural poet; "words came from him like flour from a mill." Like Moore he aestheticizes easily, ranging through dizzy transitions from Wagner to Plato to Veronese, from the music halls to Pierrot. "Pierrot!—there is music, there is poetry in the name. The soul of an epoch lives in that name, evocative as it is of shadowy trees, lawny spaces, brocade, pointed bodices, high heels, and guitars." If Mike goes to a "gambling hell" his luck goes with him and he cannot lose.

Mike seeks in Lily a Platonic mistress after the model of Villiers' Sara and Poe's Annabel Lee. "I have dreamed of a woman," he says, "to whom I could bring my poetry," poetry which has been lifted out of *Pagan Poems*. Hitherto he has been "given some more or less imperfect flesh," but now he longs for a vestal who could comprehend all sorrows. First Lily's purity must be tested, however; hence his invitation to her to visit his rooms:

"She is coming!" Mike cried, and laying down the opera glasses he took up the scent and squirted it about the room. . . .
"When I saw, or thought I saw, that you loved me, I was God. . . . Give yourself, make this afternoon memorable. . . ."
"No, good bye! . . ."
"This is cruel of you. I dreamed of you madly, and why do you destroy my dream? . . ."
"Love! you profane the word; loose me, I am going."
"No, you are not going, you must remain." There was an occasional nature in him, that of the vicious dog, and now it snarled. "If you do not love me, you should not have come here," he said interposing, getting between her and the door. . . . Lily screamed piercingly. "No one will hear," he said, laughing hoarsely. . . .[8]

Lily has survived the test; "mastered, he followed her down the long stairs." Now his love is unlike any previous love. "The sensation is delicious—like an ice or a glass of Chartreuse." Lily remains unapproachable and virginal, and these qualities are soon enhanced by pulmonary tuberculosis, which she makes known to Mike with some bluntness: "Have you not heard? . . . I have only one lung left. Do you think I'm looking very ill?" In the course of the novel she does finally pass away, closing off the main avenue along which Mike has sought to escape from his aggravated case of *Weltschmerz*.

The commoner roads to salvation are blocked for Mike at the outset. Family pride has no meaning to him, since he is an illegitimate son. Domesticity is impossible:

> If I were married, even if I were married to Lily, I should insist on having separate rooms. . . . One day I should be sure to surprise her washing herself; and I know of no more degrading spectacle. . . . Degas painted it once. I'd give anything to have that picture.[9]

He cannot stomach alcohol. Conventional religion is attractive but for him impossible; his reason tells him that Christianity is merely an inferior offshoot from the original religion of the race. But many other possible solutions to his overwhelming question present themselves, and one by one they are tried and discarded.

He engages in roistering with young British peers, disturbing the respectable households of the West End with Offenbach serenades in the early morning hours, dashing about the country with a coach and four like the proud seigneur in *A Tale of Two Cities:*

> "What care we for that pale mother and her babe, or that toiling coster whose barrow is too heavy for him! If there is to be a revolution, it will not be in our time; we are the end of the world. . . ." The great Lord Muchross is shouting derision at the poor coster. . . . See the great Muchross, the clean-shaven face of the libertine priest, the small sardonic eyes. Hurrah for the great Muchross! [10]

These adventures quickly pall, and Mike abandons his slow-witted, lordly, sporting friends.

He tries a return to nature. One sortie into the idyllic country-side of Sussex ends when he finds that his bank balance has fallen very low; a second try, undertaken after he has inherited a great fortune from his former mistress, is wrecked by ennui. But the search for natural innocence goes into a third stage, when Mike attempts to live with Bedouins in the desert. This also fails. "The scent of the white woman's hair and skin was in his nostrils; the nostalgia of the pavement had found him and he knew that he must leave the desert."

He tries to find salvation in social uplift work. He joins the Parnellites and stands for the House of Commons, winning his election easily, of course. Disenchantment, however, comes faster than usual:

> Always impressed by new ideas, rarely holding to any impression long, finding all hollow and common very soon, he had been taken with the importance of the national assembly, but it had hardly passed into its third session when all illusion had vanished, and Mike ridiculed parliamentary ambitions in the various chambers of the barristers he frequented.[11]

He throws himself into social work among delinquents in the East End but leaves it soon afterward, disturbed that his attempts at reformation do not diminish the supply of delinquents.

He thinks he might find salvation in "work"—and by work he means the composition of a novel—but he discovers that he is already too old to start. He sighs unhappily for his missed opportunity and says to Lady Helen, wife of the "mean cad" Lewis Seymour, the hero of *A Modern Lover*, "If you had been my mistress or my wife you would have been happier; you would have worked, and in work, not in pleasure, we may cheat life. You would have written your books, I should have written mine."

He turns at last to depravity and crime. "Before I kill myself," he says, "I will kill others." Henceforth, walking about London, the sight of a pretty girl on the street will cause him to turn, pull at his mustache, and murmur: "Not bad!" He turns his rooms in Temple Gardens into a gambling den, and there he invites his victims for fleecing: race-horse owners, actors, peers of the realm, Members of Parliament, and young men who say reproachfully to each other, "You never admire anything I wear." Mike's face takes on a strange contradictory cast, his violet eyes still soft and beautiful, his chin and mouth wrinkled and goatlike. He tires of playing at Mephistopheles; ennui, "like a pure fire," consumes him. One day he says, "I'm weary of life," whereupon he takes a pistol and blows out his brains. "And who," asks Moore of his readers, "reading of Mike's torment is fortunate enough to say: 'I know nothing of what is written here.'" [12]

The fact that *Mike Fletcher* was a degradation of his talent penetrated Moore's consciousness slowly. The effect of burlesque, which the *Confessions of a Young Man* had manipulated with such masterful art, emerged out of *Mike Fletcher* as a total surprise to the author and a perpetual embarrassment. All the hundreds of Moorisms were apparently composed unconsciously. Moore's discovery that *Mike Fletcher* was a near-fatal blunder was not long postponed after its publication, however. Frank Harris, who had encouraged him to think that the novel was indeed, as he was convinced it was, "the best thing I have done," suddenly deserted him and joined with the chorus of detractors. Moore was at this time carrying on a chatty, Platonic, transatlantic correspondence with a marquise, Clara Lanza of New York. He wrote her that he felt that Harris' abuse was "overstating the case against the book," because he was satisfied that "it is impossible that a man who writes as well as I have done, and am still writing, should be the author of three hundred pages of twaddle." [13] Yet that very conclusion seemed inescapable. In the preface to his next novel he confessed that he was not capable of judging his own work.

The suspicion that he was destined to suffer the torments of a near-great, not-quite-great artist distressed him for some time. His character, Lewis Seymour, had suffered from the malady, and Moore's eloquence in depicting it was striking. Lewis was filled with great vague visions, but these impalpable things "faded into nothing when he attempted to reduce the unapparent reality into apparent pictures." He "suffered all the pains of this terrible child-bearing without the supreme happiness of deliverance." [14] And, in the same letter which boasted of the excellence of *Mike Fletcher,* Moore wrote his mother that he had his doubts too, and symptoms identically like Lewis':

> The bitterest thing is what I think of myself:—it is not the work of genius, nor that of great talent. It is the work of a man affected by the most terrible of all maladies, a dash of genius.[15]

He wrote to his brother Maurice of his sense of abject failure, based on the shame that *Mike Fletcher* now caused him. "I have the sentiment of great work, but I cannot produce it. *Voilà ma confession,* what I strictly believe to be true." [16]

Anxious to make the best of the situation and dogged by his relentless drive to go on working, he thereupon turned with a certain pluck and ingenuity to composing a novel about a writer who had the sentiment of great work but who could not produce it. This novel was *Vain Fortune* (1892), which turned out to be another financial disappointment, though it was a vast improvement over *Mike Fletcher* and superior, too, to most of the other fair-to-mediocre novels of this period with better reputations, such as *Spring Days.*

Vain Fortune is a pathetic story of an artist *manqué,* who can neither write nor give up writing. In the first part of the novel, Hubert Price, the hero, is shown in futile pursuit of art—that is, the creation of art—at the cost of poverty, abuse, and wretchedness. He blames poverty for his failure. But an unexpected inheritance suddenly ends his poverty. Comfortable and secure for the first time, and established in a luxurious country house, he continues the pursuit of art with even greater unsuccess and wretchedness. He loses confidence in his talent and falls into a condition of chronic exhaustion, brought on by the pangs of frustrated composition, a malady which Moore describes with considerable feeling and freshness of detail. The story of Hubert's travail gives the clearest statement in all of Moore's work of the sort of experience he had in mind when he spoke of "sacrifice for art" or called himself an "art-tormented" Saint Augustine of literature:

> [Hubert's] pain lay at his heart's root; he could not pluck it forth, and its gratification seemed more than ever impossible. . . . See him reading and re-reading the few lines he has written, knowing them to be worthless, tortured by a prescience of the perfection required, and maddened by the sight of the futility that is. See him rising from his writing table with blank despair upon his face, unable to bear any longer the mocking ghastliness of the sheet of paper. He throws himself on the couch, absorbed in despair, and then a curious painful look creeps round the corners of the mouth, and looks out of the eyes— the pained, pinched look of impotent desire.[17]

Such are the miseries of creation; but for some there is reserved "the supreme happiness of deliverance," and one day Hubert finds himself transported, caught up in a euphoric frenzy that he believes to be creative inspiration:

> He wrote on for some hours, rested, and then returned refreshed and ardent to his work; and it was not till four o'clock that he had exhausted himself, feeling he had done enough for the day.
> He lit a cigar, and threw himself in his armchair, happy in the sensation of accomplishment. Never had he written so fluently before— only a shadow of a doubt lingered; and he felt sure of being able to achieve his play in exactly the manner he had intended; he even thought it likely he would exceed his ideal. And as he blew the fragrant smoke from his lips his happiness grew irresponsible—bird-like in a new sense of wings, and like a bird in a warm June garden, his soul wandered through a fair region of fancy, and everywhere through the sweet air came intoxicating odors of ultimate success.

In the midst of this warm self-congratulation, Hubert's thoughts turn to literary tradition. He begins to examine it critically, to place it beside his own work for comparison, and to evaluate it afresh. He discovers that there is no art except what he has himself created:

Vague and furtive remembrance of the literature of all ages passed through his mind, and he was astonished at how little had been done. Infinite possibilities seemed to open up before him, and he only asked for time and health to achieve an entirely new literature—dramas peopled with human souls, strangely true, intense, subtle, and strong! He analyzed masterpiece after masterpiece, finding all defective. *Romeo and Juliet* was only a love song; *Hamlet* ought to have ended with a philosophic suicide. . . .[18]

There follows a long interlude of aestheticizing in which Hubert Price, like the co-author of *Martin Luther,* runs up and down the garden paths of the English drama searching unsuccessfully for acceptable flowers. Hubert concludes that it is really surprising "how little had been done" in the English drama:

Then a little giddiness came into his brain, and the dramatic literature of the world seemed paltry, a mere plot of kitchen garden. But *The Gypsy* [his own play]? This play seemed to unite all qualities in one perfect whole. It was realistic, romantic, psychological. And the story? Surely it would be difficult to invent a finer one.

Having thus disposed of all rivals that might compete for his affection against his own brain child, Hubert then returns to his thoughts about the ultimate satisfactions of art:

Overcome with self, he pitied the toilers whom the want of a little money never allows to realize the high ideals that haunt their souls. They must remain unknown; but he was a great man—he could hear his own heart singing the words, "A great man"; and he felt strangely happy—strangely at rest—strangely at harmony with his own surroundings—strangely thankful for all that fate had done for him.[19]

The correspondences between the author and his hero are too many to leave any doubt that Hubert Price's labor pains are a remembrance of Moore's own torment on one of the days when Æ saw him come from his writing desk "pale with anguish" or that Hubert Price's ample store of self-satisfaction is a description, now objectified, of Moore's own manic phase, when he dreamed that he had created a work the equal of *Mademoiselle de Maupin* or *Marius the Epicurean.* This was his mood when he wrote his mother that *Mike Fletcher* was the best thing he had ever done and when he confessed to Gosse that he considered *Martin Luther* his supreme accomplishment. Out of this mood arose the notoriously incautious judgments he made on the value of his own work: "I invented the aesthetic novel," "I invented adultery," and so on. Finally, Hubert's systematic disparagement of all the important figures of literature shows precisely how Moore's nihilistic critical method came into existence. Moore found his satisfaction in the production of art, not in its consumption. One is reminded of Ibsen's reply when asked what he had been reading: he had been reading nothing, he was a *writer.*

Hubert Price's elation is only momentary. He soon discovers that all his effort is wasted; *The Gypsy* is an imbecility. The novel concludes on a wistful note of quiet resignation, with Hubert hoping weakly that he can find in domestic life some reason for living, some substitute value to replace art, whose seductive and deadly charms will never be won by his mediocrity.

The ailments of Moore's imagination in the period of his discipleship to Walter Pater are not yet quite completely described. The year following the publication of *Vain Fortune,* he published a play never performed, called *The Strike at Arlingford.* His preface cautioned the reader to beware of the conclusion that the author had any interest in strikes. "In my own conception of my play, the labor dispute is an externality to which I attach little importance." The play concerns the love of a labor agitator, Reid, for the owner of a strike-bound mine, Lady Anne. The agitator is frequently thrown into despair by this unhappy circumstance, and he composes Swinburnean poetry for the release of his feelings. The play opens with this exposition *selon la formule de M. Scribe:*

STEINBACH: (*to Lady Anne*) And in the following years you married Sir Francis Travers. Five years ago he died leaving you a rich widow, and your old lover heads a strike of miners, little thinking that Lady

123

Anne Travers is the Anne that he loved. You were a lovely girl! how much you must have meant to him!

There is no need to set out all the painful details of this work. Inevitably it drags to the only possible denouement, and with it closes another phase of Moore's career. He had now composed five failures in succession, four novels and one play. His embracement of the new Cyrenaicism had not brought him any notable advantage. Pater himself had been displeased, finding excessive wildness in his disciple, but his warnings were not heeded as Moore drove himself on toward the disaster of *Mike Fletcher*. Pater's opinion of *Mike Fletcher* is not known, but that strange work, so clearly derived from him and yet so utterly foreign to him, could not, if he read it, have contributed to his peace of mind during the last two years of his life.

Out of tact, Moore's contemporaries were impelled to silence on the subject of his novels and spoke only of his critical essays. Moore wrote to Clara Lanza: "My book, *Impressions and Opinions,* continues to be well received here. Everybody likes it, and it is being said that I am much better as an essayist . . . than as a novelist. I shall disabuse them of that idea presently. There is more in me than they think." [20] His feeling was sound and his prediction correct. Already he was meditating the subject of *Esther Waters,* and, having now worked many volumes of nonsense out of his system, widened the range of his experience, and chastened himself with a bitterly honest probe of the anatomy of his failure, he was ready to start his most famous work.

Low Life and High Life

> *"I think your forte is rather among the lower classes*
> *than the upper," [Vizetelly said]. But I am gentry, said*
> *I to myself, and I shall be able to write about gentry,*
> *and Vizetelly, guessing my thoughts said, "It is the*
> *gentry who write best about the lower classes."*
>
> —A COMMUNICATION TO MY FRIENDS

HE MONOTONOUS chain of unsuccessful efforts was broken at last by the appearance of Moore's most famous novel, *Esther Waters,* which turned its back upon the world of Mike Fletcher and "pre-Raphaelite nastiness" to treat such congenial Victorian subjects as the triumph of mother love, the maladministration of eleemosynary institutions, the methodical beastliness of foundling homes that "took care" of illegitimate babies, and the mathematically probable results of continued betting on horse races. All this was intermingled with jolly scenes depicting life in public houses and racing stables. "An English Story," the subtitle reads, and Moore's penchant for hyperbole led him to call it "more English" than any other novel in the language. Gladstone announced his approval in the *Westminster Gazette.* The novel sold in such numbers as to excite the envy of the great circulating libraries and to force the partial abandonment of Mudie's and Smith's ban on Moore's work. Moore believed that the novel inspired legal action to outlaw the "baby farms" it describes, and that it led philanthropists to endow nursing homes for unmarried mothers, an ironical achievement for the chief English pupil of Théophile Gautier's doctrine of aesthetic amorality.

Moore had long planned to write a novel about the lower classes, an idea he treated at some length in *Confessions of a Young Man,* where he described his morning chats with the charwoman who cleaned his bedroom in a rooming house in the Strand. "Awful Emma" and "the horrible servant" he called her in the first edition of *Confessions,* though he deleted the epithets in the editions published after the success of *Esther Waters.*[1] As originally conceived, the subject appealed to him because of its possibilities for shocking philistines, who were apparently disturbed to read a novel on any subject other than "pleasure in evening dress," as the Goncourts complained. *Mike Fletcher* mentions the projected novel, "the hero of which was a butler and the heroine a cook," in a context showing that Moore considered it equivalent in impudence to writing "insolent letters addressed to eminent people" and similar devices for astounding Victorian respectability and for titillating Mike's circle of intellectuals.

Objectivity was to be the dominant note of the projected "study." "I studied the horrible servant," he said, "as one might an insect under the microscope," and he envisioned a final product that would give England its first novel in the grim tradition of the Goncourts' *Germinie Lacerteux* or Huysmans' *Marthe:*

> The lodgers sometimes threw you a kind word, but never one that recognized that you were akin to us, only the pity that might be extended to a dog. And I used to ask you all sorts of cruel questions, I was curious to know the depth of animalism you had sunk to, or rather out of which you had never been raised. And you generally answered innocently and naively enough. But sometimes my words were too crude, and they struck through the thick hide into the quick, into the human, and you winced a little; but this was rarely, for you were very nearly, oh, very nearly an animal: your temperament and intelligence was just that of a dog that has picked up a master, not a real master, but a makeshift master who may turn it out at any moment. Dickens would sentimentalise or laugh over you; I do neither. I merely recognise you as one of the facts of civilisation. . . . Yes, you are a

mule, there is no sense in you; you are a beast of burden, a drudge too horrible for anything but work; and I suppose, all things considered, that the fat landlady with a dozen children did well to work you seventeen hours a day, and cheat you out of your miserable wages. . . . And you were taken by this fat landlady as 'Arry takes a rose and sticks it in his tobacco-reeking coat; and you will be thrown away, shut out of doors when health fails you, or when, overcome by base usage, you take to drink. There is no hope for you; even if you were treated better and paid your wages there would be no hope. That forty pounds even, if they were given to you, would bring you no good fortune. They would bring the idle loafer, who scorns you now as something too low for even his kisses, hanging about your heels and whispering in your ears. And his whispering would drive you mad, for your kind heart longs for kind words; and then when he had spent your money and cast you off in despair, the gin shop and the river would do the rest.[2]

A novel on this theme would have harmonized well with the "Ode to a Beggar Girl" in *Pagan Poems* or with *Mike Fletcher* and *Parnell and His Island*. But this was not the novel Moore wrote; instead he wrote *Esther Waters*, a novel commonly assumed to be closer in kinship to *Adam Bede* and *Oliver Twist* than to *Germinie Lacerteux* or *Marthe*. It is clear that, some time after drawing his sketch of "awful Emma" in the *Confessions*, he altered his original intent.

Practical motives for the sudden shift of Moore's point of view are not hard to find. The collapse of his reputation was much on his mind in the early 1890's, and there is abundant evidence that *Esther Waters* was, among other things, a gesture of appeasement to the British reading public. In later years he recalled his dismay at his failure to hold readers after his break with Zola, after *Spring Days* and "another novel which shall be nameless," meaning the unspeakable *Mike Fletcher*, of course. A late preface to *Impressions and Opinions* attributed his rescue to those critical essays, a fanciful but unwarranted theory. The readers of his essays were perhaps fit, but certainly few, whereas his object was Balzacian "conquest" and a broad, popular hearing. While composing *Esther Waters* he confessed to his brother

Maurice that he hoped to achieve fame with the new novel, complaining that their brother Augustus, whom he now disliked, was making out of scurrilous journalism no less income than he was making from sacrifice to art. Success, he recognized, demanded a radical shift in the tone of his writing, and he wrote to Clara Lanza: "My next novel will be more human. I shall bathe myself in the simplest and most naive emotions, the daily bread of humanity." [3] The human pigsty was forgotten for the moment as "awful Emma" stepped aside to make way for Esther Waters.

This is cogent information, yet behind such a collection of evidence lies a suggestion of "insincerity" that belittles the scope of Moore's achievement, the truth and originality of which must be tested by reference to the novel rather than to external evidence. The external evidence itself is contradictory. Havelock Ellis had reason to believe that Moore's sentiments in the novel were genuine. He reported that Moore had stopped him on the street to tell "with deep emotion" and "tender human sympathies" of his discovery that young girls in London were being forced to destroy their illegitimate babies. Even Malcolm Elwin, a vigorous detractor of Moore's work, veers toward the view that Moore's feelings expressed in the novel were not factitious. He observed that *Esther Waters* was written under the spell of Mrs. Pearl Craigie, an American patent-medicine heiress and very proper grass widow, herself a writer, whom Moore was courting with unwonted abandon at the time. Elwin suggests that Moore's normal perversity was placed in temporary eclipse by the respectability and piety that enveloped Mrs. Craigie. She did indeed find the novel admirable, and the strength of her conviction is indicated by the fact that she continued to praise it even after Moore, following the end of the courtship, had begun to circulate petty innuendoes against her in London drawing rooms.

Moore's direct comments on the novel are extraordinary for the violence of the duality they betray. Even before the novel was published, his thoughts about it show him to have been afflicted with a total prostration of his judgment. In the midst of composition of the novel he wrote Maurice that "the servant girl" was "the most serious" attempt he had yet made to "do a real piece of literature"; but another letter followed in the next mail to correct the false impression given. It would, he said, "take the wind out of every sail"; still he was not satisfied: "The impression . . . that my last letter seems to have conveyed is somewhat grandiose. It reminds me more of a book I am minded to write than of the book I have written." [4] He added that the most satisfying part of the novel was the description of the race-track crowds on Derby Day, a small technical experiment in which he tried out his skill in handling the self-imposed problem of omitting horses, grandstand, and paddock from Esther's and William's day at the Derby.

After the publication and the success of the novel, his most common public remarks about it were broadly farcical. Whenever the issue under discussion concerned his popularity or his humanity, nothing pleased him more than a reference to "the good book," *Esther Waters*. His solicitor was the kind of person he delighted in teasing with praise of the novel that seemed unbecoming in the author. He would ask, "Don't you think it better than anything Dickens ever wrote?" (The answer was, "Candidly, I don't.") The novel became a favorite source of Moorisms. In later years, after he had taken up the role of the elderly satyr of Ebury Street, he liked to announce to his friends, "I have just read it; it has done me good, it radiates goodness." He blandly informed a reporter from the daily press that the novel had been written out of "a love of humanity, a desire to serve humanity"; at other times, however, he insisted that it was "pure of all intention to do good—that is, to alleviate material suffering." Whenever he came under attack for wickedness and misanthropy, he would charge forth righteously waving a copy of *Esther Waters*. Thus when his cousin, a Carmelite nun, asked him in the name of holiness to burn all his books, it was *Esther*

Waters that she was reminded of in the letter of reply, a copy of which was sent to the newspapers. He was not hesitant in asserting that it had "perhaps done more good than any novel in my generation" and was pleased to drop into any conversation a reference to the existence of a refuge for wayward girls which he understood to be the charitable gift of a man who had just read *Esther Waters*.

This puckishly grandiose manner toward the novel alternated with frank disparagement. Some time after publication he called it "worthless," a "bad book." He was fond of comparing it unfavorably with his minor and unsuccessful work. He thought it inferior to *The Lake* and held even the tepid *Spring Days* in higher esteem. When Robert Ross told him that *A Mummer's Wife* was his one work most likely to live, he said: "If I had lived herebefore, Jupiter knows what I would have written, but it would not have been *Esther Waters*." [5] Just before he died he conceded in the last of many prefaces to the novel that it alone had kept him "in renown" through all the years, but confessed that Esther afflicted him with an overwhelming boredom.

A characteristic statement on the novel appeared in his last memoir, *A Communication to My Friends*, which recalled the way the novel came about:

> I fell to thinking that there is nothing in this world more lonely than an author without a subject. To dispel the gloom that was beginning to settle upon me I bought a newspaper and read as I walked, jostling the passengers; I heard mutterings behind me, but I did not mind them, for I was interested in the article I was reading—an article on servants. The author had the courage to ask the readers of the hour if they ever thought of the manifold services that we demanded of servants, to the performance of which we summoned them by bell-pulls. I heard them in my thoughts mutter in the pantry and the kitchen, "Ah! that's the old girl's bell again, her bell is very lively this morning." But I did not pursue the servants to the upper floor of the house. My thoughts had galloped away on something that looked like an inspiration from the Muses. I was asking myself if servants, who in English literature are never introduced except as comic characters, might not be treated

as the principal characters of a novel. After all, they are human beings like ourselves, though reduced by riches to a sort of partial slavery. Before I reached St. Clement Danes in the Strand, I was asking myself whether the hero of my new book should be a footman or should I take a cook for a heroine, and before I reached the Law Courts I decided that it could be neither. A footman could not be a pleasing object in the love passages and it is hard to think of a good-tempered cook, though no doubt there are such beings. A cook is too old, but not a scullery maid. Ah, there I have it! A scullery maid, said I, she shall be. And I asked, What is the story of this scullery maid? [6]

This recollection possibly distorts historical fact, for Moore was inclined to foreshorten and reweave actualities to improve the narrative quality of his memoirs. But as an embodiment of his feelings toward the novel it is accurate and apropos. Flattery is missing here. His recollection degrades the novel into a merely mechanical affair of desperate searching and the chance discovery of a subject whose sole virtue was that no rival had ever exploited it. The condescension that lay behind his interest in the scullery maid cannot be missed: "After all, they are human beings like ourselves." Yet the novel itself belies, at least in part, this condescension and coldness and mirrors a vigor and breadth of feeling and commitment that would be extremely difficult to simulate; and it asserts, as being indubitably Moore's own, the very values he elsewhere loudly denied.

Moore's inconclusive doubts about the worth of *Esther Waters* arose out of the same conflicts that had dominated his literary life since his Parisian days. He required popularity, yet the very success of the novel brought on pangs of guilt. *Vain Fortune,* written during an interlude after he had begun composition of *Esther Waters,* shows Hubert Price struggling with dilemmas of artistic morality analogous to Moore's own. Hubert had written a realistic problem play called *Divorce,* whose plot is, amusingly, the plot of Ibsen's *Doll's House.* Hubert is savagely attacked in the press, one reviewer observing: "Always the same relentless method; the cold, passionless curiosity of the vivisector; the scalpel is placed under the nerve, and we are called upon to watch the quivering flesh." [7] This is a reasonable forecast of the response Moore could have expected if he had proceeded with "awful Emma" and written the first English *Marthe*. In *Vain Fortune* Hubert Price is crushed by these attacks and sets about rewriting his second play, *The Gypsy*, in order to "secure the sympathies of the public." Thereupon, so relentless is his dilemma, he incurs a violent attack from the novelist Harding, who informs him that his cowardly emendations have deprived his characters of their "original humanity." *Vain Fortune* thus depicts Moore himself in the act of weighing the decision that led to *Esther Waters* and of deciding to yield to the public's seemingly shallow judgment, though convinced that the choice he made had entailed a breach of his integrity as an artist. At mid-career and at the height of his energy he was incapable of respecting any piece of work, even his own, which departed from the manner of *Mike Fletcher* and *Pagan Poems*, though these he could not respect either, as his conscious and unconscious desecration of his models demonstrated. He still understood Huysmans' "ten superior persons" to be in perpetual, categorical dissent from the rest of graceless mankind; and Gladstone's praise of *Esther Waters* became a subject for his most sardonic wit.

He was troubled by the suspicion that *Esther Waters* uttered doctrines and expressed affections inimical to his aesthetics. In the interest of combating such tendencies, he took pains to explain that Esther's "goodness" grew directly out of her illiteracy. Conversely, her companions in the servants' quarters are shown to be degraded in proportion to their literacy; like Kate Ede in *A Mummer's Wife* and Emma Bovary, they prepare themselves for their downfall by the compulsive reading of romantic novels. Moore was thus able to repeat once again his cherished belief that the Education Acts were subverting civilization and that salvation was only possible through a "renaissance of illiteracy." In its narrow application this half-comical notion is not a particularly important component of the novel. While it may have flattered his sense of integrity to have included it, he did not bring much artistic energy to its support, and it stands in the novel as a casual, and slightly odd, foreign object. But, considered more broadly, Esther's illiteracy seems to have symbolized for Moore a sort of primordial, almost protoplasmic, strength which would survive all persecutions and outlive her persecutors, an attitude similar to William Faulkner's conception of the Negro servant, Dilsey.

Moore's perplexity in handling his new commitments is exposed in several striking imaginative lapses which give parts of the novel a slight thinness of tone. Katherine Mansfield reviewed the novel and attacked it for its coldness and externality and based her judgment, apart from her philosophical distaste for the realistic method in general, upon citation of some of these lapses, where Moore had seemingly had to drive himself to get on with the disagreeable business. One such seizure of banality led him to write Esther's explanation of her pregnancy to Mr. Barfield: "I shouldn't have touched the second glass of ale," and so on.[8] The opening chapters of the novel are especially stark and tedious, suggesting that Moore did not enter upon his new subject and manner easily. The feebleness of Esther's introduction and of her first troubles at Woodview becomes clear when compared with the richness and power of the opening of a typical mid-Victorian novel or a typical Hardy novel, such as *Tess of the D'Urbervilles*, with its magnificent initial action leading to the death of the Durbeyfield horse on the highway at midnight.

And yet *Esther Waters* shows Moore in possession of abilities that were absent both in the classical Victorian novelists and in Hardy. He was fully aware of the nature and scope of his originality, but chose to mark out his claim by indirect devices. He praised himself principally by the devious method of castigating all Victorian predecessors and contemporaries. In these fulminations he was able to highlight weaknesses of other writers in skills in which he was himself strong and to show up blindness where he was notably perceptive. So he saw Hetty Sorrel's destiny as plain falsehood beside Esther's plain truth: "George Eliot sought a subject in Hetty Sorrel's murder of her child. A woman's moulding of the subject, a true moulding, would be Hetty living to save her child." [9] Esther lived to save her child. But it was not *Adam Bede* that he liked to consider he had surpassed; it was *Tess of the D'Urbervilles,* which was published while *Esther Waters* was being gestated.

All of Moore's contemporaries were puzzled by his denigration of Thomas Hardy, which involved attacks so violent that they were generally judged to be infamous, or even demented. When Moore was pressed for evidence to support his charges, he would invariably cite as Hardy's unpardonable aesthetic sin the scene in which Tess confesses her past sins to Angel Clare, a scene that so deeply imprinted itself in Moore's mind that it supplied him with daily conversation for forty years. The passage that received such close and protracted scrutiny consists of the last part of Section IV, ending as follows:

> . . . pressing her forehead against his temple she entered on the story of her acquaintance with Alec D'Urberville and its results, murmuring the words without flinching, and with her eyelids drooping down.

Moore's objection to the incident was that Hardy had prepared his readers for some climactic illumination; then, through "brain paralysis, something of the sort," had frustrated this expectation by a retreat into a bare exposition followed by an abrupt termination of the scene.

> The husband is sitting in a chair, his wife at his knees; and then in a few pages, and in the third person, Hardy disposes of it all. This incident, to which everything should lead up, which we should never be allowed to overlook, is over almost as soon as we realize it has begun. [10]

This was his statement to Geraint Goodwin in 1930, but his attack upon the scene had begun even before *Esther Waters* with a parody inserted into *Vain Fortune* in 1892, the year following the publication of *Tess*. At the close of the novel,

Hubert Price on his wedding night begins, like Tess, to make a confession about his friendship with an actress:

> Then, passing his arm round his wife's neck, and with her sweet blonde face looking upon him, and the insinuating warmth of the fire about them, he told how Rose had lent him five shillings to buy a hat.[11]

In *Esther Waters* the stage is set once more for this scene, when Esther must confess to Fred, her Salvation Army suitor, that she had been seduced and abandoned by William. Now Moore set out to show Hardy how he might have done the scene:

> "I've got a child. There, you have it now, and you can take your hook when you like."
> It was her blunt, sullen nature that had spoken, she didn't care if he left her on the spot—now he knew all and could do as he liked. At last he said:
> "But you've repented, Esther?"
> "I should think I had, and been punished too, enough for a dozen children."
> "Ah, then it wasn't lately?"
> "Lately! It's nearly eight years ago."
> "Then if—"
> "I don't want no ifs. If I am not good enough for you, you can go elsewhere and get better; I've had enough of reproaches." [12]

A related but broader criticism of Hardy's limitations was contained in Moore's weaving of the ironic turn of his main narrative line in *Esther Waters,* a totally new departure from Victorian ways and a genuine "modern" note, though a similar irony had been suggested in *A Mummer's Wife* in the characterization of Dick Lenox, who, as his stolen wife turns from innocent to degenerate, himself mutates from degenerate to innocent. The plot complications of *Tess* and *Esther Waters* are identical. In both, the central figure is a girl possessed of dignity, amiability, and strong impulsiveness. In both, the girl is seduced and deserted and brought to disaster. In both, a "good

135

man" thereupon appears and offers security and affection. In both, the seducer reappears to jeopardize the girl's chance for recovery of happiness. At this point Hardy's action turns to Tess's total ruin, her melodramatic revenge, and the melodrama of society's retribution. This is a simple inversion of the Hetty-Arthur plot of *Adam Bede*, and, when Moore spoke of Hardy as "one of George Eliot's miscarriages," he seems to have intended some such comment on his "rival's" limitations. At the same turning point Moore's narrative leaves the beaten path, never to return. After her desertion Esther had struggled for years to save her child and had come at last to the threshold of respectability and comfort. One day, by chance, she meets her seducer on the street. Almost without hesitation she chooses to follow him once again. The ménage turns out to be not at all unsatisfactory, and it thus violated at once the Anglo-Saxon tradition in fiction and the moral expectations of evangelical readers. Esther finds her proper niche as the mistress of the King's Head Tavern and achieves a measure of peace and happiness in her new life with William and their child. At last, however, William's business is destroyed by the revocation of his license to sell spirits, his punishment by the law for making book on horse races. Finally he contracts tuberculosis. Esther nurses him in his fatal illness, buries him decently, and returns at the end of the novel to work as the servant in the "big house" in Sussex where her story had first begun. Such a treatment meant the end of standard plot of the Victorian novel, which found its new form, not in the rebellions of Ernest Pontifex or Bathsheba Everdene or Eustacia Vye, but in Esther Waters' lucid choice to follow her first lover, to do what she must do.

Moore's handling of this fable is in important ways clearly superior, even if we grant the virtue of Hardy's own typical insights. Moore intended Esther's second meeting with William to denote cosmic chance, "a mere accident," or, to use Hardy's own unhappy phrase, "one of life's little ironies," according to a statement he made to Barrett H. Clark when he refused to allow Clark to weaken the fortuitous aspect of the incident in adapting the novel to the stage. As a cosmic accident Moore's incident is the better integrated and more clear in its implications, if less striking as separate incident, than the famous mischance of Tess's letter slipped under the rug. Moore's turn in the narrative line allowed him to avoid the sentimentalization of William's villainy, after the manner of the unspeakable Alec D'Urberville. Esther's reasonable recognition of the principle that it takes two to make a seduction made her return to William a perfectly natural choice, while Tess's key decisions required elaborate rhetorical preparation and dubious resort to Gothic mechanisms. Moore's "good man," Fred, is perfectly clear and convincing, avoiding the grotesque demeanor of Angel Clare toward Tess. Finally, the bloody denouement that Hardy's narrative line forced upon him at the end of *Tess* (and not for the first time) was excelled by Moore's muted story of William's quiet and unavailing struggle to find money enough to buy his own life, which his doctor told him could be prolonged only by a winter trip to the Mediterranean, and by Esther's coming to the full turn of the circle with her return to Woodview, following the pattern of eternal recurrence that Moore had first described in *Pagan Poems*. Moore's special and superior skill lay in his ability to tighten the consecutiveness of his narrative, no small virtue among novelists concerned primarily with the unfolding of a deterministic world.

Thus Moore's variations on Hardy's story represent a real mutation in insight. In spite of his stated dislike of Esther's world, in spite of his habitual condescension to the lower classes—"after all, they are human beings like ourselves"—the act of composing *Esther Waters* had somehow neutralized his repulsions. A barrier had fallen away for the most part, and he achieved a real and original, if incomplete, identification with that remote world of poverty, degradation, and misery. His ability to make the identification was limited, of course; and Moore's success remains, despite his greater technical brilliance

137

and his solider sense of the consecutive, inferior in ensemble effect to Hardy's cruder but certainly more pulsating creation in *Tess of the D'Urbervilles*. With Moore, as with Dickens, Flaubert, Maupassant, and Baudelaire, affections could scarcely be aroused except by remembrance of some member of the servant classes, usually a childhood nurse. Yet, for the times, even to represent that relationship without sentimentality was not easy or common. To appreciate the importance of Moore's effort to broaden the world of his affections, one need only compare *Esther Waters* with the usual "lower-class" novels of his time. Moore's publisher, Vizetelly, had introduced him to the paradox that the gentry, lacking cockney prejudices, might write best about the lower classes, and his achievement was perhaps one that awaited his special talents and viewpoints. "Dickens would sentimentalize or laugh over you," his original sketch of "awful Emma" said; "I do neither. I merely recognize you as one of the facts of civilization."

Moore never again cast upon Esther's world more than a casual glimpse, such as he would later give to Heloise's stylized Balzacian nurse. House hunting in Dublin some years later, he was to declare that a view of the slums was not a defect in the residence of a man of letters—"he sharpens his pen there"; but this was a Moorism which both made a mockery of his success in creating Esther and recognized that his achievement would survive the barb. Esther was his farewell to realism; the net that he was now to cast was "woven of fine silk for the capture of dreams, memories, hopes, aspirations, sorrows, with here and there a secret shame," and we see him hurrying through the telling of an anecdote of furniture packers at work, anxious to avoid falling into his earlier realistic habits. "I will say no more than that I was out of the house one morning early, lest I should see a man seize the coal-scuttle and walk away with it." [13]

But if Esther's world had escaped from the range of his interests, the narrative line of her story had not. In 1894, the year of the publication of *Esther Waters*, he wrote a preface to a translation of Dostoevski's *Poor Folk,* explicitly affirming as doctrine the philosophy of narrative implied in the organization of his own novel. It is clear from his preface that he had no comprehension of Dostoevski but read him as another version of George Moore, or rather of Turgenev, though more uncouth, "more linen than fine silk," a judgment necessary to his new conviction that Turgenev was "the greatest artist that had existed since antiquity." In both Russian writers Moore found the rare skill to manage the endings of their narratives, the same skill, that is, that his own current success had just demonstrated:

> We must drop into a minor key if we would increase the effect [of the ending]. Only by a skillful use of anti-climax may we attain those perfect anti-climaxes—sensations of inextinguishable grief, the calm of resignation, the mute yearning for what life has not for giving. In such great pauses all great stories end. And *Poor Folk;* in what sad and solemn harmony does the theme find rest? [14]

Such skillfully contrived semitragic anticlimaxes—"suspended cadences," he called them later—he first mastered in *Esther Waters,* and his adroitness in their manipulation would characterize all his subsequent work.

Esther's story put Moore under a great strain, and with the novel finished he turned, like an alcoholic to the bottle, to his old aestheticisms, far removed from "the common bread of humanity." For some months he occupied himself with composing two novellas which, together with a shortened version of the rewritten *A Mere Accident,* were published in a single volume called *Celibates.* One story deals with the familiar figure of the artist *manqué,* represented here by a painter, a girl named Mildred Lawson, who is afflicted, like so many of Moore's characters, with "that most terrible of maladies, a dash of genius." The tale ends with Mildred suffering from failure and frustration, lying sleepless on a hot summer night and crying to herself: "Give me a passion for God or man, but give me a passion. I cannot live without one." The other new story, "Agnes Lahens," is a sketch of the type of sexless, will-less,

Poe-like heroine who had previously appeared in *Martin Luther,* *Vain Fortune,* and *Mike Fletcher.* The great adventure of Agnes Lahens' life is to return home from convent school to discover the evil in which her parents are enmeshed and to flee back timidly to the safety of the convent, where the nuns play with their doves and chase the ball down the gravel paths.

These tales were a minor effort, as he recognized, and in a short time he was at work on an ambitious new "aesthetic novel," a tale of primitive musical instruments and a Wagnerian soprano, of Berkeley Square and a baronet said to be drawn from Sir William Eden, the father of the British Prime Minister, of a mystical Celtic poet and a suave society priest, of nuns and nunneries in abundance, out of which he hoped to weave his greatest story. The task occupied him longer than any previous project, and three years of labor resulted at last in the publication of *Evelyn Innes* (1898). His letters of the time describe his normal feelings of insecurity and halting reservations toward new work but also report a rapturous flow of narrative. One of the letters said:

> The subject unfolds itself like the dawn. Light is breaking in every direction and I am dreaming a lovely dream. But will any of my dreams transpire? Shall I communicate my dream? I often ask myself the question.

At about the same time he reported to his brother Maurice:

> It is a pleasure to write this book. Hitherto I have had to drag myself to the writing table, now I can't drag myself away. I am making myself ill. The composition of this book is a pure joy. I cannot think what has come over me to write like this. It must be very bad or very good. I shall do a great book this time or cut the whole thing.[15]

The last sentence, with its grim resolve to succeed "this time," leaves no doubt about his current dissatisfaction with *Esther Waters.* Meanwhile, his new enthusiasm was identical with his earlier assurance of the "greatness" of *Mike Fletcher.* Once again, in turning back to enjoy the seductions that had always

140

brought him to the verge of artistic disaster, he seemed "this time" bound to succeed.

Moore's joy in composing *Evelyn Innes* is at first puzzling, since the story confronted him with difficulties that would have stopped most writers before they had begun. At the outset, there was the staggering problem of recreating the musical world he had chosen for his setting. One imagines that only a wealth of musical knowledge coupled with a depth of musical feeling could induce a writer to undertake a novel about music, and one takes it for granted that novelists like Mann or Rolland had these qualifications at the start of their tasks. But Moore had not. The evidence from his biography indicates that he was probably not tone deaf but was otherwise almost nonmusical. Except in the writing of *Evelyn Innes* he never pretended otherwise. In a letter to his brother he described himself as "rotten" with Wagnerism, and added: "I daresay I do not understand [the music] but what does it matter? I regard music as other men regard a game of billiards." [16] After the publication of *Evelyn Innes* one of his public confessions dwelt upon the same shortcoming: "My ear only allows me to hear the surface of the music, the motives which float up to the top, the transforming effect of a chord upon a melodic phrase." [17] He heard Wagner, that is, like the casual tourist in Bayreuth, and like any other amateur he was swept off his feet by the English horn solo at the opening of the last act of *Tristan*.

His musical deficiency was overcome by summoning experts, almost collaborators, whose assistance now became a permanent adjunct to his way of working. Specialists were found, on Palestrina, on the viola da gamba, on Purcell, on Wagner, on Mathilde Wesendonck, and were induced to disgorge all pertinent knowledge. The chief among these was Edouard Dujardin, an eccentric Parisian journalist, Moore's only important personal contact with French artistic life after his break with Zola in the late 1880's. Dujardin was later to provide the historical material for Moore's venture into Palestinian lore in

The Brook Kerith, for among his diverse achievements were Biblical exegeses, the last one of which Joseph Hone discovered to be dedicated jointly to Lenin and the Aryan racist, Houston Stewart Chamberlain.[18] Dujardin was the author of an experimental subjective novel called *Les Lauriers sont coupés* which Moore knew and admired, a novel whose possible contribution to James Joyce's technical development is the subject of an interminable literary discussion. Dujardin was above all, however, a fanatical Wagnerite and had founded *La Revue Wagnérienne* as an organ for Wagnerian and symbolist journalism. He overflowed with both enthusiasm and information on all Wagnerian matters and was able to enrich the notes and recollections that Moore had brought back from his own pilgrimages to Bayreuth. He seems to have served Moore also in the meticulous chore of scrutinizing the manuscript of his musical fiction to catch the howlers that Moore, in his ignorance of music, could not discover.

Besides talking about music, Moore was also anxious to project the esoteric doctrines of Celtic-Rosicrucian mysticism, in which one of his characters was immersed neck deep. Yeats apparently supplied him with information on this subject. This task was carried out considerably less cleverly than Moore's Wagnerian reconstructions, judging from the impressions derived from a reading fifty years later; yet Yeats was not dissatisfied with Moore's portrait of himself and his projects, and, that being the case, who should complain? To the specialized contributions of his informants Moore added his own epigrammatic phrasings and a veneer of ninety-ish sophistication reminiscent of the genial arty chitchat of his friend James Huneker. Echoes of the "aestheticizing" of *Mike Fletcher* and *Confessions of a Young Man* are frequently heard in *Evelyn Innes,* but carrying a new tone. Moore had decided that the bare-bones style of *A Mummer's Wife* and *Esther Waters* must be abandoned, and in the new novel he began to experiment with aesthetic talk couched in a fantastically lush style:

In *Parsifal* there was only the second act which he could admire without enormous reservations. The writing in the chorus of the "Flower Maidens" was, of course, irresistible—little cries, meaningless by themselves, but, when brought together, they created an enchanted garden, marvellous and seductive. But it was the duet that followed that compelled his admiration. Music hardly ever more than a recitative, hardly ever breaking into an air, and yet so beautiful! There the notes merely served to lift the words, to impregnate them with more terrible and subtle meaning; and the subdued harmonies enfolded them in an atmosphere, a sensual mood; and in this music we sink into the depths of soul and float upon sullen and mysterious tides of life—those which roll beneath the phase of life which we call existence.[19]

The hurried reader, retreating before this verbal bombardment, would almost fail to perceive the factitiousness of Moore's musical sentiments or the meaningless verbiage of "the phase of life which we call existence."

His ambitions for *Evelyn Innes* turned out to be excessive. The novel had a modest run, caused no sensation, and brought no enhancement to his reputation. Moore's masterful handling of motivation was still in evidence, if one sought it, but most of his skill and taste were drowned out by a blatant, rococo aestheticism and by the clever jargon—musical, occult, and pantheistic—in which the assertedly fierce passions of his dedicated characters were expressed. In particular, his treatment of Sir Owen Asher, the Berkeley Square hedonist, with his yacht, his *avant-garde* taste, his Oscarian wisdom, and his Manet—"the most beautiful thing that Manet ever painted, the most beautiful in the room, and there are a great many beautiful things in the room"—all this led to snickers among his contemporaries, Wilde not the least among the critics. Subsequent aging has hardly diminished the absurdity. Once again, sadly, Moore had to admit a new failure. There were revisions and rewritings, but his enthusiasm was gone. Although Liveright persuaded him to include this novel in the last American collected edition, Moore neglected to supply the affectionate, nostalgic preface

143

that normally accompanied all his reprinted work; and the last collected English edition omitted *Evelyn Innes,* judging it to be unworthy to stand beside *Esther Waters, A Mummer's Wife,* and *Confessions of a Young Man.*

After the completion of *Evelyn Innes,* Moore had still on hand a great mass of unused notes, particularly relating to a concert singer's life, and a sequel seemed in order. The new novel was *Sister Teresa* (1901), which traced the further adventures of Evelyn Innes with her two aesthetic lovers and recounted her final retirement from art, love, and the world by taking the veil and vows of a nun in a contemplative order. *Sister Teresa* presented some of the same practical problems as *Evelyn Innes.* Moore's ignorance of convents and monastic orders was profound, though nuns were plentiful among his cousins. He sought for help in his difficulty from the editor W. T. Stead, for reasons that remain mysterious, since Stead's surviving fame connects him principally with a poorly timed public campaign for increased sexual freedom. Two undated letters to Stead survive. In one Moore said:

> I am considering a story the great part of which passes in a convent of cloistered nuns. I shall write the story if I can obtain certain necessary information regarding the discipline of such convents. . . . If I can get the information—I don't like the word but I can't think of a better one for the moment—I think I can do something with the convent subject.[20]

This sounds like the first step toward another factitious creation. As it turned out, however, *Sister Teresa* was to become a thoroughly competent piece of work, Trollopian in setting and movement and delicately conceived and wrought within its coherent low-keyed limits.

Moore's real subject in Evelyn's story had finally revealed itself to him. It was not, as he had at first supposed, a breezy tour through Wagnerian *Schmalz* and tweedy pantheism, not even the depiction of religious moods, about all of which he was without profound understanding, a mere onlooker. It was the onlooker as such who now took the center of his stage, as Evelyn Innes suddenly discovered herself to be incorrigibly uncommitted and hence, necessarily, a lost soul. This was a subject in which Moore was no ordinary expert. His desecration of the aesthetic pieties that he considered his most sacred beliefs, and his compulsive profanation of the artistic vocation, which had turned the first half of his story into farce, now were suddenly silenced. Into their place came Evelyn Innes' perfectly equilibrated dilemmas, her elaborate self-deceptions, ironically repeated, her pointless achievements, and her slow lapse into quietly resigned defeat—all lucidly seen, perfectly understood, and depicted with new-found stylistic skill and force.

But all in vain; despite its sudden discovery of competence the novel was another failure. The sequel novel could not be separated from its unhappy predecessor; and the leaden weight of *Evelyn Innes,* with its heavy load of Moorisms, dragged *Sister Teresa* down. The delightful house of the childishly ingenuous nuns at Wimbledon, their little vanities, their small anxieties, even their festive *papier-mâché* elephant—all sank into oblivion as the two novels disappeared together from the last collected edition of Moore's works.

The Wild Goose Goes Home

It is for Ireland to admire us, not for us to admire Ireland.

—HAIL AND FAREWELL

ONCE AGAIN artistic defeat had overwhelmed Moore. Press time for *Evelyn Innes* was passed in misery, and he wrote to Dujardin that he seemed to have "given three years to the concoction of an imbecility." The two new novels were less absurd than some of his earlier failures, and they enjoyed a short, fashionable vogue; but they were clearly not likely to enhance his fame or to sustain his self-respect. They had demonstrated for the third time, and with finality at last, the incompatibility of his doctrinaire aesthetic line with serious narrative composition, and he confessed that his career as a novelist was ended unless he could discover a fresh stimulus for his imagination.

A "return to the soil" suggested itself as a possible way around his artistic impasse. For several years he had observed that, while his own work was sinking into debility and "cosmopolitanism," other artists had exploited phases of folk culture to vitalize and solidify their work. Folk aestheticism had begun to interest him as early as *Modern Painting* (1893), when he had written:

> To the select few the great artist is he who is most racy of his native soil. . . . In art, eclecticism means loss of character, and character is everything in art.[1]

The opening phrase, "to the select few," was not a slip of the pen but stated, implying that no one could think otherwise, that the folk movement in art would naturally imply a superior sophistication. This was a portentous assumption, bluntly broaching the most delicately sensitive of all the practical issues to beset the career of the Irish literary revival. In the same mood he had found in the *Punch* cartoonist, Charles Keene, the strength that grew from roots in the English soil. Moore drew the unexpected conclusion from Keene's work that "foreign travel should be eschewed; we should turn our eyes from Paris and Rome and fix them on our own fields; we should strive to remain ignorant, working our lives mole-like, burrowing in our own parish soil." He denounced the Victorian painter George Frederic Watts for not manifesting more interest in his home soil and informed him that, if "he would find the eternal type, he must seek it in his own parish." He observed that even Turgenev, who was later to supply him with his models for the production of "rooted" literature, had included in his work an insufficient feeling for his native land.

In these thoughts of the early 1890's Moore sounded already convinced of the power and charm of folk art. But several barriers were to hold him back from participation in the folk movement for almost another decade. To begin with, his Parisian masters had been silent on the subject, and their permission to proceed was not to be had: "Folklore was unknown in Montmartre." [2] Moreover, he had invested years of work in propagating the opposite artistic ideals of exoticism and artificiality; it was not easy for him to turn upon his own past, to "sneer at artistic accomplishment and to praise the rude and rough manifestations of untutored genius." The most serious barrier of all was his active prejudice against folk and peasants. Folk to Moore meant Irish folk, and the author of *Parnell and His Island* was naturally reluctant to embrace as brother the "rat-faced" Mickey Moran. For several years he cautiously weighed his decision:

. . . I began to wonder . . . if it were true that whoever cast off tradition is like a tree transplanted into uncongenial soil. Turgenev was of that opinion: Russia can do without any one of us, but none of us can do without Russia—one of his sentimental homilies grown wearisome from constant repetition, true, perhaps, of Russia, but utterly untrue of Ireland. Far more true would it be to say that an Irishman must fly from Ireland if he would be himself. Englishmen, Scotchmen, Jews, do well in Ireland—Irishmen never; even the patriot has to leave Ireland to get a hearing. We must leave Ireland; and I did well to listen in Montmartre. All the same, a remembrance of Edward Martyn's conversation could not be stifled. Had I not myself written, only half conscious of the truth, that art must be parochial in the beginning to become cosmopolitan in the end? [3]

The dedication of *Evelyn Innes* in 1898 was made jointly to Yeats and Symons, "two contemporary writers with whom I am in sympathy," but, while one of these young men looked to the Irish soil and the Irish peasant for the forces that would rejuvenate English literature, the other still looked to Paris. *Evelyn Innes* and *Sister Teresa* reveal a creeping intrusion of Irish paraphernalia into Moore's composition, and his free borrowings from Yeats's stage properties—rooks, reeds, curlews, Druids, et cetera—are mixed into his habitual talk about Manet, Wagner, Franck, and Veronese. Those novels and their equivocal mixture of incompatibles had decisively failed. Moore concluded that he must abandon his timidity and his scruples and take the plunge with Yeats, embracing Ireland without compromise or reservation. He was ready to lose his soul to find his soul:

> Even if I am to end my days in the workhouse I must go, even though . . . [I] may break up the mould of my mind. The mould of my mind doesn't interest me any longer, it is an English mould; better break it up at once and have done with it. [4]

As it turned out, he broke up no molds in Dublin but became more essentially and purely himself as he took up the cause of the Irish literary revival in the same inimitable spirit in which he had once espoused Baudelaire, with a hearty fanaticism equivocally compounded of mingled piety and disaffection and passing through minute shades of transition into Moorisms and burlesque.

148

The excesses that would dominate his Irish adventures commenced at the moment of his conversion. Prompted by Yeats, he had just learned to identify England with "vulgarity and materialism" when the Boer War broke out. His hatred of England suddenly flared into a violence totally out of proportion to his usual response to such issues. It is known, for example, that he held rather strong views on the Dreyfus case, but apparently he had no difficulty maintaining silence on the subject, for one will search his collected writings in vain for a single reference to it. But about the Boer War he could not be silenced, and he spent his days insulting old friends who disagreed with him, making scenes in public places, and writing inflammatory letters to the newspapers. "On the subject of the war, I think I am going a little crazy," he wrote to his brother Maurice, who was serving at the time as a British colonel in the field in South Africa. In the countenance of strolling Englishmen he read "a repugnant, sensual cosmopolitanism," "a shameful and vulgar materialism." The city of London, which he had affectionately described in all of his earlier works, drawing upon Whistler's colors for his tones, now became merely "a great sprawl of brick on either side of a muddy river, without a statue that one could look upon with admiration." Sometimes the thought occurred to him that the Boers might themselves be unworthy, that is, unartistic, "speaking a Dutch dialect in which no book had yet been written, a people without sentiment of art." But these doubts came rarely, for he had now fixed his eye on Ireland as the shining antithesis to the baseness of England. Yeats had told him: "Folk is our refuge from vulgarity," and he was convinced. So it came to pass, as every reader of *Hail and Farewell* will remember, that one day in Chelsea Road he heard "a Voice" call to him, saying: "Go to Ireland! Go to Ireland!" He fled from London as from the cities of the plain, fled to Dublin, where he established his little ménage, his cook, his cat, his Aubusson carpet, and his impressionistic paint-

149

ings, in a charming Georgian house just off Stephen's Green, his residence for the greater part of the ensuing decade.

Dublin in 1900 had become irresistibly attractive to Moore. Like Paris in the 1870's, it was tuning its fiddles, and a sensitive ear could catch the excited sound from as far away as Victoria Street. Yeats had long since put away his impulse toward exile and was daily demonstrating himself to be one of the most potent leaders in English letters as he moved about Dublin, Galway, and Sligo, promoting, organizing, stimulating. Æ and his bicycle were exploring the rural lanes, carrying directly to the folk the fused gospels of poetry and the co-operative egg. Douglas Hyde, a mixture of peasant, poet, and philologist, had put his energies behind the organization of the Gaelic League and had set himself the task of driving the language of the foreigner from the Irish soil and restoring to the Gael his ancient and virtually defunct tongue. There was no novelist at hand as yet, but a dozen poets were at work on Irish subjects, a dozen translators were busy reworking the mediaeval stories of the Red Branch and the Fianna. Yeats was experimenting with Irish plays, and there was talk of an Irish theatre. Ireland was witnessing the start of the Irish literary revival, one of those rare and unpredictable outpourings of extraordinary artistic energy that occasionally ornament the history of man's affairs.

All this energy was recognized to be somehow connected with Irish politics. Ireland was moving toward sovereignty, and the nationalistic emotions of a resurgent people had reached intoxicating potency. The fall of Parnell in 1891 had checked the Home Rule movement without destroying the separatist impulse; the moderates who had seized control of Parnell's organization were obviously defensive in their moderation. A small circle of Fenians who had survived all the Crown prosecutor's efforts toward their extermination now sensed opportunity in the air. Tom Clarke was just out of prison after fifteen years, and in his little Dublin tobacco shop he had resumed his revolutionary agitation just as though it had never been interrupted. Arthur Griffith had just begun publication of *The United Irishman* and was shortly to announce the creation of a new type of political organization for "ourselves alone," Sinn Fein. MacBride was off fighting for the Boers. A chain of portentous events had been set in motion, and it would lead in time to Easter Week, to the Black and Tans, to the bloody legends of Childers and Collins, and the prosaic visage of Mr. De Valera.

The artists and the politicians met often in Dublin to converse and argue, and a half-friendly, half-suspicious association arose between them. There was a feeling that all were moving together in the same direction, somewhat vaguely defined as the good of Ireland, and there was much agreeable talk about the legendary Cuchulain, the martyr Wolfe Tone, and the lofty and antimaterialistic Gaelic soul. Yet a sense of alienation was also felt, for the two groups held profoundly incompatible views on the important question of the location of the final authority of their movement. The artists thought of the resurgence as basically "spiritual," that is, aesthetic; they thought of Wolfe Tone as a literary possession, as what would now be called an embodiment of the myth of the sacrificial hero. They looked upon the politicians as moderately useful subordinates. "We must accept the baptism of the gutter," said Yeats privately to apologize for the poet's interest in politics, and with equally innocent condescension he declared that Ireland "has need of the violence of the mob that it may sometimes tear the subtle net." The politicians, meanwhile, showed the impatience that men who are daily intimate with the direct forms of naked power typically display toward mere words and ideas. They were quick to confess, if anyone cared to raise the issue, that they thought the poets more than a little odd, and simultaneously dangerous and ineffectual. The classic statement of this conviction belonged to Standish O'Grady, a journalist whose florid translations had made the stories of the Red Branch mythological cycle available to all Irish school children. At a memorable banquet given by the *Daily Express* to celebrate the founding of the Irish Literary Theatre, O'Grady arose very drunk to propose a toast to the arming of the Irish Boy Scouts, defending his proposal with an extraordinary prognostication, which ran, according to Yeats's recollection of the incident, as follows:

> We have now a literary movement, it is not very important; it will be followed by a political movement, that will be very important; then will come a military movement, that will be very important indeed.[5]

But in 1900 such a cavalier dismissal of the poets sounded crude and arrogant. Not that all was harmonious between the two wings of the resurgence. Long before Moore's return to Ireland, Yeats had fought a skirmish with the politicians over the issue of whether good incendiary propaganda might be properly designated by the term "art." Yeats seemed to have won his point in defense of the purity of art; subsequently he had joined the Fenian brotherhood and had taken the secret oath, though he had not been happy in the midst of Fenians and had drifted away from them without feeling or incurring enmity. Most of Yeats's oratory at the end of the century was for the unity of the poet and the politician, for a calming of ungenerous fears, and for the common cause. He had succeeded in reducing the latent conflicts to a state of mere suspense. It was into this atmosphere that Moore walked, fanatically convinced of the superiority of art to all other activities whatever, especially to political activity, and "without enough talent to be obscure." "I think I am going to teach the Irish what art and politics are," he said, and, hoping that few would remember what he had written in *Parnell and His Island,* he readied himself to "strike a blow for Ireland."

Moore's official contribution to the Irish literary revival was important, though not prolonged. In 1899 Yeats, Martyn, and Moore founded the Irish Literary Theatre, the forerunner of the Abbey Theatre. According to Yeats's testimony, the new theatre could not have been set in motion without Moore, whose practical knowledge of the stage and of the rudiments of plot construction forestalled early collapse of their project through the sheer ineptitude and ignorance of the organizers. Moore was the stage director for the theatre's first great success, Martyn's somber twilight play, *The Heather Field,* produced with professional London actors brought over in the second-class coaches while Martyn, as befitted a Maecenas, indulged himself in the luxury of a first-class passage. Another of Martyn's plays was rewritten by Moore and produced in 1900 under Moore's name as *The Bending of the Bough.* In the same year Moore delivered a famous speech in the Dublin Rotunda on behalf of the revival of Gaelic, the one and only oratorical adventure of his entire career. In the year following, Moore and Yeats collaborated in writing *Diarmuid and Grania,* produced on the Dublin stage October 21, 1901. Meanwhile the three individualists of the original theatre had inevitably fallen out with one another and parted; Moore is our source for the epigram, which he attributed to Æ, on cooperative aesthetic enterprises: A literary movement is a small group of writers who live in the same town and hate each other cordially. Before the rise of Synge's star, Moore and Martyn had already withdrawn from the theatre, leaving Yeats and Lady Gregory in full command for the glorious years that lay just ahead. After the severance of Moore's official connections with the movement, he took up the role of independent Irish sage.

For a short time it appeared that he had indeed been mystically transfigured by his return to Ireland. The mood of the Celtic twilight seemed to obliterate his former self, and he could scarcely set pen to paper without falling into the trancelike rhythms and ethereal images of the seer. No writer in Dublin spoke so ecstatically of the inner life of the Irish soul. Gautier's visible world sank into the mists, leaving no trace. "In the visible," said the new convert to spiritualism, "the worldling finds amusement, unsatisfactory distraction; whereas spiritual man finds continual consolation in the invisible—in an imagined world." He renounced his championship of the music halls, once his last hope for bringing the English to culture, and he gravely informed his Irish countrymen that there is "nothing in life so low as musical comedy, for in the musical comedy the meaning of life is expressed in eating, drinking, betting, and making presents to women." [6] He wrote an introduction to Martyn's play, *The Heather Field,* and, after first comparing it favorably with *Hamlet,* he continued:

> The idea . . . is that silvery beauty which survives in the human heart, which we see shimmering to the horizon, leading our longings beyond the world, and we hear it in our hearts like silver heartstrings, sounding seemingly of themselves, for no hand is by. The morning light, the hoar frost, the moonlight wandering among the mountains are the natural symbols of this divine beauty. . . . To triumph thus over common instincts and infect the reader with sympathies and longings which lie beyond the world is surely to succeed.[7]

It was prose of this texture that doubtless led Yeats to demand the sole right to determine "the final words" of the Irish play he wrote jointly with Moore. To his friend J. E. Blanche, the French portrait painter, Moore wrote in high spirits that he had said farewell to his "artificial life." "The wind off the sea and from the fields makes me feel another man."

This phase did not hold Moore captive long. Before many years had passed, his detached and prosaic vision of Ireland had returned. The hero of *The Bending of the Bough* expounds his orthodox Dublin spiritualism in a curiously hard-minded and factitious tone:

> No race has looked so long and so steadfastly through the shells of things out into the beyond as our race, it will be the first to attain this supreme end; we know the end is union with something beyond, though words may not further define it; we feel it throbbing always like a pulse within us.

If Moore's Dublin contemporaries had possessed a more suspicious ear for rhetoric, they might have caught hints of his impending defection in Moorisms of this sort and might have saved themselves the surprises that came with the publication of *Hail and Farewell* eight years later. In any case, Moore's revulsion from the ideals of the Irish literary revival seems to have been well advanced by 1905, the year of the publication of *The Lake*. His adherence to the movement had scarcely begun before it was finished, as he found himself overfed, according to his subsequent explanation, with "Irish hallucinations." He began to wonder "if it might be that through excessive indulgence in dreams for over a hundred years the people had at last dreamed themselves and Ireland away." He was panic-stricken, he said, by a sense that he was losing his grip on reality, a fear that had once seized him while listening to a lecture given by one of Yeats's Indian mentors:

> The homely earth that I knew had faded, and I waited expectant among the peaks, until at last, taken with a sudden fear that if I lingered any longer I might never see again a cottage at the end of an embowered lane, I started to my feet and fled.[8]

Now his thoughts about Ireland lost their sanctimonious tone; and his fishlike, cold, china-blue eye was cast upon the Dublin scene, in keeping with the principle recommended by his great compatriot and contemporary. He began to meditate upon the tragicomedy of the return of the wild goose to Ireland and at last, with the start of the composition of *Hail and Farewell,* to create one of the great satiric works of our language.

Besides the attraction and repulsion of the intense Celtic inane, some frankly mundane impulses lay behind Moore's Dublin arrival and departure. A search for relief from specific literary ailments had contributed a strong motive toward his return. Chief among his ailments was his fear that his creative impulse had burnt itself out; and he predicted with confidence that Ireland could restore his loss by providing him with a virginal language and a true audience. Both expectations were frustrated by realities that he did not fully anticipate and that Yeats could not warn him to prepare for, since Yeats, no less than Moore, had still to discover the full force of the hostility that could be generated in Ireland to oppose an independent, heretical, and passionately uncoordinated artistic activity.

On the language question Moore's highly individual views were maintained with such seeming force of conviction that their eccentricity was not immediately perceived in Dublin. At the outset he had scornfully rejected the drift of Yeats, Lady Gregory, and Synge toward apotheosis of the so-called Kiltartan dialect of Anglo-Irish, the language of *The Playboy of the Western World* and *Spreading the News*. Synge might think that Kiltartan gave to literature the flavor of nuts and apples, but Moore considered it vulgar, identifying it with the brogue and, in turn, with all his deepest prejudices. Moreover, he thought it a timid compromise of the language issue, a view in which he saw eye to eye with Edward Martyn, who had attacked it in the press as a bastard speech, neither English nor Irish. Moore heard Kiltartan as a mere mechanism, "tricks of speech a parrot can learn," capable of manufacture in any quantity, like journalese:

> When we look into the beautiful speech that Lady Gregory learnt as she moved among her people, we find that it consists of no more than a dozen turns of speech, dropped into pages so ordinary, that redeemed from these phrases it might appear in any newspaper without attracting attention.[9]

Synge's achievement, Moore decided, consisted mainly in learning the twelve turns of Kiltartan speech; and, to demonstrate that his own aversion to it did not arise out of his inability to learn them himself, he wrote a specimen paragraph mocking Synge's memory in Kiltartan:

> And morebetoken, his language in the same book is as bald as the coat of a mangy dog, and trapsed along over a page of print like the clutter of a horse that was gone in the legs. It's many a heart scald this same must have given to my bold Yeats, for it's the grand judge entirely he is of the shape and color and the sound of words. "Give up your schoolmaster words that have no guts left in them, and leave

off thinking of Loti and his barley-sugar, and go down into County Wicklow and listen to what the people do be saying to 'other when they're at their ease without any notion of an ear cocked to carry off what they say. I hear tell that they speak a language that isn't worn out yet, and that has some of the youth of the world in it." [10]

The last gibe parodies Moore's own words, originally borrowed from Yeats, on behalf of the revival of the Gaelic tongue. The disabilities of Kiltartan, Moore had decided, were not shared by Gaelic. It was certainly not vulgar: "There is a great difference," he said, "between the Irish language and the English as spoken with a thick brogue. One I love, the other I have no objection in confessing I hate." [11] Gaelic was a drastic cure for a radical ailment; nothing less would serve, for Kiltartan was still English and English was moribund, "worn out like a coat," "corrupt," "polluted," expressive only of "commercial platitude," the dead language of the destined "universal suburb, in which a lean man with glasses on his nose and a black bag in his hand is always running after the bus." [12]

Sometimes Moore explained his impulse toward Gaelic more crudely. He was dismayed by his conviction that in English "everything had been already written," and that his chances of "adding to English literature" were not great. His friend Dujardin had abandoned musical composition for the interesting reason that he estimated he could never outdo Wagner. Balzac's and Zola's vision of artistic "conquest" never altogether lost its appeal to Moore; but in the year his Irish adventure began, he confessed morosely to his brother Maurice that he had come too late to conquer:

> . . . Shakespeare absorbed dramatic poetry, Balzac the novel, Wagner absorbed dramatic music—we are the moths that flutter in the light of suns that shall have no setting.[13]

The conclusion to be drawn was plain enough. He would establish a connection with a language in which "the volume" of literature was small.

What could suit his purpose better than Gaelic? Mickey

Moran's language was one in which not everything had already been written, in which, indeed, very little had been written. The first literary fruit of Moore's return to Ireland was named *The Untilled Field*, a title that contains a note of self-congratulation on his good luck in staking an early claim upon the art of the Irish folk. The problem of the Irish peasant, which had resisted economic and political solution for centuries, was suddenly unraveled by aesthetics, according to Moore's explanation to William Archer, in which he used the analogy of the American Negro:

> The American wonders what to do with the Negro population. The Negro in America is the seed of the future literature; for when the journalists have killed the language, when it becomes incapable even of journalese, the Negro will be inventing new idiom. . . . The Negro will invent the new language; the man of letters will apply it to literary purposes.[14]

This argument might suggest a justification of the literary use of dialects, even of Kiltartan, but Moore did not so understand it. His explicit statement in the Rotunda speech of 1900 was that Ireland must make up its mind to be bilingual, "to use English as a universal language, and to save our own as a medium for some future literature."

Since the Irish patriots and politicians clearly envisaged other employment for the revived language, it would have been strange if they had let Moore's singular position stand without some sort of a rejoinder; and it is true that he was more suspiciously eyed in Dublin than the rest of his aesthetic compeers. A heckler interrupted the Rotunda speech: "It isn't that sort of sophisticated stuff we want," he shouted, even before the orator reached the paragraphs of his manuscript in praise of Walter Pater. Later, after the publication of *Hail and Farewell*, which many of his fellow countrymen read as an insult against the national honor, Irish patriots would feel themselves revenged by reciting Susan Mitchell's little counterattack against Moore's patriotic conversion:

Some day you'll all discover how respectable I am,
How I revere the marriage state, believe in Abraham,
And for the Gaels and their Revival don't really care a damn.[15]

But this merely discovered the second convolution of Moore's meaning. The further depths were unperceived, and would remain so until Joyce and Yeats, a decade later, followed him in exploring the infinite regression of irony and pathos that were emerging out of Irish history.

Moore's Gaelic fantasies were troubled from the start by two near-fatal difficulties. In the first place nobody knew Gaelic. Even among Irish peasants the tongue had all but disappeared except in a few wild and remote glens in Connemara and in Aran and the other western islands. If a masterpiece should appear in Gaelic, it would necessarily blush unseen. Moore was inclined to disregard this obvious fact, however, citing his favorite dogma that "there is no such thing as a beautiful unknown line of poetry," and pointing to the example of Ibsen. Irish writers, he assured his friends, need only produce great work in Gaelic and it would soon "travel all over Europe."

More disconcerting still: he knew no Gaelic himself and was at the stage in life in which it was hopeless to expect to learn it. This would seem to have been a fatal flaw in his language project, and indeed he was never quite able to cope with it seriously. One of his responses to the difficulty was to urge Gaelic upon his nephews, Maurice's sons. The peroration of the Rotunda speech spoke of this patriotic scheme:

> I have no children and am too old to learn the language, but I shall at once arrange that my brother's children shall learn Irish. I have written to my sister-in-law telling her that I will at once undertake this essential part of her children's education. They shall have a nurse straight from Aran; for it profits a man nothing if he knows all the languages of the world but knows not his own.[16]

This Moorism was too broad for anyone to miss altogether, and Susan Mitchell's verses caught the note of self-mockery, if not the parody of Irish patriotism:

I've puffed the Irish language, and puffed the Irish soap;
I've used them—on my nephew—with best results, I hope;
For with this older, dirtier George, I have no heart to cope.

Translation offered a second possible way of surmounting the language barrier. Masterpieces could be composed in English and earmarked exclusively for translation into Gaelic. Moore seems to have studied this possibility seriously, and his well-known farcical anecdote about the writing of *Diarmuid and Grania* is a characteristic desecration of an idea with which he was clearly identified: the plan was, he said, that the play should be composed by Moore in French, translated by Lady Gregory into English, translated by Taidgh O'Donoghue into Gaelic, translated by Lady Gregory back into English which, now purified by its "bath in Gaelic," would "have the poetry put on it" by Yeats. But his special interest in translation was genuine and long outlived his Irish adventure.

The Rotunda speech contained an announcement that the Irish Literary Theatre was planning a performance of Yeats's *Land of Heart's Desire* in Gaelic, in a translation prepared by Douglas Hyde. Said Moore to his listeners: "Alas! there will be fewer in the theatre who will understand the Irish text than a Latin or Greek one." Anticipating the rejoinder that such a project was foolish on the face of it, he readily confessed the truth of such a contention and, like Tertullian on faith, embraced the foolish as his special wisdom:

Our desire may be foolish, unpractical, unwise, according to the lights of the English nation at the present moment; but our desire is our desire, our folly is our own, and if we wish to start ill equipped in the business race of the world, knowing no language which is understood outside of Ireland, shall we be gainsaid like children?

"Our folly is our own"; this was good Hibernian oratorical language, but if one thought about it for a while it might begin to sound suspiciously like the words of Baudelaire: *"Hypocrite lecteur, mon semblable, mon frère."* Susan Mitchell's wit could give no catharsis for the shock of that discovery.

160

But Moore's folly was his very own. His plan to serve the Gaelic League was so original that he shortly found himself a leader without a following. "There has been no more disinterested movement than the Gaelic League," he said; "to believe that a movement distinguished by so much self-sacrifice could fail, would be like believing in the failure of goodness itself." The word "disinterested" was an equivocal one. The reader of *Confessions of a Young Man* will recall the highly personal meaning that Moore attached to it: a thing was "disinterested" if it helped George Moore toward the achievement of his aesthetic object of the moment. The Easter Week martyr Padraic Pearse also meditated on the work of the Gaelic League and came to quite another conclusion: "The Gaelic League will be recognized in history as the most revolutionary influence that has ever come into Irish history." Behind similar rhetorical masks Moore and Pearse were each declaring themselves to be the ultimate manipulators of the symbols of authority embodied in the Gaelic League. And if history did not prove Pearse's estimate absolutely correct, it did prove Moore's to be absolutely mistaken.

"I came to give Ireland back her language," Moore announced to Æ, who thought Moore should take on the role of the Irish Voltaire instead, leaving leadership on the language front to Irishmen more plainly qualified for the work. But Moore already had projects sketched on paper. One, based on a suggestion from Goethe, was to organize a little group of strolling actors to go through the countryside playing folk drama in the Gaelic tongue from the tail gates of their wagons, an idea that had the force of myth in Moore's imagination and that recurred in his novels from *A Mummer's Wife* to *Aphrodite in Aulis*. This project came to nothing; for practical minds pointed out that the Irish peasant would need to learn Gaelic before Gaelic folk plays could be understood, and that teachers, rather than playwrights, were the need of the moment. The second project brought more solid results for literature if not for Ireland. He

161

volunteered to compose literary works especially for the Gaelic League. They would be translated from his corrupted English into the pure liquidity of Gaelic, adding, so he hoped, aestheticism to the League's proselytizing appeals. Two charming little stories were written, "The Wedding Gown" and "A Play-House in the Waste," and duly translated into Gaelic by T. W. Rolleston. Moore experienced a moment of childish delight in seeing his name on the title page after undergoing its bath in Gaelic: *Seorsa O Morda.* But the officials of the Gaelic League could envision no advantage their movement might derive from the aesthetic approach to the problem. They did not even display the little booklets in their window, and according to Moore's estimate scarcely a hundred copies found their way into circulation.

So ended Moore's scheme for the recovery of his innocence through exposing himself to the unfamiliar sounds of Gaelic. The Rotunda speech bore a strong resemblance to absurdity, and only slight changes of emphasis were needed to transform his linguistic projects into unmitigated satire, which he now began to practice with full vigor, assigning to himself the role of the chief *farceur.* He had a vision of making the long pilgrimage to Aran; "a large, bright cottage with chintz curtains" he would have there, "and homely oaken furniture, and some three or four Impressionist pictures, and the restless ocean my only companion"; and he thought of himself returning to civilization ten years later a master of Gaelic and totally de-aestheticized. He suggested to John Eglinton that, since Gaelic was "dead beyond all hope of resurrection," the Irish peasant might still be of some use to literature if he could be taught the second person singular. "Even the Gaels could learn to *thou* and *thee* each other; *thou* and *thee* would become a Gaelic banner and afterward would be adopted by English writers." He went dutifully to Galway with Martyn, Yeats, and Lady Gregory to listen to the traditional folk singers at a Gaelic feis. Like Matthew Arnold at the Llandudno eisteddfod, he was arrested, bewildered, and at last not a little wearied by hours of strenuous recitation in a foreign language he could not comprehend and would never learn:

> I listened to the singer, but could catch only a vague drift of sound, rising and falling, unmeasured as the wind soughing among the trees or the lament of waves on the shore, something that might go on all day long, and the old fellow thatching his cabin all the while.[17]

He went on the Dublin quays to catch the music of the speech of Breton sailors, the linguistic cousins of the Gael. He said to one: "Doesn't it seem odd to hear Celtic speech while you are climbing in the ship's rigging high above the stormy seas of Cape Horn?" The Breton answered, "Not at all, sir; all of us are Bretons." Moore walked away muttering, "To be sure, to be sure," his folkish sentimentality deflated and another anecdote stored away for use in *Hail and Farewell*.

Moore's aesthetic demands on Dublin were not confined to linguistics. He hoped to find in Ireland a fitting audience for his work and to bring to a close at last his perpetually frustrated search for acceptance and appreciation on his own terms. Years later he told Geraint Goodwin that Dublin was "searching for a new literature" in 1900 and that he "decided to give it to them." After the objective inaccuracy of this statement is discounted, it remains a valid recollection of his excitement in believing that there were people, his own people, who wanted him, a feeling that none of his earlier literary associations had ever given, not even the Nouvelle Athènes. During the first phase of his return home his writing occasionally suggested a Tolstoian impulse that might faintly threaten to turn Moore Hall into an Irish Yasnaya Polyana. Thus the first versions of *The Untilled Field* find him confessing in a passage later deleted that "all your interesting utterances about the Italian renaissance would not interest me half so much as what Paddy Durkin and Father Pat would say to me on the roadside."

James Joyce, who was a derisive Dublin adolescent in the

early years of the Irish literary revival, understood that the theatre of Yeats, Moore, and Martyn was some sort of a concession to the multitude, and in an angry little pamphlet called "The Day of the Rabblement" he scolded Moore for coming home in search of a mob for his audience, taunting him with the accusation that the new Dublin theatre had "surrendered to the trolls." Joyce had been misled; the surface of Moore's folk enthusiasms had obscured his true position. Whatever else he might have been forced to surrender on his return home, he had no intention of compromising his fundamental aesthetic conviction that art is for the few. In the excitement of the literary revival he merely added an amendment: art is for the few—as always—but it has need of the many for its cultivation. He had dreamed that the population of Dublin and of all Ireland was a waiting audience, ready to appear to watch the new plays and to read the new poems and stories that would be composed to express the Irish soul; an audience that would be enthusiastic at the requisite times and always grateful but that would not be asked to understand or even to approve, since approval implied the right to disapprove, the art that in some puzzling way required them as witnesses.

Moore's most lucid statement of this extraordinary attitude is to be found in *The Epistle to the Cymry,* a version of the Rotunda speech recast for presentation to Welshmen at a time when his Gaelic enthusiasms had grown feeble. The epistle urged the Welsh to cherish their countryman, Moore's friend Lord Howard de Walden, who could already, so Moore reported, "speak a little Welsh; he can write it. . . . He may write a play in Welsh." Against this eventuality Lord Howard had tried to anticipate what accessories would be wanted, and he had come to an important conclusion: "There is one thing that a theatre cannot do without—an audience." Such being certainly the case, the duty of the Welsh was clear: they must constitute themselves into Lord Howard's audience. "Be his audience," Moore pleaded with his Welsh listeners, "and make him proud of you and of the original step he has taken." As a crowning achievement the Welshmen who supplied Lord Howard with his missing ingredient would "practically guarantee that anyone who writes a meritorious play will have the pleasure of seeing it acted." Out of all this activity would necessarily arise, according to natural law, the greater glory of Wales and of Welshmen.[18]

This last step in Moore's line of thought was one that Irish logic could not follow, and who can say whether it was Moore or his intended audience who eventually proved to be the more arrogant and unbending? Dublin had no waiting audience to offer; on the contrary, Dubliners would repeatedly demonstrate either indifference or open enmity to their talented fellow countrymen who wrote plays, poems, and novels in their midst. The Irish literary revival opened in hostility, when Yeats's *Countess Cathleen* came under a surprise assault from theologians who considered that the heroine's offer to sell her soul for the relief of her famine-stricken peasants was a heresy dangerous to the faith of Irishmen. Moore was still officially connected with the Dublin theatre at the time of the *Countess Cathleen* disturbance, although he was not present in the theatre to hear the pious hecklers. He prepared himself for another historic battle like his skirmish against Mudie's library. The battle never materialized, however; the objection was withdrawn; the play was saved; and the issue was soon forgotten. In the latter years of Moore's Dublin sojourn, rotten vegetables, thrown to defend the honor of Irish womanhood, would halt the speeches of the actors in *The Playboy of the Western World*. Lady Gregory might refer to these hooligan outbursts as "lovers' quarrels," but Moore thought otherwise. When he saw the haste with which Martyn, T. P. Gill, and other enlightened Dubliners abandoned their aesthetic convictions in the face of orthodox resistance, he concluded that Dublin did not possess sufficient courage or intelligence to support an artistic movement.

Meanwhile, his own new Irish literature was neither welcomed nor attacked. His two plays were moderately successful, but his stories were ignored. His first Irish story, "The Wedding Gown," was innocuous enough from the patriotic point of view, dealing with such unexceptionable matters as the pathos of old age, the recurrent cycle of generations, and the supernatural awareness of the presence of death à la Maeterlinck and Yeats. Yet its public reception was scarcely even lukewarm. In his next story, "A Play-House in the Waste," he aimed to touch upon more lively and striking subjects, but in so doing he began to intrude into the forbidden: into illegitimacy, murderous superstition, rural depravity, eccentric priests, in this case one who believes that the celibate rule should be relaxed. A vicious circle was now set in motion. An ordinary Irish reader, if he read Moore's second story at all, would have found it disturbing. His hoped-for Irish following failed to appear; his irritation at the indifference of his Irish welcome increased accordingly; his writing became in turn more belligerent still. *The New Ireland Review,* edited by a Jesuit, Father Finlay, a friend of Moore, was in a short time forced to close its pages to his work. His high hopes of finding a waiting audience in Ireland had collapsed. His fellow countrymen had lain too long, he said, "under the spell of the magicians" to care for the art that he was prepared to bring them.

The emotion that previously had been channeled off into hatred of English materialism and English bullying of the Boers now suddenly found a new outlet in anticlericalism. Convinced that the aesthetic apathy of the Irish people was irremediable in the existing state of affairs, he initiated a ceaseless discourse upon the interrelation between Catholicism and the degradation of Ireland. The subject occupied all his conversation, all his correspondence, all his thought. His stories all ran in the well-worn channel. Now he envisioned Ireland as "a western Tibet"; he saw cathedral and nunnery brooding malignantly over the dirty cottages "like one great cloud." Now he forthrightly affirmed nineteenth-century progress, and he

castigated its detractors as superstition mongers and obscur-
antists:

> . . . for the sake of the fruit of the tree of knowledge, all the fences
> that the clerics had erected were broken down one by one; and during
> the nineteenth century a great feast was held under the tree. But
> after every feast there are always ailing stomachs; those denouncing
> the feast go about in great depression of spirit, surfeited feasters, say-
> ing the branches of the tree have been plucked bare; others complain
> they have eaten bitter fruit. This is the moment for the prowling
> cleric.[19]

One of his characters in a story called "The Wild Goose," included in *The Untilled Field,* takes the ship out of Howth into
exile crying: "Better to die than to live here."

In his private life Moore began to dramatize his new *idée fixe*
with elaborately contrived symbolic incidents that would eventually find their way into the pages of *Hail and Farewell.* He
sought out Michael Davitt and, forgetting their ancient enmity
from the days of the Land War in Mayo, he lionized the old
agitator as a fellow anticlerical. He caused a great fluttering in
the dovecotes by sending a letter to the Dublin press announcing
that he had "discovered himself a Protestant." He undertook a
long and unrelenting assault upon the Catholic beliefs of his
brother Maurice. With ironic hints of analogous dispositions
required in mixed marriages, he commanded Maurice to bring
up his children as Protestants and threatened to deny them their
expected inheritance of Moore Hall if his command was ignored.
Maurice did refuse, and Moore willed his property to other
Catholic nephews and nieces. A large part of the last of the
three volumes of *Hail and Farewell* is devoted to a colloquy
between the two brothers on the subject of art and Catholicism,
with George maintaining, and Maurice sullenly assenting, that
Catholics had produced no art since the Council of Trent.

He began a new novel, *The Lake* (1905). It retraced all the
marches and countermarches of faith and doubt across the
battlegrounds of *Sister Teresa* but with a significant new ending

which renounced religion, self-denial, and the "light from without," in favor of—what? The visibility of the visible world, individual freedom of choice, hedonism, and art. The novel tells of a priest in an Irish village who, as the story opens, has just driven from his parish a beautiful and intelligent young unmarried mother. The priest opens a correspondence with the girl, having deceived himself with the excuse that he must not shirk his responsibility for the salvation of her soul. Actually he has been overcome with remorse at the inhumanity of his action, as his correspondent very deftly and quickly forces him to admit. The girl turns out to be no ordinary writer of letters. Her letters soon seize the moral ascendancy from the priest and overwhelm him with eloquent affirmations of pleasure, honesty, and freedom. In due time she even begins to "aestheticize" and to supply the priest with information on Wagnerian *leitmotifs*, summaries of the librettos of *The Ring*, and Spenglerian comparisons between Ruysdael and Spinoza. The priest is so effectively routed by the correspondence that he begins to doubt his vocation; a crisis ensues, and he is at last converted. The novel closes with his renunciation of the priesthood and flight to America. To give the appearance of drowning, he leaves his clothes on the shore of the lake and swims across to the far shore, where secular clothing, freedom, and anonymity await him:

> . . . he laid his priest's clothes in the middle of a patch of white sand where they could be easily seen. He placed the Roman collar upon the top, and, stepping from stone to stone, he stood on the last one as on a pedestal, tall and gray in the moonlight—buttocks hard as a faun's and dimpled like a faun's when he draws himself up before plunging after a nymph.

The dive of the naked faun brought Moore back to the position he had occupied twenty years before in *Confessions of a Young Man*, a fact acknowledged indirectly through his growing preoccupation with recurrence and the feeling of always having passed this way before. *The Untilled Field* contains a story on the subject, called "So On He Fares," a story that so satisfied him that he once called it with characteristic exaggeration the best story ever written. It is a fable about a little boy who was hated and tormented by his mother Catherine, i.e., Ireland. "His mother was always telling him not to do something." One day she punishes his disobedience by putting a bee inside his shirt. Screaming with pain and anger, he runs out of the yard and hides on the bank of the canal that runs to the Shannon. There he cajoles some bargemen to take him away. He finds a kindly widow, i.e., France, who takes him in and he is "loved by his chance mother as he had been hated by his real mother." Ten years later he feels an impulse to "see what they are doing at home." He goes on board a barge and heads back. His mother now has another son whom she loves as much as she hated the older child. When she sees the returned wanderer, she says: "Oh, it's you. Why we thought you were drowned." Her heart is still set against him; and, when his little brother asks him to tell tales about sailing ships, he replies, "But mother hates to hear my voice." He waits for another barge to the Shannon and goes aboard; "the green country flowed on"; and on he fares.

Yet Moore's recurrence did not bring him exactly back to his earlier self. The "Aristophanic joy" of his youth was gone, and its place was taken by another tone, stoical and solemn, described in "So On He Fares" as a bitterness growing out of the hold life had taken upon him. The new tone was Irish in its expression; and, as Moore had certainly gone home to find, among other things, "metaphors for poetry," he might with justice have attributed his mastery of it to Ireland, as the one literary achievement of his return.

The mood of the Celtic twilight profoundly affected Moore's imagination. Even in the first days of his enchantment he was never stirred by patriotic sentiments, nor by the roll call of heroes whose names "have gone about the world like wind," nor by Red Hanrahan, nor by the cruder expressions of patriotic bravado; but only by twilight images: ruin and weed, the soughing of the wind on lonely bogs, the wan skies, the melancholy gray Irish eye, and Ireland's unlit lamp and ungirt loin. In one of Moore's Irish stories called "The Way Back," someone asks Harding why he planned to go home and receives this lugubrious reply:

> Looking across a park with a view of the mountains in the distance, I perceived a pathetic beauty in the country itself that I had not perceived before; and a year afterwards I was driving about the Dublin mountains, and met two women on the road; there was something pathetic and wistful about them, something dear, something intimate, and I felt drawn towards them. I felt I should like to live among these people again.

The Irish patriots might well have watched this predilection and inquired why it should be that, whenever Moore's imagination turned to cast a poetic glow on Ireland, his voice took on the mournful tone of keening.

But one need not remain in Ireland to savor the charming melancholy of the Celtic twilight; indeed, it was enhanced by absence, and that was a fortunate thing, "Ireland being a fatal disease, fatal to Englishmen and doubly fatal to Irishmen." The sacrifices that seemed to him to have wasted the lives of his great-uncle and his father were on his mind, and he began to tremble for fear that "the terrible Cathleen ni Houlihan" would overtake him.

> . . . as in a vision I saw Ireland as a god demanding human sacrifices, and everybody, or nearly everybody crying: Take me, Ireland, take me; I am unworthy, but accept me as a burnt offering. Ever since I have been in the country I have heard people speaking of working for Ireland. But how can one work for Ireland without working for oneself? [20]

Since Ireland would not "forego her superstitions for the sake of literature" and had thereby made herself "a slut among nations," Moore decided that he must go once again into exile, like Wilde and Shaw, like Joyce and Gogarty, Colum and O'Casey, like every "brave-hearted" Irish lad who cried: "Now, off with my coat so that I may earn five pounds to take me out of the country."

Back in London with his cat, his carpet, his paintings, and his antique clock, he could conjure up in comfort the images of those wistful Celtic folk "with eyes as sad as the waters of western lakes." He had failed to remake himself into an Irish Tolstoi, but he could become an Irish Chekhov; and *Hail and Farewell* closes with the fateful sound of the axe upon the trees of Moore Hall, where "the landlords have had their day" and where "all that was, has gone or is going."

The White Birds
Of Recollection

When a great genius is declining, the special token of old age is the love of marvellous tales.
—Longinus, ON THE SUBLIME

. . . one's existence from day to day came to be like a well-executed piece of music; that "perpetual motion" in things (so Marius figured the matter to himself) according itself to a kind of cadence or harmony.
—Walter Pater, MARIUS THE EPICUREAN

MOORE RECOGNIZED that he would have to leave Dublin before the publication of *Hail and Farewell* in order to avoid meeting the victims of his satire on the street. But he wanted to delay his departure as long as possible in order to allow himself the fullest time to study his unsuspecting models. The logical moment for packing his *objets d'art* and catching the exile's boat to England came in the spring of 1911, just three months ahead of the release of the first volume of the trilogy. Back in London he found himself, in his sixtieth year, ready for the sixth time in his career to turn his back upon the past and to start life afresh. The new phase following his Irish adventure was to be his last. He established a fixed and final address at 121 Ebury Street in Pimlico, in the lee of the smoke from nearby refineries and rubber factories, and symbolically located, as he observed, half-way between bohemia and Belgravia. Immediately he set to work on new literary projects that were to occupy him without further revolutions or transfigurations for the last twenty-one vigorous years of his life.

Moore was now in full reaction against an art that concerned itself with folk sentiment, topicality, tendentiousness, "impurity," or other aesthetic sins, as he thought them, flourishing in Dublin. His writing turned toward a search for the "universal," and his taste began to approve highly of the culture of antiquity. He did not recant in his worship of Balzac or Pater, but he began to speak more often and more enthusiastically of other masters, ancients or imitators of the ancients. References to Theocritus, Apuleius, and Longus began to drop into his letters and his criticism. He announced that the most beautiful passage in all literature was a sentence from Andrew Lang's translation of Bion's *Lament for Moschus:*

> Ah me, when the mallows wither in the garden and the green parsley, and the curled tendrils of the anise, on a later day they live again, and once we have died, in hollow earth we sleep, gone down in silence; a right long, and endless, and unawakening sleep.[1]

The facet of antiquity that had caught his imagination was its occasional mood of sweet and quietistic pessimism. It will be recalled that this was the mood of his grandfather, George Moore the historian, as his languid gaze fixed on the "melancholy line" of the misty blue mountains that lay across the wan lake at the foot of his Georgian park. It was the official mood of the Celtic twilight and of the young and lugubrious Yeats, wandering beside another desolate water "where the wind cries in the sedge." It was very close to Moore's own definitive statement of the Irish soul in *The Untilled Field:*

> I heard a shepherd playing this folk tune. Listen to it. Is it not like the people? Is it not like Ireland? . . . It is the song of exile; it is the cry of one driven out into the night—in a night of wind and rain. It is night, and the exile is on the edge of the waste. It is like wind sighing over bog water. It is a pathetic echo and final despair of a people who knew they were done for from the beginning.[2]

173

If one removed the borrowings from *Die Walküre* and *Tristan* from this paragraph, not much residue would remain. But to Moore it sounded Celtic; the erstwhile Celtophile was now a Celtophobe, and these images of wind-swept bog no longer interested him. Antiquity alone, he now insisted, knew reality; and antiquity alone understood the pathos of existence or knew "the poetry of life to be in our consciousness of its passing from us always."

This mood of secret inquietude, he decided, was the "universal" theme and the source of the greatness of all great art. Writers who had never expressed the mood he dismissed as "surface writers," devoid of all sense of the eternal and of the hidden essence of existence. He looked for it in vain in Fielding, Thackeray, Trollope, Kipling, even George Eliot; and as for Hardy, he dared not speak his name in the same breath with the melancholics of antiquity, pessimist though he was, since his knowledge of the secret inquietude of life lacked both refinement and poetry. "That verse about the dog on the grave" irritated Moore; it was "an example of how to make pessimism trivial"; and as a general proposition: "Hardy popularized pessimism and coaxed his readers into drinking from an old tin pot a beverage that had hitherto only been offered to them in golden and jewelled goblets."

The universal theme, which he now designated by the "beautiful word 'nympholepsy,'" had been served, he thought, by very few devotees in the nineteenth century. In painting there was Ingres, whom he idolized as the perfect reincarnation of the ancients, and Corot, who "lived in the depths where all is still and quiet." Hence, "he who has seen Corot has seen all the universe," for we could never find "in the furthest star" a greater beauty than "evanescent cloud and nymph gathering summer blooms where the larch bends and the lake mirrors a pellucid sky."

Among writers, Walter Savage Landor, to whom he had given passing praise years earlier, now became his first enthusiasm.

No man of letters has ever championed Landor's work as vigorously as Moore; some readers indeed have found his praise so excessive as to suggest a lurking trap or Moorism. The British literary public was astonished to hear that Landor was greater than Shakespeare, not only for his creation of the Duchesse de Fontanges, Bishop Parker, Horne Tooke, and other figures in *Imaginary Conversations* but even for the verse in which he warmed his hands before the fire of life, and for:

> Rhaicos was born amid the hills wherefrom
> Gnidos the light of Caria is discern'd,
> And small are the white-crested that play near,
> And smaller onward are the purple waves.

Kindred talents won his unhesitating praise; he was awed, for example, by Joseph Bédier, the French academician who had collated the Tristram legends, and by Pierre Loti's unctuous Levantine travel sketches. "It is the indecisive and lovely hour," said Loti's universal prose in Moore's translation, "when amid limpidities which are neither day nor night our odorous fires begin to burn clearly, sending up their white smoke to the first stars."

In fiction Moore's new likes and dislikes were even more sharply indicative of the changed bent of his mind. The sort of Faustian dramatic incident that had once fascinated him in Balzac—Rastignac's defiance of Paris, or Rubempré's adolescent cry for love and fame—these were now half-forgotten as his imagination came under increasing domination by leisurely, anticlimactic tales of frustration, such as Flaubert's story of Frederic Moreau and Mme. Arnoux in *L'Education sentimentale*. He demanded a fiction that would accord, both in form and subject, with the proposition, now his steadfast conviction, that "the sadness of life is the joy of art," and what he sought he found typically embodied in his own work, naturally, and, beyond that, in the work of the great nineteenth-century Russians, Dostoevski excepted.

Chekhov had the sense of the universal. Moore had stumbled

upon a synopsis of one of his tales, as he told Geraint Goodwin, one in which a man, meeting a stranger, a woman, in a restaurant, begins to relate all his life's troubles to her. The woman is sympathetic, and, after she has left, the man decides he would like to marry her. But she has left. Such a story, Moore added, was one which would "suit me very well," and he resolved to ask his parlormaid to read more of Chekhov and retell the stories to him. Chekhov was not absolutely "pure," however; he had been unable to forego the gratuitous and banal morality, and of *The Cherry Orchard* Moore asked: "Why does Chekhov try to spoil his plays with those dreadful pieces of philosophy? 'Do you know why I am here? Am I here? I don't know why I am alive. Am I alive?' " [3]

Tolstoi also grasped the universal theme, Moore thought. Natasha's anticlimactic domesticity and her absorption in the "disgusting little ailments" of her children contained ironies that were not wasted on Moore. He was also moved to approbation by Tolstoi's picture of the landed gentry struggling with their dilemmas and groping for some meaning in their lives, by Levin's unbidden tears at the thought of the sadness at the heart of things, and by Nikolai Rostov, whom Moore remembered not quite accurately as "standing on the balcony watching the small rain that the thirsty oats are drinking up greedily, thinking that he must be, after all, no more than a commonplace man who married an ugly princess." But in *Resurrection* the Christian moralist had run amuck, spoiling a perfect story out of Nature's loom, which Moore retold as follows:

> A judge who had tried a Finnish girl for stealing told Tolstoi how one of the jurymen, a man who had never shown any interest in ethical questions before, was so overcome by the thought that he and eleven other sinners were called upon to condemn a thirteenth that he obtained permission to visit the girl in prison. He offered himself in marriage, and the girl accepted his offer gladly, seeing in a rich marriage endless gratification of her desires. But perceiving in time that she did not understand the sacrifice he was making, the man withdrew. Some years afterward he married a girl of his own class,

one who shared his ideals, but it appears that he did not succeed in living happily with her.[4]

The tone of this story is identical with that of the Chekhov tale, with Moore's own characteristic tales, *A Vain Fortune, Esther Waters, Sister Teresa,* and "So On He Fares," all out of the past, and with *The Brook Kerith, Heloise and Abelard,* and *Ulick and Soracha,* that were yet to come.

Turgenev, said Moore, would instantly have recognized the beauty of the story on which Tolstoi based *Resurrection,* but he would not have perverted it. He "would have judged himself the humble reporter." Turgenev, who with Corot made "twain souls, the most beautiful born of woman," was the supreme master of the universal theme, and the most perfect expression of his genius was in the *House of Gentlefolk.* There is an unhappy marriage, the wife takes lovers, and the husband leaves. After many years he gets news that she is dead. He meets another girl, the two fall in love and plan to marry. Then the wife returns, and the girl sends her lover back to his wife. "No more than that," said Moore, "yet it is out of this trite and commonplace material that genius speaks in telling how Taveretski comes back after many years and finds a new generation" and how the old man, sitting on a bench in the sun, begs the children to play somewhere else and to leave him alone with his memories. The image of the old man who had surrendered all his faculties to time and mutability except the last resource of recollection— this was for Moore the universal theme in essence and the source of the extraordinary beauty he saw in Turgenev's story.

Moore's own choice of subjects for his last novels might be thought to have violated these principles that he urged so strongly upon other writers. His stress upon muted pathos and anticlimax as the keystones of narration would not seem clearly to recommend the story of the crucifixion in *The Brook Kerith,* the mutilation of Abelard in *Heloise and Abelard,* or the picture of the devastation of mediaeval Ireland by the marauding armies of de Burgo and Robert Bruce in *Ulick and Soracha.*

In all three of these novels, however, the luridness of the central situations was foreshortened and fogged over by Moore's manner so skillfully as to suggest that he may have deliberately chosen to demonstrate the worth of his principles by a brilliant application of them to the most difficult of cases. However that might be, he was able, without violating the melodramatic traditions that lay behind his last stories, to cast over them all a tone recognizably derived from the tone of the model stories he had found in Chekhov and Turgenev.

Moore insisted that the universal theme of literature should be enacted in narrative upon a universal stage, purified of local color and capable of loosing from one's shoulders the burden of "universal education, bimetallism, free trade, electric light, and wood paving." Only those settings were deemed worthy which man had known these ten thousand years: camels, for example, for man had ridden camels "for ever and ever," or at least since Abraham. Unfortunately Kipling had overdone camels. Other approved impedimenta are easily identified by their recurrence in Moore's last novels, where they appear constantly before the reader. Among them are rooks, magpies, rowan trees, great rivers, forest journeys, Bedouins, strolling players, vineyards, voices (Go to Ireland! Go to Aulis!), wolves, barnyard procreation, cockfights, sheepfolds, shepherds, and indeed all the paraphernalia of sheep husbandry, and, above all, ewes, which Moore insisted on calling "yoes" on the grounds that this word suggested the female sheep as no other did. It is clear that Moore's preferred settings, almost exclusively pastoral in origin, were highly charged personal symbols based ultimately on the recollection of childhood emotions but purified by transposition from their original form into traditional literary guise. Hence, his imagination did not recreate the Mayo countryside realistically; in Moore's childhoods there were few wolves, forests, vineyards, or even sheep in Connaught, and certainly no Bedouins or camels. Even in *Ulick and Soracha,* where county Mayo is directly described, the local was carefully avoided to suggest a more timeless scene.

The same impulse led Moore to seek his new subjects in the simpler, more "universal" societies of the past, feudal societies, to use the term he habitually applied to the Mayo of his boyhood. "I must go back in time," he said, "when people lived as men and women, not as standardized machines." His last vehicle was the historical novel, which he took up in his own special way. He did not surrender the view he had long held that "the essential quality of the historical novel and of the historical picture is that it should contain no history," an attitude that had once led him to rebuke Zola for not throwing history to the winds in *La Débâcle* and to praise Flaubert for setting *Salammbô* in ancient Carthage, about which neither he nor anyone else had any precise knowledge that might hamper the imagination. It is true that in Moore's historical reconstruction he did worry a good deal about accuracy in the details of costume, manners, and especially topography, as is attested by a large and solemn correspondence he carried on with antiquarians and travelers on such issues as the precise date of one of Robert Bruce's minor skirmishes in Connaught in the fourteenth century or the route that might be taken by a nun fleeing from a French convent in the Middle Ages: could she have gone by canal boat from the Garonne to the Mediterranean, or must she go by horse? But these details never challenged the rule of his master preconceptions. When someone objected to the disproportionate emphasis given to the courts of love in *Heloise and Abelard* and to Moore's naïveté in taking the rhetoric of a fanciful literary convention as a literal report of behavior, his reply was that in such matters his own intuition was a better guide than the dead compilations of historical scholars; so much for the hampering facts of history. Operating in such fashion he found the historical novel the ultimate release for his imagination. It allowed him perfect freedom to pursue his fancy without disturbance from the harsh importunate clamors of either the present or the past.

With the publication of *A Story Teller's Holiday* in 1918, Moore initiated a policy of publishing only in a limited edition, thus allaying somewhat the threat of court action for blasphemy, indecency, or what not and freeing himself from all immediate concern with popular values in the novel. This move implied no final break from the general reading public but merely a shift of strategy: his aim was now set upon immortality rather than popularity. This symbolic withdrawal was accompanied by a quieting of all the frenzied disorder of his emotional relations with the rest of mankind. The announcement of his new publication policy did not sound like the brash young blade of *Confessions of a Young Man* but was quiet and weary in tone, merely stating that "somebody" had brought legal action against *The Brook Kerith,* that the failure of the action had not protected him from gratuitous insult, that he was herewith retiring into the "dignified privacy" of a "literary arcanum" where the philistine could not follow.

He had come to the conclusion that "sympathy" is, after all, an essential component of the immortal works of art. With a trace of self-consciousness he set about to make it an ingredient of his last work. "The true artist," he said, "captures the world with broad human sympathies and woos and wins his fellows with his craft"; by "fellows" he meant fellow craftsmen. In this mood he denounced Anatole France, whom he had previously admired, as a "specialist in gibes," as "utterly loathsome," like a "draught of foul air." *Thaïs,* he said, was cheap sniggering at a man who had "given up his life for an ideal," and he drew the lesson from France's career that "a man continually skeptical toward not one thing but everything never gets far." Those contemporaries of his who liked to reply to this sort of opinionizing by reminding him of his own bohemian excesses had missed his point. As he understood himself, his life had been devoted to an ideal, to the assertion of the most precious of all values, the value of art, and never so religiously as in his old age.

Moore's new "sympathy" was no more restricting than his new "history." The world of his last novels was essentially the patrician world of Wordsworth and Scott, with the evangelical priggishness extracted; a past which had been rearranged, as one critic has said in another connection, so that it would not again generate the present; a world in which sympathy arises as a reward to the lower classes for their instinctive acceptance of their inferiority. In his last years Moore was told about Aristotle's political views, and the principle of hierarchy appealed to him as so sensible that he announced himself an Aristotelian, arguing that the world had fared best when the slave remained a slave and when the peasant stuck to his toil in the fields, refusing education and achieving dignity through their unconscious nearness to art.

Kebren, the old father in *Aphrodite in Aulis*, explained this theory to his two sons. Pointing to a peasant driving his plow in the crabbed uplands of Attica he said, "His labor in the field is not unworthy, Rhesos, inasmuch as it allows thee to labor upon a statue for the adornment of a temple. Without the oxen and the plow, and the peasant with the goad behind the oxen, the walls of the Parthenon could not be raised." [5] This sentiment carries echoes of a Victorian bromide, and the expectation of a hidden Moorism is not disappointed, for the very next sentence observes: "The boys did not answer, thinking silence was the best weapon of defence, and they rode on without speaking."

In his youth Moore's views on mankind had been turbulent and muddied by crosscurrents of fear, repulsion, charity, impatience, and guilt. In old age he achieved a certain clarity and calm as his emotional attitudes were burned out by time and experience. Moore's symbolic shepherd tending his "yoes" does bear a sort of resemblance to Carlyle's Gurth the Saxon swineherd. Yet Moore was incapable of the meanness contained in Carlyle's vision, just as he had been incapable, in the blustering reactionism of his youth, of the paranoiac singlemindedness of a "patrician" like Léon Daudet. In old age Moore saw only boredom in the social issue, and he put it out of his mind in order to devote his energy to his ancient pursuit of art and to a new interest, an intense absorption in the perfection of a new style that might fittingly express his universal fables and describe his universal settings and carry his name to immortality.

Moore's famous later style was woven of strands that he had been gathering for a couple of decades. When Edward Martyn first persuaded Moore to make the aesthetic pilgrimage to Bayreuth in the 1880's, he had sensed that Wagner's musical form had possible literary usefulness, even though at the time he could find no means to apply it. *Evelyn Innes* had exploited the more obvious messages that Bayreuth brought to Moore, such as Wagner's affection for the illicit and the exotic, his theoretical exaltation of strongly sensual artistic effects, his "difficulty." Meanwhile Moore pondered the problem of adapting Wagner's form to narrative, and Wagnerian language entered into his critical vocabulary as early as *Confessions of a Young Man,* where he may be found rereading Zola as primarily a formalist:

> I had read the *Assommoir,* and had been much impressed by its pyramid size, strength, height, and decorative grandeur, and also by the immense harmonic development of the idea; and the fugal treatment of the different scenes had seemed to me astonishingly new—the washhouse, for example: the fight motive is indicated, then follows the development of side issues, then comes the fight motive explained; it is broken off short, it flutters through a web of progressive detail, the fight motive is again taken up, and now it is worked out in all its fullness; it is worked up to *crescendo,* another side issue is introduced, and again the theme is given forth. And I marvelled greatly at the lordly, river-like roll of the narrative, sometimes widening out into lakes and shallow meres, but never stagnating in fen or marshlands.[6]

This language reveals not only the Wagnerite but also the writer who had cut his teeth on Balzac instead of Dickens, acquiring a taste uninhibited by the expectation of plot and episode that are cherished by the ordinary Anglo-Saxon reader. The music of Wagner and the narratives of Flaubert tended to fuse in his mind. Hence, before he had found any practical solution to his problem, he was meditating on the kinship of *Tristan* to *L'Education sentimentale,* seeing them both as built up out of "echoes, transformations, modulations, never a full close, always a suspended cadence," and seeing in the novel, where Flaubert himself saw only flatness and failure, a work of consummate skill in the weaving of ironic anticlimax and irresolution of incidents.

In 1897 Moore read his friend Dujardin's novel, *Les Lauriers sont coupés.* This little volume attracted a certain oblique fame as the first "stream of consciousness" novel but is more precisely an experiment in the elaboration of a narrative by the device of leitmotifs. It concerns a young man-about-town who has become enmeshed in a foolish pursuit of a clever, mercenary chorus girl. There are three simple motifs, the cash payment in advance, the anticipatory frenzy, the rebuff. In musical analogy the novel could be described as a progression of thematic statements, contrasts, and variations, concluding with a resolution with brasses blaring. Dujardin thought of the novel as Wagnerian, and as such it was a fertile discovery, certainly helpful to Moore and probably helpful to Joyce, though for reasons other than the one usually stated. Joyce's tributes to it were, it is true, somewhat enigmatical; but Moore's approbation was unequivocal. He wrote to Dujardin: "In *Les Lauriers* you have discovered *the* form, the archetypal form, the most original of our time."

But in retrospect Moore tended to forget Dujardin and to attribute to Wagner his discovery of his final narrative form. It was from Wagner, he said, that he had first learned

> . . . how a story might be woven from start to finish out of one set of ideas, each chapter in suspended cadence always, never a full close; and as an example of the kind of book that comes out of such ideas as these, I will name *The Brook Kerith,* for the story begins like a brook; the old woman telling stories to her grandchild may be com-

pared to "The Fanfare of the Rhine"; and the brook widens out as it flows, a smooth current, not very rapid, but flowing always, turning sometimes east, sometimes west, winding, disappearing at last mysteriously like a river.[7]

Moore was perhaps overgenerous in allowing himself none of the honor of his discovery. The sense of *flow*, the essential trait of Moore's style in his last novels, the quality referred to in the statement just quoted as the "smooth current" of the brook widening into a meandering river, may have been suggested by listening to the motif of the Rhinemaidens in *Das Rheingold* but was only achieved by following an altogether different lead picked up during his stay in Dublin. The opening pages of *Ulick and Soracha* hint that Moore had imitated the rambling, hypnotic stories of the shanachies, poor strolling Gaelic bards who were occasionally heard about the kitchen fire at Moore Hall in the days of George Henry Moore. The statement romanticizes a debt which was actually due to more sophisticated sources. The writers in the nineties were fond of complaining about the decadence of the written word; Wilde had observed that "the trouble with writers is that they write too much," and he thought that "the age of the ear may be returning." Yeats had built an elaborate philosophical case for the recovery of spoken rhythms both in poetry and in narrative fiction; and it was from Yeats, rather than from a recollection of the shanachies of the 1850's, that Moore took the impulse to tell his stories viva voce, dictating to a stenographer, an experiment in composition undertaken some time shortly after his return to Ireland in 1900 and leading ultimately to the startling discovery of a new style, unlike Moore's previous way of writing and unlike anything else in English prose. The scheme was later elaborated into many steps. First Moore would dictate a rough draft to his stenographer. Next morning he would take the rough first copy and dictate from it, testing and recasting freely from yesterday's sentences. The next day he would take the redraft and dictate afresh from it; and sometimes the process would continue through as many as twenty drafts before Moore's ear was satisfied with the mellifluousness of his narrative.

Such were the origins of the "melodic line," the personal trademark of Moore's last novels, paradoxically discovered in a search for an anonymous prose that would show no trace of the personal jargon that he was distressed to find in Carlyle, Stevenson, and Meredith. An illustration will show its qualities; the sentence which follows is taken from a description of Moore's breaking up housekeeping in London to move back to Ireland, as related in *Hail and Farewell*. He is just taking leave of his cook:

> She cooked me excellent dinners, making life infinitely agreeable to me; a present of five pounds was certainly her due, and a sovereign was more than enough for the porter, whom I suspected of poisoning my cat—a large, grey, and affectionate animal upon whom Jane, without the aid of a doctor, had impressed the virtue of chastity so successfully that he never sought the she, but remained at home a quiet, sober animal that did not drink milk, only water, and who, when thrown up to the ceiling, refrained from turning round, content to curl himself into a ball, convinced that my hands would receive him—an animal to whom I was so much attached that I had decided to bring him with me in a basket; but a few weeks before my departure he died of a stoppage in his entrails, brought about probably by a morsel of sponge fried in grease—a detestable and cruel way of poisoning cats often practiced by porters.[8]

This may be taken as a fair example of Moore's ideal of "the long sentence." In later years he would praise another writer with whom he had no common artistic interests—Hall Caine— merely because he had written a story containing sentences "three inches long." Moorisms apart, the new device was necessary for the objectives he had set himself in his last work. The long sentence, the skillful repetition to strengthen coherence, the incessant use of appositives for linkage, and the modulated rhythms accomplished the smoothly running flow he sought.

"The old story tellers," he said, "always looked for their stories by running water," and he seldom spoke of his melodic line without suggesting the metaphor of the river.

His new ideal was the antithesis of the standard of *le mot juste* and of Flaubert's inevitable word, once his model. His tone tended rather more to the languid than to the scintillating, as befitted the mellow disenchantment of the admirer of Corot and Landor. The strained and agonized tone of such writers as George Eliot and Henry James—who composed much more quickly and freely than he—was almost totally absent, and his paragraphs give the impression of having been composed without effort. Not that they actually were. An intense strain of nerve and energy was required to produce his effects, so that his style is a sort of ultimate case of the art to hide art.

His most intense concentration was upon the stylistic problem of weaving an effortless continuity of narrative. "My specialty, my gift if I have one," he said, was the "power to link up a story." No rivals for supremacy in this special skill suggest themselves. His technical virtuosity in building narrative linkages became so masterful that eventually he was able to make a natural transition from anything in creation to almost anything else.

The melodic line made him a more certain master of his incidents and effects, allowing him to win unquestioning assent for turns of action that would have been incredible or foolish in a less skillful telling. The momentum of the melodic line carried *The Brook Kerith* easily through the delicate task of rewriting the story of the crucifixion without falling into indignity and of presenting as credible a story in which Christ escapes alive from the cross and eventually meets Paul face to face, the two denouncing one another as madmen and impostors. The melodic line allowed Moore to heighten the effectiveness of his ironic anticlimaxes; of the fate of Joseph of Arimathea in *The Brook Kerith*, for example, who occupied the central position in the novel throughout the entire first half but dropped from the story shortly thereafter, like Gorki's Clim Samghin, with a casual mention of his murder. The melodic line was also capable of building a strangely moving sense of cold-blooded cruelty or of inexorable stupidity in such incidents as the loss of Heloise's little boy, who, disobedient to his mother, listened to the allurements of an insane friar, then fell into step with a band of children toddling toward Marseilles to join the Children's Crusade and was never heard from again.

There was an important practical advantage for Moore in his new skill. His imagination had always been more astringent than ebullient in the creation of incident. He knew what it was like to stare at a blank page for hours, for days, until he wondered whether his brain had not softened. His disability was in part overcome by the new style, which allowed him to embrace all sorts of unrelated and low-charged incidents and to incorporate them into the woof of the melodic line without conveying too obvious an impression of indecorum. When his friends and disciples paid him public homage on his eightieth birthday, their testimonial to him said: "You taught the narrative to flow again and anecdote to illuminate it as the sun a stream," language that shows intimacy with Moore's late aims and ideas. But the anecdotes were sometimes so oblique that, like young Abelard's defense of salad at the family supper table or the Argenteuil Prioress' thoughts on the winter storage of apples— "after Christmas decay begins," [9] they illuminated the stream only by virtue of the compelling sense of monolithic unity conveyed by the new stylistic manner.

A related but more important function of the melodic line was "poetic." Since the over-all effect of Moore's style was oneness and concord, all his material was always kept orderly and coherent, and the nonsyntactical confusion of other contemporary experimenters was avoided. But since his stylistic power allowed him to force the admissibility of material at will, he was left utterly free to pursue any of the richly colored associations that arose in his imagination. As with Proust, whose novel he shrewdly refused to read, sensing kinship and fearing influence, his creative energy was now largely engaged in reworking and reordering the most profoundly emotion-laden images and incidents accumulated in a lifetime's experience:

> The present is no more than a little arid sand dribbling through the neck of an hour-glass: but the past may be compared to a shrine in the coign of some sea-cliff, whither the white birds of recollection come to roost and rest awhile, and fly away again into the darkness. But the shrine is never deserted. Far away up from the horizon's line other white birds come, wheeling and circling, to take the place of those that have left and are leaving.[10]

But Moore's white birds did not fly in Proust's patterns. At a time when other novelists were engaged in a variety of self-conscious attempts to shatter time, after the fashion of Joyce and Gide, relying only upon leitmotifs to restore order, or were interested at least in tinkering with the flow of time in the manner of *The Magic Mountain,* Moore was developing a narrative mode based on absolute surrender to the consecutiveness of time. His last novels are built of pure motion, pure pageant, repeating endlessly Heloise's constant question to Abelard: "And afterwards?" Sitting in his Pimlico study dictating to his stenographer year after year in the last phase of his life, Moore had always a single, paramount object: constantly to enrich his fable with myth-laden digressions but never to let the continuity of the thread snap, not even at the end, for the end too, he concluded, should be only another suspended cadence. The last two sentences of *The Brook Kerith* depict Paul preaching to the multitudes: "He spoke from morning to evening. The rest of the story is unknown." So on he fares.

Back in the 1880's Moore had observed that Flaubert had subordinated everything in his novels to narrative, so that "description is narrative, analysis of character is narrative, dialogue is narrative; the form is ceaselessly changing but the narration is never interrupted." He added, however, that he did not think that this discovery was very wonderful after all, an opinion he suddenly reversed two decades later, when he began to rewrite old publications to conform to the rule of continuity of action. Royal A. Gettman's study of Moore's revisions points out that originally we are told that Esther Waters went for a walk and then are presented with a description of a bit of Essex scenery, whereas the 1920 revision says, "Esther was surprised to find herself in front of so much wild country." All new work, of course, conformed to the new rule. When Moore referred to his last work as "epic," he seems to have been thinking of the uninterrupted movement of his narration; this appears to be the meaning, if there is meaning, in his statement to Charles Morgan that there were but two "prose epics" in the English language, *The Brook Kerith* and *Heloise and Abelard*.

Moore's absorption in the problems of narrative continuity was more than a stunt or mechanism. Anyone who believes that his effects were merely the product of a mechanical procedure, in the sense that Hemingway's creation of innocence by literal translation from Spanish is mechanical, might try a bit of dictating himself or, more fairly, compare Moore's effects with those of other writers who dictate, Steinbeck or Wyndham Lewis, for example. Moore's new style gave him some sort of ultimate creative satisfaction, some sense that he had discovered at last the secret ritual by which an indifferent world could be lived in, even wooed and won. It was unquestionably associated with his growing fascination with the story of journeys. All his last novels are woven principally of accounts of journeys; all open and most close in journeys. How many scores of journeys are related in the unreeling of the melodic line: up and down the Seine, the Jordan, the Shannon, the Garonne, across the Euxine, the Aegean, the Irish, the Galilean seas, on "mule-back, ass-back, camel-back," sometimes afoot. On a journey one moved through a gently changing scene, one let its qualities flow in upon the senses and register their presence; later one arranged these into an arabesque, like Stephen Dedalus on the train to Cork, forging the clicks of the wheels upon the rails into a cosmos. Finally, one contemplated the pattern that had emerged, for it was art and the supreme value of existence.

Ulick and Soracha was built up mainly out of picaresque elements. It returns casually to the theme of the escaped nun, and it traces the sullen, senseless compulsions of the great, warring mediaeval dukes to reduce Ireland to utter devastation, a theme doubtless inspired by Moore's meditation on the parallel destruction of Ireland by the Anglo-Irish war and the civil wars raging at the time of writing the novel. But these interests are subordinated to the endlessly dovetailing journeys which, though often groping through "a crapulous wood, full of newt and frog and tadpole pools, stinking rooks and nettles," still bring Sir Ulick and his old servant Tadgh back at last to the parish of Balintober and the reedy shores of Lough Carra. There the master, like Moore's priest in the novel set beside the same lake, swims out into the gray moonlit waters and is seen no more. The servant, granted by his wife Biddy the same sight that Gwennie Lloyd permitted to Lewis Seymour at the opening of Moore's first novel, comes likewise with the fullest satisfaction into his own last port.

This summary perhaps overstates the quietism of Moore's final artistic manner. Actually, the main journeys of his last novels led to significant moral destinations. Behind his suave and unctuous manner, Moore remained the same militant child of the enlightenment that he had always been, loving color and freedom and life, and hating the cruel, the niggardly, the ignorant, and the drab. In *The Brook Kerith* Jesus is originally seized by an overweening zeal and an urge to asceticism, both "blasphemies against life," but in the end he has learned to repent his sins in full humility, while his first life-denying ambitions are taken up by Paul and passed to posterity in a poisoned stream. *Heloise and Abelard* is deeply involved in the same moral problem, the murderous curse cast upon pagan innocence, represented by Heloise and Abelard, by the Pauline theological temperament, speaking through the hard mouths of Abbé Suger and the evil Canon Fulbert. Moore's impatience with the sentimentalism of the mediaevalist was not as fulminous as Mark Twain's—except in his private conversations—but it was as earnest and as telling. The somber end of the journey for Heloise and Abelard found him maintaining precisely the same liberated position he had held all his life, but with a more muted and less equivocal rhetoric:

> . . . he must return to Brittany and never ride to the Paraclete again, lest his enemies, seeing him going thither, should mock and jeer, saying in their beards: the old wether still hankers after his yoe. So they would speak of him, being pitiless, and he sought for words whereby he might break the news to Heloise that they might hope for nothing in this world, but that God would recompense them in the next for unmerited suffering. A shade came into his face, for Heloise had suffered, he feared, without much belief in an eternal recompense; yet she had ceded to his prayer not to take poison but to put her faith in God and live her appointed life however empty it might be. It would be lonelier for her than for him, for he still cherished the hope that divine philosophy would prevail in the end, bringing all the world into God's fold. Faith was the antique shepherd, Reason was the new. But Heloise had not philosophy, and if he were taken from her was he sure that she would be able to endure life? and if she were not, then indeed they would be separated. Then he put to her the question: What hast thou done with the poison? and she answered that she had emptied the phial into the street's mud. For having obeyed thee, Abelard, always, I was moved not to disobey thee in the end, for to do so would spoil all; and he answered that she had done well, saying (knowing well that it would please her to hear him say it): Heaven would not be heaven for me without thee; thou wert my heaven on earth and wilt be my heaven hereafter, if we gain heaven. As all hangs on that, let us devote, as I said before, whatever years of life remain to us in gaining heaven. It was surely wisdom to spare no pains to accomplish our love, for when we meet in heaven there will be a fulfilment of love such as has not befallen us here; though our love was very great on earth, it will be greater in heaven. . . .

There were still some miles to ride before they reached the next village, and Abelard and Heloise rode immersed in the sad belief that their lives were wasted and that their last hope was heaven. Abelard believed in heaven, therefore Heloise believed, and, united at last, they rode to Troyes, thinking how they were to live out the few years that remained for them to life, thereby gaining an immortal happiness, the letters germinating in their minds as they rode, hints of them appearing in their talk as mile after mile went by.[11]

The letters "germinating in their minds" were the inception of salvation through art; but the mood of the passage is nevertheless grim and defeated, a gloomy and unpagan note on which Moore did not care to close his career. He had talked a great deal in the course of a long lifetime about paganism, but he had never undertaken to write a pagan novel peopled only by men and women who had never even heard of Christianity. He was minded to close his accounts with such a novel; and for apprenticeship he began a translation of *Daphnis and Chloe*, using a Renaissance French translation for text, since he knew no Greek. After a careful library reconnaissance of Periclean Athens, he began dictating *Aphrodite in Aulis*, which was finished, in spite of a near-fatal attack of uremic poisoning, in 1931. The novel shows strong evidence of illness and fatigue, not to mention age, but it is marvelously ingenious in construction, and it succeeded in recreating a believable pagan world, freed at last from Swinburne's sadism, Gautier's exotic taste, and Pater's effeminacy. His fable was a fitting one: the seer Daricoeus foresees apocalyptic destruction of Aulis unless the godless people build temples to the gods. Lacking the evangelical bent, the people set out to meet the requirements in a direct and sensible fashion. They know of no way to worship the gods except through beauty; they will erect the most handsome temple, therefore, that their talented sons can create. The temple is to be dedicated to Aphrodite, and, for a model for her statue, who more fitting than Earine, spied bathing one day by young Rhesos, whose sculptor's eye immediately judges her to possess the "most perfectly modeled bum" in all Greece. The temple is built and adorned and given to the festive public; and amid echoes of "aestheticizing" by Socrates, Euripides, Aristophanes, and Phidias, Moore's last finished novel, and his final statement on art as the new yet ageless religion of mankind, moved to a close.

But Moore understood that "life should never cease to unfold," and in a short time he was again at work on a new novel. It was to be called *Madeleine de Lisle* and was to deal with the escape of a nun, ending, like *Sister Teresa*, with her voluntary return to the convent. "I still encourage the hope," he said, "that if I live till ninety and keep my health and intellect all the time I shall be able to write . . . nearly as well as I should like." He was literally unable to find the place to conclude his pursuit of art. When the novel palled after the completion of the first draft, he turned to composing the charmingly unveracious *Communication to My Friends*. In mid-January, 1933, he finished revising the first half. On the fourteenth he wrote to his old Irish friend John Eglinton: "I am very ill today and feel inclined to abandon the project of writing anything more. I have written enough." [12] Seven days later, before the end of the month that brought both Roosevelt and Hitler to the center of the world's stage, he was dead, aged eighty years and eleven months.

The Craftsman as Critic

I don't believe in books.
—George Moore to James Huneker

M OORE WAS easily the most hated of the important literary figures of his time, but a search of his novels discloses very little to contribute to his infamy. Even *Mike Fletcher* was more ludicrous than disagreeable; and, although the melodic line might lead Yeats to talk about toothpaste squeezed from a tube, who could conceivably take offense from *Heloise and Abelard* or even *The Brook Kerith,* except from external considerations? The animosities that Moore inspired among his contemporaries grew mainly out of his critical writings, particularly those of his last, or Ebury Street, phase. It was the critical work of the aging Moore that led John Middleton Murry to cry: "Fool, fool that he is, why could he not refrain? This senile indecency will be remembered against him forever." Malcolm Elwin found Moore as critic "contemptible," "posturing for cheap effect," "sensation seeking," a poseur absorbed in "petty malice." Another contemporary found Moore's criticism that of a "self-centered, conceited egotist, vain, ignorant, and totally unappreciative of other men's genius." When one of Moore's essays caught the eye of Benedetto Croce, he labeled the author simply "a crank."

With the passing of the years these reactions have come to sound a bit excessive, yet they were not altogether unprovoked. Moore's critical opinions were designed to compel attention and showed a forthright disregard for taste, orthodoxy, or common sense. A few samples of his dicta will illustrate the captious and

THE CRAFTSMAN AS CRITIC

headstrong tone of his critical manner. "Tolstoi I have not read, but he is only Gaboriau with psychological sauce, and that of an inferior kind," he wrote.[1] Later, after learning that Tolstoi could not fit into this description, he rewrote the epigram as follows: "Tolstoi I have not read, but Dostoevski I know to be little more than Gaboriau with a psychological sauce, and that of an inferior kind." [2] His thoughts on Pinero's *Mid-Channel* remind the reader that Moore was a critic who "hadn't enough talent to be obscure": "I bethought myself of Thomas, the sculptor, who was afflicted with a tape. It is not exactly a pain, he would say, rather a feeling of great discomfort." [3] Of the novels of Joseph Conrad, whom he considered a competitor, he said: "Anyone might write this stuff about ships disappearing in a blue mist." [4]

It was inevitable in the nature of things that Moore, like Walt Whitman, should be a Baconian, and his contribution to the Shakespeare-Bacon controversy was the following argument:

> In the discovery of a name's power Bacon was before me; for he knew the importance of a name in literature, and chose the most beautiful name of all; and with each play "Shakespeare" grew more and more like his name, more elusive, more recondite; and for the sake of the name let no edition of Bacon's plays be put on the market.[5]

Moore's sensitivity to absolute irrelevancies was one of the odder quirks of his critical mind. His condemnation of the novels of Thackeray was based in part on the fact that the name "Thackeray" sounded to his landed gentleman's ear like the name of a valet, and in part on the fact that Thackeray, unlike Moore, disliked cats. His intuition into the significance of names extended beyond literature even into military science: he had no fears for Britain in the first World War because the Royal Navy was commanded by a man whose name was Jellicoe.

Ignorance never deterred Moore from critical opinionizing. He was certain that Russian novels were "not inferior to Russian poetry," though he knew nothing whatever about Russian poetry. His familiarity with John Gower was probably no greater, but he was positive that Gower had written in three languages "with equal facility and equal mediocrity." Moore was incapable of suppressing an urge to take flight upon the flamboyant "aestheticizing" surveys of boundless scope that had begun with the preface to *Martin Luther* nearly half a century before he took up the role of the aesthetic sage of Ebury Street. Hence, as late as the year of his return to Ireland, he summarized the history of English letters in the following uninhibited and unconventional manner:

> In Elizabethan times England was young, blithe, careless, interested in ideas rather than in facts, and neither in social customs nor in adventures in the South Seas did our early poets find subjects for their poems; the human heart was their adventure, and the Elizabethans span their poems out of the passions. A nation in its youth may be compared with a fountain which, bursting through the loose earth, scatters all the summer a refreshing brightness amid embowering trees. The birds come down from the branches and drink, with sweet movement of head and throat, and flowers brighten beneath the refreshing shower. The sun's heat cakes the earth, but still the water flows, loosening it, and the grass and flowers renew themselves until the first frost marks a deadly change in the season. But even at the end of September in October, after the first frosts, summer may come again; a gentle, inactive summer, with here and there a day that is most June-like. And a beautiful St. Martin's summer happened at the beginning of this century. Our fountain of song burst forth again, the late summer lasted until nearly two-thirds of the century were done, and in the seventies were seen the last days of summer weather. November came with the eighties, a wheezy, asthmatic bard with gray in his beard. In December, in the nineties, the English garden was white; the diminishing water from the fountain ascended for the last time; and now it stands stiff and cold in the air! [6]

The idea presented in this survey has a Yeatsian sound. Yeats took pride in the fact that he had discovered the decline of the west by himself without the guidance of Spengler; and Moore was very likely rephrasing Yeats's view here. Yet nobody but Moore was capable of reducing the idea to such willful verbiage as the "St. Martin's summer" of Wordsworth and Keats, or of inventing the Moorism contained in the concluding image of the erect column of frozen water.

All of these odd little fragments are less extraordinary than the total impact of Moore's criticism. His foremost critical project was to leave the English literary tradition, as viewed by the orthodox reader and the academician, in wreckage. A great part of his critical writing consisted in a search for literary merit under conditions that guaranteed the hunter would always come home empty handed. When he had finished sifting the accumulation of English poetry, he announced that only about three thousand lines of miscellaneous verse were acceptable to him; all the rest he rejected. Rejected from the canon of the English novel were the works of Fielding, Smollett, Scott, Charlotte and Emily Brontë, Dickens (with reservations), Bulwer-Lytton, Thackeray, Trollope, George Eliot (except *The Mill on the Floss*), Meredith—("*Diana* I liked better [than *Rhoda Fleming*] and had I absolutely nothing to do I might have read it to the end"), Stevenson, Henry James, Wilde, Hardy, Conrad, Galsworthy, and all post-Edwardian novelists except Bennett, Charles Morgan, and David Garnett, author of the little Kafka-like fantasy, admired by Moore, called *Lady into Fox*. When one removed from the roster of novelists all the offending names, plus the names of those whom he simply ignored, such as Gissing, Samuel Butler, and H. G. Wells, whose work is not mentioned in all of Moore's writings, the acceptable novelists in English would be found to consist of Richardson, Jane Austen, Anne Brontë, and Walter Pater, besides the three younger novelists mentioned. The record of the English novel was in his opinion largely one of weakness and failure: "Masterpieces are written only by first-rate minds. . . . only the inferior or—shall I say— the subaltern mind has attempted prose narrative in England." He was driven at last to the conclusion that the only bright pages in all the dismal library of English fiction were to be found in the novels of George Moore.

Toward continental and American novelists his general attitude was similar, though somewhat less virulent. His adulation for Balzac and Turgenev was almost, but not quite, unqualified, and he praised Dujardin, Huysmans, Loti, Gorki, and Chekhov. He privately confessed an admiration for Hugo's hunchback. Like all good children of Montmartre he frequently asserted his admiration for Poe, believing himself more sensitive toward Poe's charms than were Poe's own compatriots. But he ridiculed Hawthorne. In his youth he praised Flaubert, Zola, and Tolstoi, as we have seen, but in old age he savagely denounced all three. He made personal attacks upon the Goncourts and Maupassant. He was not impressed by Dostoevski; his preface to *Poor Folk* reminded his reader of his statement about Dostoevski and "psychological sauce," and added: "When I read the second volume [of *Crime and Punishment*], perhaps my opinion will alter." He denounced Anatole France and Proust.

Moore's critical judgments add up to a sweeping attack upon the artistic tradition to which he was himself attached. To his contemporaries he seemed to be fouling his own nest, and an imputed charge of artistic treachery lies behind the animosity he generated among fellow writers and critics. Most of his detractors relieved their feelings by attributing his judgments to the perverse animus of an artistic failure who had been outdistanced by his "rivals." Even Sir Edmund Gosse, who thought himself charitable to Moore's criticism, apologized for him by arguing that no artist can tolerate his contemporaries, a view derived from Oscar Wilde, who had said: "A great artist cannot recognize the beauty of work different from his own. Bad artists always admire each other's work. They call it being large-minded and free from prejudice." But Gosse's well-intentioned argument only explained Moore's attacks upon Hardy, James, and Conrad; as for the classics, which he attacked no less vigorously, their lack of appeal for Moore required some other explanation, such as John Middleton Murry's charge that "it is a law that sincerity cannot be penetrated by insincerity."

As Moore's enemies contended, his criticism undeniably showed an occasional streak of childish peevishness. His sensitivity to the personal weaknesses of rival writers might well arouse suspicion. He accused Yeats of stealing the plot of "The Unicorn from the Stars" from him. In the 1880's, as he later recalled, he had outlined to Henry James the scenario of *A Modern Lover,* and he was quick to catch a look that he interpreted to be envy pass fleetingly across "the vast face" of his distinguished listener. Both Yeats and James reciprocated the accusations: James referred to Moore as the most adept writer in London to pick a brain, and Yeats called him a literary thief.

Moore's fatuous side, though generally subdued in most of his novels, found freer scope in his criticism. There he felt it appropriate to be himself, and to be himself, he said, he must play nothing but light comedy. James Whitall has given a typical account of an afternoon spent with the uninhibited elderly Moore, who performed all his little tricks for his temporary disciple: a contemptuous reading from *Tess of the D'Urbervilles,* a sentimental lecture on Gérard de Nerval, a scene on the street with a woman walking a Great Dane on a leash, another scene on the street with two nuns, and a loud pronouncement in the theatre on the incompetence of all actors.[7] In the special genre of literature that has arisen to relate the details of Moore's perversity, none of the anecdotes portrays the essential quality of his personal extravagance quite like his own story of his last parting from the patrician Mrs. Craigie shortly before her death. That stern and marmoreal woman had first encouraged Moore's courtship but had later humiliated him by refusing a firm offer of marriage, a refusal motivated perhaps by her dislike for "that coarse levity which passes all too easily, in these days, for courage," to quote from her review of the "immortal" *David Harum.* Years later she met Moore in a London park and the two exchanged angry words about a play they were trying to write together. As she turned to walk away down the wooded path, she received, he said, his foot "nearly in the center of the backside, a little to the right. . . . It was inevitable, I said, part of the world's history, and I lost sight of all things but the track of my boot on the black crêpe de chine."

But after taking full account of all the nonsense in Moore's make-up, one is still hardly wise to dismiss his aesthetic nihilism as arising only out of personal folly or malice. His fierceness was not so much *sui generis* as traditional, learned originally from his French teachers but known in England in the course of time through the behavior of a dozen important post-Victorian rebels, most of them anticipated by Moore: Shaw, Wilde, Samuel Butler, Norman Douglas, Frank Harris, Max Beerbohm, Lytton Strachey, and all the Bloomsbury ironists of the post-Edwardian generation.

The lowest common denominator of the rebellious tradition was a simple mechanical formula of dissent which Moore had picked up in Paris and perfected in London, under the guidance of his brother Augustus on *The Hawk*. Moore described it in *Mike Fletcher* as follows:

> The formula of criticism . . . was to consider as worthless all that the world held in estimation, and to laud as best all that the world had agreed to discard. . . . Virgil was declared to be the great old bore of antiquity, and some three or four quite unknown names, gathered amid the Fathers, were upon occasion trailed in triumph with adjectives of praise.
>
> What painter of Madonnas does the world agree to consider the greatest? Raphael—Raphael was therefore decried as being scarcely superior to Sir Frederick Leighton; and one of the early Italian painters, Francesco Bianchi . . . was praised. . . . There is a picture of the Holy Family by him in the Louvre, and of it Harding wrote—"This canvas exhales for us the most delicious emanations, sorrowful bewitchments, insidious sacrileges, and troubled prayers."
>
> All institutions, especially the Royal Academy, St. Paul's Cathedral, Drury Lane Theatre, and Eton College were held to be symbols of man's earthiness, the bar-room and music hall as certain proof of his divine origin; actors were scorned and prize-fighters revered; the genius of courtesans, the folly of education, and the poetry of pantomime formed the themes.[8]

The barb of this curious passage is obviously directed against Moore himself. As a confession it scarcely does justice to the sound and creative achievement of the post-Victorian skeptical rebellion in exposing and destroying the dead force of cultural inertia that the Victorians loved to designate by the word "cant." Before one becomes too solemn about such matters, however, one should recall that his typical discursive rhetoric was the Moorism, a deceptive device in which his "sincere" beliefs were either directly satirized or dramatized with such bombast that they became absurd, thus allowing him within a single assertion to embrace and to reject a contentious point of view and to become, like Emerson's paradoxical Brahma, both the slayer and the slain.

One must be especially alert for Moorisms in examining the tangled question of Moore's credentials to speak as a critic. Among his detractors there is unanimous agreement, encouraged by innumerable admissions on Moore's part, that he had read almost nothing and that he was thus without direct knowledge of the works of literature on which he opinionized so freely. Yeats thought that Moore's acquaintance with the cultural tradition was derived mainly from conversations with experts—with Dujardin on Wagner and Palestinian archeology, with John Eglinton on English literature, with Yeats himself on the folk as a refuge from vulgarity. Moore himself said, "I would lay aside the wisest book to talk to a stupid woman," agreeing enthusiastically with Yeats's intended condemnation. The rest of Moore's knowledge Yeats thought he derived from looking at paintings; and here too Moore freely agreed. In an address delivered in Paris on "Shakespeare and Balzac," he confronted his listeners with a defiant refusal to read literature prior to discussing it:

> I make no pretense of having explored the depths of the literature of the Renaissance; but one can very well grasp what there is in any literature without having to read it from one end to the other. . . . We lack time for all this reading. . . . It takes less time to look at

pictures than to read books. . . . The Renaissance was a pagan movement. . . .[9]

A considerable part of Moore's criticism might be classified
under the heading "books never read" or, more commonly,
"books abandoned in the middle." It is a curious fact that, when
Susan Mitchell wrote her little book about Moore for the Irish
Men of Letters series, the only part Moore took exception to, or
seems to have noticed, was a sentence in the first paragraph on
the first page. The only reference he ever made to specific incidents in *L'Assommoir* was to the fight in the laundry, which
appears in the opening pages of the novel. The only specific
mention of incidents in *Marius the Epicurean* was to the second
chapter, "White Nights." One of the more engaging bits of
information in *Hail and Farewell* deals with Moore's reading of
the manuscript of Synge's *Playboy of the Western World*. The
opening speeches had convinced him that "Ireland had at last
begotten a masterpiece," and with every speech his admiration
increased until he had finished the first act, crying, "A masterpiece!" But the second act interested him less, and the third
act he never did find time to read: "My dislike of reading is so
great that I overlooked it."

Moore's insistence on his literary ignorance seems to have
had a multifold purpose. It was a real confession, no doubt, but,
as always with Moore, a confession in the Baudelairean manner,
on behalf of his readers. *"Nul ne commet un crime,"* said Rémy
de Gourmont, *"dont son frère ne soit capable,"* and where would
this principle hold more firmly than in the matter of books left
sinfully unread? The tendency of literary experts toward this
secret vice had always amused Moore, and in reaction he went
out of his way to advertise his own seeming illiteracy, shouting,
"I shudder at the name of *Felix Holt*" and slyly asking John
Eglinton to explicate for him the line: "A man's a man for a'
that." Sinners were tricked into pursuing him self-righteously,
discovering only later that the butt of the joke was themselves.
Sometimes Moore reversed the tactic and achieved a similar

satiric effect by a fake pedantry. He had noted that the academic literary mind sometimes concealed its limitations by using small bits of specialized knowledge offensively, and he adopted the trick himself, turning it into burlesque. Thus he announced to John Eglinton one day that he had just discovered "the best English prose that ever came out of Ireland," and could Eglinton, a noted scholar, guess who it was? No, it was not Swift. No, not Goldsmith. No, it was not Skelton—"who is Skelton, and tell me what he has written." The answer was only revealed after his victim had spent several weeks in futile guessing: it was Edward Berwick's *Life of Apollonius of Tyana*.

Moore's claim to literary ignorance also served him philosophically, giving exaltation to the pure act of artistic creation as the center and circumference of aesthetics. The Victorians had praised "the great reader" and saw such men as Macaulay or, later, Saintsbury or the Gissing of *The Private Papers of Henry Ryecroft* as their cultural heroes. But Moore remembered that Degas had wanted to spend a lifetime learning to "indicate" fingernails, and he regarded the mere reader of books as little better than a parasite. Art was for the artist alone. John Eglinton, who knew Yeats, Æ, and Joyce as well as he knew Moore, observed that this was not an "uncommon attitude toward books in those whose time is mostly spent in writing them." Richard Ellman also discovered an amusing parallel in Yeats, whose response to Joyce was precisely the same as Moore's reception of Synge's "masterpiece." Yeats was willing to pay Joyce the most extravagant praise, but he could never bring himself to read Joyce's book.

It must not be forgotten, finally, that much of Moore's claim to ignorance was plain hoax. He may have confused Schiller with Schopenhauer in his youth and thought in old age that Proust was trying to plow up the fields with knitting needles; nevertheless he did know a respectably wide range of literature, and what he knew he knew extraordinarily well. His insights were characteristically fresh and sharp, the responses of a writer who knew nothing except what he had found out for himself. "Blessed are the innocent," he once said, "for theirs is the kingdom of art," and his criticism carried a true ingenuousness, much like the Chaucerian freshness he sought to capture in his last novels. But behind the seeming naïveté was the mind of a master craftsman who spoke on his art not only with innocence but also with wisdom; or, if not, he at least avoided the inconsequential and factitious technical garrulity of other unwise commentators. His real credential as a critic was that he took literature seriously, if one understood his rhetoric properly, and, though his point of view was commonly limited, it was always significant even in its shortcomings, because he spoke with the authority of a writer who had staked all the values of his life on the discrimination of literary judgments.

Moore's critical rationale grew by slow accretion. In the beginning was the simple denunciation. The argument to support the denunciation was often merely an afterthought, sometimes omitted altogether. His first volume of critical essays, *Impressions and Opinions,* was woven of long quotations interspersed with short emotional ejaculations, like the work of the less gifted. As time passed, however, he learned to spin complex and subtle arguments in defense of his positions. When he was at work on *Avowals* in 1919 he wrote:

> Criticism in England is very dumb at present; people like books and dislike them, but none is able to say why. Matthew Arnold was the last critic who could explain himself. *Avowals* will prove, I think, that there is another who can tell why he likes and why he does not like certain books.[10]

In the process of "telling why," the aesthetic principles that he had been practicing for decades as a novelist took on a conscious and rational shape and substance.

Moore's criticism showed a marked bias toward formalism, a tribute to his masters, Gautier, Flaubert, and Whistler. Oscar Wilde had stated the rule clearly: "Start with the worship of form," he said, "and there is no secret in art that will not be revealed to you." The same idea was echoed by Roger Fry, whose apprenticeship was *fin de siècle* and whose maturity was *entre les deux guerres*. "It seemed to me that the emotions resulting from the contemplation of form," Fry said, "were more universal . . . more profound and more significant spiritually than any of the emotions which had to do with life." From Gautier to Fry, form was the key to the arcanum of art, and in Moore's time to be preoccupied with form was to be "in the movement." Concern with form was one of the stigmata by which Moore first recognized the artistic sensibility, the distinguishing mark that set apart Huysmans' ten superior persons in the universe from the bumblers who only knew what they liked; for Moore well understood the principle, later stated by Arnold Bennett, that the average reader is characterized above all by the total absence of a sense of form and unity in his experience of a work of art.

But, regardless of this sponsorship, formalism came naturally to Moore because of his role in the history of the English novel. As a rebel against the middle-class myth which formed the substance of the Victorian novel, he was necessarily driven to abandon its form as well. The teleological cosmology and the teleological plot machinery of his predecessors were inseverable. He could hardly use the forms that George Eliot had developed for her parables illustrating the moral balance of the universe to project a view of the human predicament such as he had stated in *A Mummer's Wife*: "Our lives run in grooves; we get into one and we follow it out to the end." Working without the security of an established English tradition, he was forced to devise his own form out of recollections of the French novelists and the fruits of his own painful experiments, piecing them together as best he could as he went along. It was not possible for him to avoid an absorbing concern with the technical problems of narrative form.

The critical principles that arose out of this special interest were the common dogmas identified with *l'art pour l'art*. He defined the novel as "a rhythmical sequence of events described with rhythmical sequence of phrase," an epigram that might sound flippant if one did not remember how many years of travail lay behind the simple little phrase, "a rhythmical sequence of events," and what an absolute break from the Dickens-Thackeray tradition it marked. In painting he took the position that "there are no merits except technical merits." His defense of Martyn's Irish play before the British public merely asserted that *The Heather Field* possesses qualities of balance, design, sequence." His advice to J. E. Blanche, the painter, on how to write resembles some of Flaubert's aesthetic brainstorms; the author, Moore told Blanche, must always make his composition "firm in line, like one of Ingres' pictures," and above all he should never forget that "the sound is of more importance than the idea."

Similarly, the ideal of artistic "purity" absorbed Moore throughout his life. As early as *Confessions of a Young Man* he had become infatuated with a curious distinction between "ideas" and "things" and had concluded that literature would be pure if it could avoid ideas and deal only in things. If only Shakespeare "could be freed from his ideas," he said, "what a poet we should have." In the latter Ebury Street days the notion was still with him, and in a few weeks of leisure between other literary chores he elaborated on the idea, still well preserved after nearly forty years of ripening in his mind. In 1924 he published a little collection of verse called *An Anthology of Pure Poetry*, introduced by an essay composed in the melodic line, an extended Moorism consisting of an inimitably personal argument on behalf of impersonal art.

The overt purpose of *An Anthology of Pure Poetry* was to exalt the "pure" poem—for example, Gautier's "La Tulipe"—over an "impure" poem like Shelley's "Hellas," which had fed on "duty, liberty and fraternity," ideas that no longer interest mankind after the age of thirty. All this is of course trivial as theory, merely Gautier's witty "the visible world is visible" made turgid. His insight did have a certain significance, however. The verses in his anthology consist mostly of isolated transfiguring images—flashes, bells, bleats, blowing horns, and the like—separated from any context that might indicate what sort of transfiguration the poet had been minded of, a distillation of the "pure," neat spirits of poetry. His fixation on these images shows him to have been groping, like many of his more philosophically gifted contemporaries, toward the distinction between "existence" and "essence," or between "presentational" and "discursive" statement, to use the vocabulary that became popular some time after his death. Unknowingly Moore was marching *dans le mouvement.* His anthology is a fitting exhibit of the age that produced the more precisely verbalized theories of the imagists and that led in the era of the cold war to the revival of Hopkins and Emily Dickinson as the ultimate poets of "thisness."

Moore's theories of "pure" narrative were similar, though somewhat less muddied. Pure narration did nothing but narrate, and required the unbroken thread, the suspended cadence, the incessant transition that had been brought to perfection in his old age in the melodic line of the last novels. In 1927 he wrote to John Eglinton:

> I am going to point out to you why all the translations of the *Odyssey* have failed. Because the translators allowed the story to sink. The *Odyssey* is an objective poem and the story is everything, and the aim of the translator should be always to keep the story right up at the top of the orchestra. . . . Metaphysics and elusive sentences are out of place; the translator must write as a pre-Raphaelite painter drew. . . . Turn to Lang's translation of the *Odyssey* and you'll find that he just translated line after line, forgetful of the story; instead of raising it up to the top of the orchestra he let it sink until it is out of sight and hearing. . . . Ideas are worthless, yours, mine, and everybody else's. Ideas are pernicious: things are the only good.[11]

His critical sensitivity was sharpest in observing the consecutiveness and development of a narrative, in watching "the music of sequence," moving rhythmically toward some destination. He found it in its "purest" form in *Oedipus Rex* and occasionally even in English novels, in *The Mill on the Floss*, for example, which he understood to possess "rhythm and inevitability, two words for the same thing." But failures were far more common than successes in his opinion, and his critical writing is filled with castigations of novels which either petered out in an aimless and fatuous ending, in the manner of *Robinson Crusoe*, or else were caught in the monotonous turning of the wheel and repeated themes over and over again without progression. Tolstoi he found guilty of the latter fault, and in one of his best known critical *mots* he imagined Tolstoi at the conclusion of his labors on *War and Peace* awakening in the night, seized by nightmare: "There must have been a night in which it occurred to him that he had not included a yacht race, and another night when he awoke screaming: 'I forgot high Mass.' " D. H. Lawrence's novels he found to contain no beginning, middle, or end, not even *Sons and Lovers*, and as for *Lady Chatterley's Lover*, he said: "It is just the same as if I was to go into the garden and say, 'I will have a spoonful of jam,' and then after a while, liking it, decide to have another spoonful and then perhaps another. A man running after a woman all day long, and a woman he doesn't even like." [12]

Impurity, indeed, he met in almost every English novel he read, but most abundantly in Dickens:

> Dickens' talent was more natural, more spontaneous, than any he would have met in France. He had more talent than Flaubert, Zola, Goncourt, Daudet; but he would have learned from them the value of seriousness. . . . A few years would have been sufficient to dissipate the vile English tradition that humor is a literate quality. He would have learnt that it is more commercial than literary, and that if it be introduced in large quantities, all life dies out of the narrative. A living and moving story related by a humorist very soon becomes a thing of jeers and laughter, signifying nothing. We must have humor, of course, but the use we must make of our sense of humor is to avoid introducing anything into the narrative that shall distract the reader from the beauty, the mystery, and the pathos of the life we

live in this world. Whoever keeps humor under lock and key is read in the next generation, if he writes well, for to write well without the help of humor is the supreme test. I should like to speak of the abuse of humor, but it would be difficult to make this abuse plain to a public so uneducated as ours, whose literary sensibilities are restricted to a belief that some jokes are better than others, but that any joke is better than no joke. . . . Rousseau attained a unique reality in literature by abstention from humor.[13]

All the facets of Moore's aesthetics are reflected in this passage. To begin with, his violent duality of purpose was nowhere more bluntly revealed, since the solemn denunciation of humor was written by a man who possessed one of the richest comic talents of his generation. Further, there is the familiar sanctification of art. There is the recurrent Horatian yearning for immortality through art—*non omnis moriar;* a writer will be read "in the next generation" if he is humorless, provided he also writes well. There is the perpetual note of anti-Philistinism; humor is commercial rather than literary. There is the subtle shift of weight from content to form, to skill for the sake of skill: "To write well without the aid of humor is the supreme test." This resembles Flaubert's ideal of writing without using the preposition *"de";* it leads to the notion that supreme literary achievement results from the omission of this, that, or the other thing, or in Flaubert's hyperbole it results from omitting everything and writing beautifully about nothing at all. There is the remembrance of Bernard Lopez' precept on unity. "To violate the unity of subject," Lopez had said, "is the negation of all art." Humor is thus condemned because it destroys the severe formal organization and "distracts" the reader from beauty, that is, from the contemplation of form.

There is, finally, the admission of two nonformal elements. The first is mystery, by which Moore meant the affective impact of pageantry, the feeling of "thisness" conveyed in the outcry— That such things should be!—and described by Moore in words borrowed from Stevenson, as the romance of destiny which casts each individual upon his own ultimate island. "Giacomo Cenci, whom the Pope ordered to be flayed alive," observed Moore in *Memoirs of My Dead Life*, "no doubt admired the romance of destiny that laid him on his ultimate island, a raised plank, so that the executioner might conveniently roll up the skin of his belly like an apron." The second nonformal admission was pathos, by which he meant the quietistic frustrations of the nympholeptic and the sadness of the last meeting of Flaubert's Frederic Moreau with Madame Arnoux, the osmazome of all literature, the tragedy of all who inherit five hundred pounds a year or upward.

The pure narrator was singularly unfree in the material he might work upon. Besides outlawing humor, Moore deplored melodrama, as found in *Far from the Madding Crowd*, whose concluding gunfire "of course does not come within the range of literary criticism." Even *Adam Bede* was disapproved of on the grounds that the story of a crime is never a good story. Moore frowned not only upon the "healthy" school of melodrama that Andrew Lang preached and Rider Haggard and Stevenson practiced but also upon the sort of bizarre subject he had himself employed in *A Mere Accident*, the novel that Pater had found too sensational for his taste. Only Balzac, he said, remembering "An Incident of the Terror," possessed sufficient tact for handling the tale of bloody terror; other writers did well to avoid terror altogether, choosing "an ordinary, everyday story, for in developing it, any originality of mind and vision [they] possess will appear to advantage." Local color was of course forbidden, and he observed that a writer like Kipling did not achieve art simply by filling his stories with "hookas and elephants." But neither could he find value in subjects derived from the low-charged, platitudinous, middle-class world, for art had no concern with Minnie who lives in Clapham or with Uncle Jim's words to the undergraduate. Trollope's concern for "the conditions of the junior clergy" particularly irritated him, for Trollope was addicted to "the vice of subject," the seemingly incurable perversion of Victorian taste. The popularity of Fildes's well-known painting "The Doctor" led Moore to lecture his fellow countrymen as follows:

> Has any critic thought of pointing to any special passage of color in this picture, or calling attention to the quality of the modelling or the ability of the drawing? No, what attracted attention was the story. Would the child live or die? Did that dear, good doctor entertain any hopes of the poor little thing's recovery? And the poor parents, how grieved they seemed! Perhaps it is their only child.[14]

The vice of subject arose out of the error of substituting "human interest" for interest in form. Moore invented a little collection of paradoxes asserting that all interesting narratives are tiresome. Tolstoi's Battle of Borodino, he said contemptuously, was as "interesting as a newspaper," and he announced to St. John Irvine that dullness is a principal component of all truly great books. John Eglinton discovered that Moore disliked all novels in which the attraction was a delightful and absorbing story; he once condemned some such novel to Eglinton saying, "You may guess how bad it was, when I had to sit up last night to finish it."

The nihilism implicit in these ferocious standards is clear. It should be said of Moore, however, that he applied the rules to himself as mercilessly as to any other writer. The harshness of his own self-discipline is now legendary. Yeats, who never praised him gratuitously, said that when in pursuit of unified construction "he would sacrifice what he had thought the day before not only his best scene, but 'the best scene in any modern play,' and without regret: all must receive its being from the central idea; nothing be itself anything." This was not an easy course. Moore was always strained to devise incidents, and his willingness to blue-pencil scenes regardless of the pain they had cost reflects the piety with which he regarded his vocation. He once told how he had forced himself to delete from The Apostle, his stage version of The Brook Kerith, a moving but irrelevant scene in which Paul bade farewell to Eunice. He reminded himself, he said, of Schopenhauer's wise saying that in great

211

art the merely charming is never found, and he composed an epigram of his own: "In art we are always sacrificing good things. A plague upon good things! for they profit us nothing in the end."

Moore's astringency necessarily had limits. One might dream of a novel that approached the condition of music and dealt beautifully with nothing at all, but a writer had to reconcile himself to the fact that narratives cannot exist without a certain substance, that is, human nature, and that they organize that substance from some recognizable point of view, separable from, and prior to, aesthetic considerations. Like all aesthetic purists Moore was himself addicted to the vice of subject, though only on alternate days of the week when he forgot that the only virtues in art are technical virtues and began to proclaim that "the more realistic you are, the better, as long as you transpose," unconsciously paraphrasing Zola's famous dictum that art is a slice of life seen through a temperament.

Moore's views on human nature were, as one might anticipate, both vigorous and individual. His psychology was a root and branch behaviorism which referred all motivation back to a few innate drives—vanity, ambition, the instinct to be free, sex, the "mother instinct," and the like. On this foundation, his characters, like Shaw's, erected a superstructure of evasion, rationalization, and window dressing or, on the other hand, if they had been granted another destiny, of courageous rituals of acceptance, which gave rise to the manifold concrete acts of their existence occupying them from the cradle to the grave. Moore's characters moved to their destinies according to the dictates of instinct alone. In mid-career he wrote:

> Our actions obey an unknown law, implicit in ourselves, but which does not conform to our logic. So we very often succeed in proving to ourselves that a certain course is the proper one for us to follow, in preference to another course, but, when it comes for us to act we do not act as we intended, and we ascribe the discrepancy between what we think and what we do to a deficiency of will power. Man

dares not admit that he acts according to his instincts, that his instincts are his destiny.[15]

Moore's novels thus never concern themselves with probing into the motives of his characters—their motives are transparent. Innate drives originate all behavior; choice is eliminated, even the illusion of choice. "I hardly knew what I was doing," said Esther Waters after her seduction. "It was like sleepwalking." With the disappearance of the drama of the sovereign free will, the focus of attention in Moore's novels fixed upon the unfolding spectacle of the behavior of given characters in given situations, moving through endless permutations like wanderers in William Morris' fantasies.

The behavior of characters in fiction ought to obey certain eternal, universal laws, Moore believed, laws whose content can be inferred from patterns presented in his own novels. He believed, for example, that like personalities attract, that pleasure arises only in invidious comparison, that the educated woman is the more erotic, that women can never be cured of dipsomania, that intelligent people are never ugly, that the unmarried observer alone knows the feminine soul—Balzac, Jane Austen, Walter Pater, and George Moore—that a lover is essential and a husband fatal for the successful playing of Wagner's Isolde. These and similar laws appear extensively in his criticism. For example, he thought Becky Sharp's behavior unbelievable; she was an "adventuress without a temperament," and therefore a contradiction in terms. The greatness of Pater lay in his intuition of feminine mentality: the Oxford bachelor perceived that "women have done some very pretty painting and written some delightful poems, but if we look into their faces we read there the sadness of the satellite." Juliet violated the law that true grief weeps with undivided mind. And so on.

Ten years before the death of Tennyson, Moore had come to the conclusion that social conduct is underlain principally by sex, and shortly afterward he made the further discovery of the sexual elements of religious emotion, a discovery which he ex-

213

ploited tirelessly in *Sister Teresa, The Lake, Heloise and Abelard,* and *Ulick and Soracha.* "To me," he said, stating his most cherished psychological law, "nothing is more natural than that a man should cross seas to release a woman from a convent." In his power to cut through pretensions of altruism and logic to root motives of egoism, ambition, and sex, a power learned by going to school to Balzac, Stendhal, and Zola, he achieved his most revolutionary anti-Victorian stroke, for it led him to dispense with the evangelical conscience as the central battlefield upon which the English novel was enacted, and to dispense with the evangelical man as the pattern of human behavior.

In view of this preoccupation, his lifelong denigration of Henry James will appear to be less a matter of jealous spite than of a fundamental incompatibility of vision. From Moore's point of view, James's delicate manner for recreating the inner quality of the experience of choice was without point or value. Rather than too much of a psychologist, James was to Moore no psychologist at all: "He mistook trivial comments about men and women for psychology; that which is firmly and clearly imagined needs no psychology. . . . The first business of the writer is to find a human instinct." The "Boston psychologist" seemed to have lost himself in trifles, in weighing "whether a woman should accept a cup of tea or reject it," in wandering through "a desert of qualifying clauses," in "bringing out a pack of fox hounds to hunt a rat." Moore missed in James what Courbet, with his "peasant's instinct," had missed in the painter Français: "Once on a time there was a painter called Français who painted landscapes spick and span as well-kept gardens, and on being asked what he thought of one of these in the Salon, Courbet answered: 'In every landscape there is a place to crap, and in Français' I can never find the spot.'" Moore would probably have raised the same objection to Conrad's novels, though he never undertook to attack Conrad with any such coherence.

The innate drives of human nature, Moore believed, are variously combined and weighted in any given personality to

214

produce a singular sort of pattern having its own unity, its own integrity, its own flavor. The writer's job is to reveal in a few simple strokes and at the outset the essence, the complex unity, of each character and to devote himself thereafter to the myriad behavior manifestations of his creation. But the first step, to "evoke the soul," was the most difficult task in all the realm of art. It could not be achieved by tricks or formulae but only by the intuition of genius. Its masters were few. In painting, Rembrandt could do it, and Hals. Later there was Degas. In literature those who had failed to evoke the souls of their characters were to be found on every hand. Zola had created but one soul, Gervaise. Meredith's characters float in shadows and "speak like lunatics." Hardy's Farmer Oak was mere "dead water"; Henry James was incapable of invoking souls; Tolstoi had created only one soul, Pierre Bezukhov. Turgenev lacked the power, and hence was confined to absolute delineation of his friends; later Moore recalled that Turgenev had created Bazarov, whom he paired with Balzac's Rubempré as the two greatest creations in all literature, the two representing, though Moore seems to have been unconscious of the fact, the classical forms of the great nineteenth-century genus that also included Moore, the genus nihilist.

But there was Shakespeare, above him Landor, above Landor, Balzac, the greatest of all, who "descended circle by circle into the nether world of the soul," revealing the whole complexity of the spinster Rose Cormon in a word or two describing the calf of her leg, revealing the spirit of youth in Lucien's single cry, creating with the utmost simplicity of means all the great dramatis personae of the *Human Comedy*, with its "innumerable and unceasing eruption of souls." Balzac had prophetically created in *Les Paysans*, written fifty years before Davitt and Boycott, "every incident of the land war in Ireland," an accomplishment which would strike "even the ordinary reader" as extraordinary. He had surpassed all other writers in seeing human nature clearly and sketching it unerringly, inimitably, instinc-

215

tively, prodigally, spitting forth "lava and ashes," peopling his "vast empire with surely a greater number of souls and ideas than did Dickens or Thackeray or Fielding or George Eliot or Turgenev or Tolstoi." "To me," said Moore ecstatically, "there is more wisdom and more divine imagination in Balzac than in any other writer; he looked further into the future than human eyes could see; and I am finishing these pages with tears in my eyes."

So Moore wrote in 1891, playing a tune that did not harmonize with the view that the novel is a rhythmical sequence of events told with rhythmical sequence of phrase. Moore never reprinted the Balzac essay, but neither did he renounce it. In the end, as in the beginning, his soul remained divided against itself, committed to incompatibles. Yet he was fundamentally an honest man, infinitely less limited than he might have been; and he sensed, even if he could never bring himself to say so directly, that his aesthetic masters, despite their command of paradox, had missed the most important paradox of all their experience: that too much sensitivity, as well as too little, may anaesthetize; that in the name of art one may either exalt or destroy art; that hatred of philistinism may transform a writer into a perfect likeness of the philistine, moving through the cultural heritage like a hooligan, like the philistine himself, finding the literary tradition only so much tiresome absurdity, seemingly demolishing it all, though not really—for only a very suggestive reader would throw his *Tess of the D'Urbervilles* or his *Vanity Fair* into the trash basket merely on George Moore's advice. One need not condescend: for its purpose, Moore's critical manner could hardly be improved upon. It is owing to George Moore as much as to any artist of his time that the formlessness, the sentimentality, the tendentiousness, the evangelical piety, the compulsive dishonesty that were once all but universal in English fiction have today disappeared from the serious novels written in our language.

216

Notes

CHAPTER 1

1. Joseph Hone, *The Moores of Moore Hall* (London: Jonathan Cape, 1939), p. 49.

2. Maurice Moore, *An Irish Gentleman, George Henry Moore* (London: T. Werner Laurie, 1912), pp. 375 ff.

3. George Moore, *Hail and Farewell* (New York: D. Appleton & Co., 1925), II, 176.

4. W. B. Yeats, *Autobiographies* (New York: The Macmillan Co., 1936), p. 345.

5. Joseph Hone, *The Life of George Moore* (New York: The Macmillan Co., 1936), pp. 26-27.

6. *Hail and Farewell*, II, 191.

7. George Moore, *Confessions of a Young Man* (London: Swan Sonnenschein, Lowrey & Co., 1888), p. 186.

8. *Confessions*, p. 187.

9. Hone, *George Moore*, p. 81.

10. George Moore, *A Drama in Muslin* (London: Vizetelly & Co., 1886), p. 95.

11. George Moore, *Parnell and His Island* (London: Swan Sonnenschein & Co., 1887), pp. 69-70.

12. *Parnell*, pp. 6-7.

13. *Parnell*, pp. 91-92.

14. *Parnell*, pp. 45-47.

15. *Parnell*, p. 52.

16. *Hail and Farewell*, II, 429.

17. *A Drama in Muslin*, p. 218.

18. *Parnell*, pp. 238-39.

19. *Parnell*, pp. 141-42.

20. *Confessions*, pp. 151-52.

21. *Confessions*, pp. 339-40.

22. *Confessions*, p. 187.

23. *Confessions* (Carra Edition; New York: Boni & Liveright, 1922-24), p. 160. This quotation was added in a late revision. Other citations refer to the London edition of 1888.

24. *Parnell*, p. 34.

25. *A Drama in Muslin*, p. 158.

26. *Parnell*, p. 234.

27. *Parnell*, pp. 184-85, 187-88.

28. John Eglinton, *Letters of George Moore* (Bournemouth: Sydenham & Co., 1942), p. 64.

29. *Hail and Farewell*, II, 423.

CHAPTER 2

1. Moore, *Hail and Farewell*, II, 207-8.

2. Joseph Hone, *Life of George Moore*, pp. 56, 78-79.

3. Hone, p. 78.

4. Hone, p. 78.

5. *Hail and Farewell*, II, 242.

6. Moore, *Confessions of a Young Man*, pp. 160-61.

7. *Confessions*, pp. 155, 224, 172.

8. *Confessions*, pp. 322-23.

9. *Confessions*, pp. 69, 80.

10. Hone, p. 71.

11. *Hail and Farewell*, I, 94-95.

12. Arnold Hauser, *The Social History of Art* (New York: Alfred A. Knopf, 1951), p. 894.

13. *Confessions*, pp. 171-72.

14. Théophile Gautier, *Mademoiselle de Maupin* (New York: The Modern Library, n. d.), p. xxv.

15. Gautier, p. 122.

16. *Confessions*, p. 191.

17. George Moore, *Avowals* (New York: Boni & Liveright, Inc., 1919), p. 109.

18. Gustave Flaubert, *Letters*, selected by Richard Rumbold (London: Geo. Weidenfeld and Nicolson, 1950), pp. 68, 108.

19. Hone, p. 171.

20. George Moore, *Modern Painting* (London: Walter Scott, 1893), p. 32.

21. *Modern Painting*, pp. 142-43.

22. George Moore, "Shakespeare and Balzac," *Century Magazine*, LXXXVIII (1914), 82.

23. Flaubert, *Letters*, p. 183.

24. Flaubert, *Letters*, pp. 179, 197.

25. *Confessions*, pp. 226-27.

26. Douglas Cooper, "George Moore and Modern Art," *Horizon*, XIV, No. 62 (February, 1945), 113-30.

27. *Confessions*, pp. 92-94.

28. *Confessions*, p. 94.

29. Flaubert, *Letters*, pp. 73, 84.

30. Geraint Goodwin, *Conversations with George Moore* (New York: Alfred A. Knopf, 1930), p. 107.

31. Hone, p. 454.

32. George Moore, "A Preface to 'The Bending of the Bough,'" *Fortnightly Review*, LXVII (1900), 321.

33. *Modern Painting*, p. 150.

34. *Avowals*, p. 32.

35. Flaubert, *Letters*, pp. 119, 218.

36. George Moore, *A Modern Lover* (London: Tinsley Bros., 1885), pp. 156, 269.

37. *Confessions*, pp. 298-305 *passim*.

38. George Moore, *Conversations in Ebury Street* (London: W. Heinemann, Ltd., 1924), p. 16.

39. Goodwin, p. 108.

CHAPTER 3

1. Clarence R. Decker, *The Victorian Conscience* (New York: Twayne Publishers, 1952), *passim*.

2. Amy Cruse, *The Victorians and Their Reading* (New York: Houghton, Mifflin & Co., 1936), pp. 225, 312, 320.

3. Thomas Hardy, *Far from the Madding Crowd*, ed. Carl J. Weber (New York: Oxford University Press, 1937), p. 368.

4. Miriam Franc, *Ibsen in England* (Boston: The Four Seas Co., 1919), p. 38.

5. Malcolm Elwin, *Old Gods Falling* (New York: The Macmillan Co., 1939), pp. 187, 193-97 *passim*.

6. George Moore, *Hail and Farewell*, I, 352.

7. George Moore, *Confessions of a Young Man*, p. 339.

8. *Hail and Farewell*, II, 243.

9. George Moore, *Flowers of Passion* (London: Provost & Co., 1878).

10. *Hail and Farewell*, II, 244.

11. Joseph Hone, *Life of George Moore*, p. 69.

12. George Moore and Bernard Lopez, *Martin Luther* (London: Remington & Co., 1879).

13. Elwin, p. 103.

14. Hone, p. 75.

15. George Moore, *Pagan Poems* (London: Newman & Co., 1881).

16. George Moore, *Memoirs of My Dead Life* (New York: Boni & Liveright, 1923), pp. 282-83.

CHAPTER 4

1. Joseph Hone, *Life of George Moore*, p. 75.

2. George Moore, *Confessions of a Young Man*, p. 99.

3. *Confessions*, pp. 112-13.

4. *Confessions*, pp. 112-13.

5. *Confessions*, pp. 127-30 *passim*.

6. *Confessions*, p. 112.

7. *Confessions*, pp. 113 ff.

8. *Confessions*, pp. 306-7.

9. Hone, p. 96.

10. Hone, p. 96.

11. George Moore, *A Modern Lover*, p. 42.

12. George Moore, *A Drama in Muslin*, p. 187.

13. *Irish Monthly*, VI (November, 1878), 610.

14. Gustave Flaubert, *Letters*, selected by Richard Rumbold, p. 95.

15. George Moore, *Literature at Nurse, or Circulating Morals* (London: Vizetelly & Co., 1885); and *Confessions*, pp. 237-38.
16. Frederick Locker-Lampson, *Letters from A. C. Swinburne to Frederick Locker-Lampson* (London: Privately printed, 1912), p. 47.
17. Hone, pp. 107-9.
18. Bess Sondel, *Zola's Naturalistic Theory* (Chicago: University of Chicago Press, 1939), pp. 52-53.
19. *A Drama in Muslin*, p. 269.
20. Matthew Josephson, *Zola* (New York: Macaulay & Co., 1928), p. 275.
21. George Moore, *Parnell and His Island*, pp. 233-34.
22. *Confessions*, p. 165.
23. George Moore, *Impressions and Opinions* (New York: Brentano's, n. d.), p. 75.
24. Emile Zola, *The Experimental Novel* (New York: Cassell Publishing Co., 1893), pp. 11-12.
25. George Moore, *Modern Painting*, pp. 117-19.
26. George Moore, *Conversations in Ebury Street*, pp. 108-9.

CHAPTER 5

1. George Moore, *Avowals*, pp. 180-81.
2. George Moore, *Confessions of a Young Man*, p. 193.
3. *Avowals*, pp. 187-88.
4. Joseph Hone, *Life of George Moore*, p. 183.
5. Hone, p. 150.
6. George Moore, *Mike Fletcher* (London: Ward & Downey, 1889), p. 81.
7. *Mike Fletcher*, p. 61.
8. *Mike Fletcher*, pp. 24-29.
9. *Mike Fletcher*, p. 178.
10. *Mike Fletcher*, p. 212.
11. *Mike Fletcher*, p. 209.
12. *Mike Fletcher*, p. 295.
13. Hone, p. 161.
14. George Moore, *A Modern Lover*, p. 157.
15. Hone, p. 150.

16. Hone, p. 167.
17. George Moore, *Vain Fortune* (New York: Chas. Scribner's Sons, 1892), pp. 192-94.
18. *Vain Fortune*, p. 163.
19. *Vain Fortune*, pp. 192-94.
20. Hone, p. 170.

CHAPTER 6

1. George Moore, *Confessions of a Young Man*, pp. 353-54.
2. *Confessions*, pp. 208-15 *passim*.
3. Joseph Hone, *Life of George Moore*, p. 162.
4. Hone, p. 187.
5. George Moore, *A Mummer's Wife* (New York: Boni & Liveright, 1925), pp. x-xi.
6. George Moore, *A Communication to My Friends* (London: Nonesuch Press, 1933), pp. 64-65.
7. George Moore, *Vain Fortune*, p. 85.
8. George Moore, *Esther Waters* (New York: Liveright, Inc., 1932), p. 109.
9. *A Communication to My Friends*, p. 66.
10. Geraint Goodwin, *Conversations with George Moore*, p. 151.
11. *Vain Fortune*, p. 266.
12. *Esther Waters*, pp. 219-20.
13. George Moore, *Hail and Farewell*, I, 345.
14. Fedor Dostoevski, *Poor Folk*, Introduction by George Moore (Boston: Roberts Bros., 1894), p. xvi.
15. Hone, pp. 204, 210.
16. Hone, p. 188.
17. *Hail and Farewell*, I, 178.
18. Joseph Hone, "Jacques-Emile Blanche," *Envoy*, III, No. 12 (December, 1950), 23.
19. George Moore, *Evelyn Innes* (New York: D. Appleton Co., 1927), p. 213.
20. Grant Richards, *Memoirs of a Misspent Youth* (New York: Harper & Bros., 1933), pp. 264-65.

CHAPTER 7

1. George Moore, *Modern Painting,* p. 213.
2. George Moore, *Hail and Farewell,* I, 467.
3. *Hail and Farewell,* I, 4-5.
4. *Hail and Farewell,* I, 328.
5. W. B. Yeats, *Dramatis Personae* (New York: The Macmillan Co., 1936), p. 45.
6. George Moore, "Is the Theatre a Place of Amusement?" *Beltaine,* June, 1899, pp. 8-9.
7. Edward Martyn, *The Heather Field and Maeve,* with an Introduction by George Moore (London: Duckworth & Co., 1899), pp. xxvi-xxvii.
8. *Hail and Farewell,* I, 217-18.
9. *Hail and Farewell,* II, 299.
10. George Moore, *The Untilled Field and The Lake* (New York: Boni & Liveright, Inc., 1924), p. xi.
11. Joseph Hone, *The Moores of Moore Hall,* p. 210.
12. George Moore, "Literature and the Irish Language," in *Ideals in Ireland,* ed. by Lady Augusta Gregory (London: Unicorn Press, 1901), pp. 45-51.
13. Joseph Hone, *Life of George Moore,* p. 213.
14. William Archer, *Real Conversations* (London: W. Heinemann, Ltd., 1904), p. 98.
15. Lennox Robinson, *Palette and Plough* (Dublin: Browne & Nolan, 1948), pp. 119-20.
16. "Literature and the Irish Language," p. 51.
17. *Hail and Farewell,* I, 438.
18. George Moore, *Epistle to the Cymry,* in *Confessions of a Young Man* (Uniform Edition; London: W. Heinemann, Ltd., 1937), pp. 235-37.
19. George Moore, "Apologia Pro Scriptis Meis," Preface to *Memoirs of My Dead Life* (New York: D. Appleton & Co., 1929), p. xxviii.
20. *Hail and Farewell,* I, 254-55.

CHAPTER 8

1. George Moore, *Avowals*, p. 92.
2. George Moore, *The Untilled Field* (Philadelphia: J. B. Lippincott Co., 1903), p. 335.
3. Geraint Goodwin, *Conversations with George Moore*, p. 96.
4. *Avowals*, pp. 161 ff.
5. George Moore, *Aphrodite in Aulis* (New York: Brentano's, 1931), p. 115.
6. George Moore, *Confessions of a Young Man*, pp. 119-20.
7. George Moore, "The Nineness in the Oneness," *The Century Magazine*, XCIX (1919), 65-66.
8. George Moore, *Hail and Farewell*, I, 346.
9. George Moore, *Heloise and Abelard* (New York: Liveright Publishing Co., 1932), I, 226; II, 99.
10. *Hail and Farewell*, I, 283-84.
11. *Heloise and Abelard*, II, 275-78.
12. *Letters of George Moore*, January 14, 1933.

CHAPTER 9

1. George Moore, "Turgenev," *Fortnightly Review*, XLIII (1888), 239.
2. George Moore, *Impressions and Opinions*, p. 48.
3. George Moore, *Conversations in Ebury Street*, p. 187.
4. Geraint Goodwin, *Conversations with George Moore*, p. 42.
5. George Moore, *Avowals*, p. 127.
6. George Moore, "Some Characteristics of English Fiction," *North American Review*, CLXX (1900), 504.
7. James Whitall, *English Years* (New York: Harcourt, Brace & Co., 1935), pp. 184-85.
8. George Moore, *Mike Fletcher*, pp. 39-41.
9. George Moore, "Shakespeare and Balzac," *The Century Magazine*, LXVI (1914), 87.
10. *Letters of George Moore*, p. 49.

11. *Letters of George Moore,* pp. 70-71.
12. Goodwin, pp. 164-65.
13. *Avowals,* pp. 79-81.
14. George Moore, *Modern Painting,* p. 53.
15. George Moore, *Evelyn Innes,* p. 85.

Selected Bibliography

The definitive bibliography of Moore's work is being compiled by Mr. Edwin Gilcher, of Cherry Plain, New York. This will supersede all other bibliographies of Moore's writings; accordingly, I have omitted Moore's own work from the selected list which follows. I am indebted to Mr. Gilcher for a number of suggestions and corrections.

Archer, William. *Real Conversations*. London, 1904.

Balderston, J. Lloyd. "The Dusk of the Gods," *Atlantic Monthly*, CXVIII (1916), 165-75.

Blanche, J.-E. *Portraits of a Lifetime*. London, 1937.

Boyd, Ernest. *Portraits Real and Imaginary*. New York, 1924.

Burdett, Osbert. *The Beardsley Period*. London, 1925.

Carthy, James. *Bibliography of Irish History, 1870-1911*. Dublin, 1940.

Clark, Barrett H. *Intimate Portraits*. New York, 1951.

Cooper, Douglas. "George Moore and Modern Art," *Horizon*, XIV, No. 62 (February, 1945), 113-30.

Decker, Clarence R. "Zola's Literary Reputation in England," *PMLA*, XLIX (1934), 1140-53.

Eglinton, John. *Irish Literary Portraits*. London, 1935.

Elwin, Malcolm. *Old Gods Falling*. New York, 1939.

Ervine, St. John. *Some Impressions of My Elders*. New York, 1922.

Farmer, A. J. "La Préparation du Mouvement décadent en Angleterre," *U. de Grenoble, Lettres-Droit, Annales*, VII (1930), 181-298.

Ferguson, Walter D. *The Influence of Flaubert on George Moore*. Philadelphia, 1934.

Freeman, John. *A Portrait of George Moore*. New York, 1922.

Gaunt, William. *The Aesthetic Adventure*. New York, 1945.

Gettman, Royal A. "George Moore's Revisions," *PMLA*, LIX (1944), 540-55.

Gogarty, Oliver St. John. *Intimations*. New York, 1950.

Goodwin, Geraint. *Conversations with George Moore*. New York, 1930.

Gosse, Sir Edmund. *Selected Essays.* 2nd Series. London, 1928.

Gwynn, Denis. *Edward Martyn and the Irish Revival.* London, 1930.

Harris, Frank. *Contemporary Portraits.* 2nd Series. New York, 1919.

Hauser, Arnold. *The Social History of Art.* New York, 1951.

Hicks, Granville. *Figures of Transition.* New York, 1939.

Hone, Joseph. "Jacques-Emile Blanche," *Envoy,* III (1950), 18-25.

———. *The Life of George Moore.* New York, 1936.

———. *The Moores of Moore Hall.* London, 1939.

Huneker, James. *The Pathos of Distance.* New York, 1913.

Jackson, Holbrook. *The Eighteen-Nineties.* New York, 1922.

Josephson, Matthew. *Zola and His Time.* New York, 1928.

MacCarthy, Desmond. *Portraits.* London, 1931.

Marie, Aristide. *La Forêt symboliste.* Paris, 1936.

Mitchell, Susan L. *George Moore.* New York, 1916.

Morgan, Charles. *An Epitaph on George Moore.* New York, 1935.

Moore, Col. Maurice. *An Irish Gentleman, George Henry Moore.* London, 1912.

O'Faolain, Sean. "Pater and Moore," *London Mercury,* XXXIV (1936), 330-38.

O'Sullivan, Seumas. *Essays and Recollections.* Dublin, 1944.

Palmer, Norman D. *The Irish Land League Crisis.* New Haven, 1940.

Pater, Walter. *Sketches and Reviews by Walter Pater.* New York, 1919.

Peyre, Henri. *Writers and Their Critics.* Ithaca, N. Y., 1944.

Phelps, W. L. *Autobiography with Letters.* New York, 1939.

Rosenblatt, Louise. *L'Idée de l'Art pour l'Art dans la Littérature Anglaise.* Paris, 1931.

Schwab, Arnold T. "Irish Author and American Critic," *Nineteenth Century Fiction,* VIII, 256-71; IX, 22-37.

Sechler, Robert P. *George Moore: A Disciple of Walter Pater.* Philadelphia, 1931.

Shumaker, Wayne. *English Autobiography.* Berkeley and Los Angeles, 1954.

Taylor, Estella Ruth. *The Modern Irish Writers.* Lawrence, Kans., 1954.

Temple, Ruth Zabriskie. *The Critic's Alchemy.* New York, 1953.

Whitall, James. *English Years.* New York, 1935.

Wolfe, Humbert. *George Moore.* New York, 1932.

Yeats, William Butler. *Dramatis Personae.* New York, 1936.

Index

229

231